INTO THE SECOND CENTURY

SURREY CCC

A HISTORY SINCE 1945

INTO THE SECOND CENTURY

SURREYCCC

A HISTORY SINCE 1945

JERRY LODGE

TEMPUS

First published 2004

Tempus Publishing Ltd
The Mill, Brimscombe Port
Stroud, Gloucestershire GL5 2QG
www.tempus-publishing.com

British Library Cataloguing in Publication Data.
A catalogue record for this book is available from the British Library.

ISBN 0 7524 3177 3

Typesetting and origination by Tempus Publishing.
Printed and bound in Great Britain.

CONTENTS

ACKNOWLEDGEMENTS

My thanks to Kit Bartlett, Michael Barton, Nigel Bennett, Brian Cowley, Jeff Hancock, Roger Knight, Michael Pearce, Gary Sutton, Paul Sheldon, Micky Stewart, Betty Surridge and Gareth Townsend for their assistance in the preparation of this book.

The majority of the photographs have been supplied from the Surrey Photo Library in conjunction with EMPICS. If any photographic source believes it holds the copyright of any photograph reproduced in this book, it should contact the publisher to rectify the matter.

FOREWORD
BY ADAM HOLLIOAKE

The last book written on the history of Surrey cricket was published in 1989, some two years before the club offered me a contract. The last fifteen years has seen considerable success for Surrey, starting with winning the National League in 1996 under the captaincy of Alec Stewart. With three County Championships from 1999 to 2002 Surrey became the premier county team in the country, which every other county strove to beat.

Moving to England from Australia at the age of twelve to live in Weybridge, I was well aware of the history of Surrey CCC, and walking into The Oval the past glories of so many famous cricketers are there for all to see. The portraits of Hobbs, Sandham, Surridge, May and the Bedser twins look down on you from the walls of the Long Room.

In this new history, Jerry Lodge points out that since the end of the Second World War Surrey have won the County Championship more than any other county, even Yorkshire. Everyone knows about the famous seven years from 1952 to 1959 and there are still plenty of people around The Oval to remind the current players about that team. The present team has brought pride back to the club by bringing success in all the four competitions that form the basis of first-class cricket in England today.

The fabric of the game has radically changed since 1945. The amateur player has disappeared and the structure of the fixture list has changed from the days when international players rushed back from Test-match duty to play the next day for their county, even against university opposition. Nowadays with central contracts for England players the county has to build their team on a squad basis, working on the premise that their international players will only play a handful of games for their county. Overseas players are under the same restraints, with the country always having first call on the player's services.

All this puts emphasis on the structure of the club and the strength of the Second XI under the coaching staff. It is no coincidence that Surrey have won the Second XI Championship outright more times than any other county. I was proud to be part of the last winning team in 1992.

My involvement with the club in the last decade has been very special, bringing me the opportunity to make numerous lasting friendships and lead a team of talented and dedicated cricketers under the management of Keith Medlycott. In my last year with Surrey I am looking forward to even more triumphs for the club to keep our numerous supporters happy. It will be strange playing at The Oval during 2004 with a vast open space at the Vauxhall End but the new development will radically change the ground and should encourage the next generation to continue playing in the great tradition of Surrey cricket.

Adam Hollioake

BIBLIOGRAPHY

Lord Alverstone and C.W. Alcock, (ed.), *Surrey Cricket, its History and Associations*, Longmans, 1902.

Bailey, Philip, Philip Thorn and Wynne-Thomas, Peter, *Who's Who of Cricketers*, Hamlyn, 1993.

Bartlett, Kit, *Laurence Barnard Fishlock, His Record, Innings by Innings*, A.C.S., 2000.

Cowley, Brian (ed.), *Surrey County Cricket Club – First-class and Limited Overs Records 1846-2000*, Surrey CCC, 2001.

Gover, Alfred, *The Long Run*.

Hill, Alan, *The Bedsers – Twinning Triumphs*, Mainstream Publishing, 2001.

Jones, Trevor, *Pursuing the Dream*, Sporting Declarations Books, 1999.

Jones, Trevor, *The Dream Fulfilled*, Sporting Declarations Books, 2000.

Jones, Trevor, *Doubling Up with Delight*, Sporting Declarations Books, 2001.

Jones, Trevor, *From Tragedy to Triumph*, Sporting Declarations Books, 2002.

Jones, Trevor, *268 – Alistair Brown*, Sporting Declarations Books, 2002.

Lemmon, David, *The History of Surrey County Cricket Club*, Christopher Helm, 1989.

Lodge, Derek, *P.B.H. May, His Record, Innings by Innings*, A.C.S., 1995.

Lodge, Jerry, *Ken Barrington, His Record, Innings by Innings*, A.C.S., 2001.

Lodge, Jerry, *Sir Alec V Bedser, His Record, Innings by Innings*, A.C.S., 1999.

Overson, Chris, *Tony Lock, His Record, Innings by Innings*, A.C.S., 1997.

Palgrave, Louis, *The Story of the Oval and the History of Surrey Cricket 1902 to 1948*, Cornish Brothers Ltd, 1949.

Root, Fred, *A Cricket Pro's Lot*, Arnold & Co, 1937.

Ross, Gordon, *The Surrey Story*, Stanley Paul, 1957.

Sissons, Ric, *The Players*, The Kingswood Press, 1988.

Stewart, Alec, *Playing for Keeps*, BBC Books, BBC Worldwide Ltd, 2003.

Yapp, Nick, *A History of the Foster's Oval*, Pelham Books, 1990.

The Cricketer Magazine.

Direct Hit – The magazine of Surrey cricket.

Surrey CCC published committee minutes.

Surrey CCC yearbooks.

Wisden Cricketers' Almanack from 1946 to 2003.

ONE

1845-1945
THE FIRST CENTURY

On 21 August 1945, Surrey County Cricket Club celebrated its centenary just seven days after the end of the Second World War. This was no time to arrange a cricket match in celebration as players were still returning from the war and The Oval was in no fit state to stage a match. Before the start of the war in 1939 The Oval was requisitioned by the government and stayed impounded throughout that conflict. Early in the war it was used as a searchlight site, before being prepared as a giant prisoner-of-war camp. However, it was never used and lay dormant. In the early years of the war London suffered badly from enemy bombing and Kennington did not escape. A considerable amount of damage was done to the pavilion and other buildings at The Oval. It was established that a large sum of money would be needed to restore the ground. The Duchy of Cornwall had extended the lease on the ground until 1984 and had expressed a wish that the ground should be used for other recreations so that it did not stay closed for half the year.

There were changes in personnel at The Oval when cricket resumed in 1946. B.A. Glanvill was now president and chairman, and Brian Castor was appointed secretary at the end of 1946. The pre-war groundsman, 'Bosser' Martin, had retired, and his place was taken by Bert Lock, who had played for the County as a medium-pace bowler in the early 1930s and was therefore no stranger to The Oval. He was demobilised from the RAF on 5 October 1945 and started work at The Oval three days later, foregoing any thought of holiday or leave. He had six months in which to make the ground ready for first-class cricket, and the task that confronted him was enormous. He describes the scene that met him at The Oval:

> The square had not been touched for six years, and was covered with long coarse grass full of weeds. The outfield was littered with miles of barbed wire supported by nearly 1,000 poles all in concrete two feet deep. There were four huts erected on concrete bases, which were one foot thick with a number of drains in between. The stands were in a shocking state of repair with hundreds of seats calling for a new coat of paint, and there were thousands of bricks from the bomb-blasted West Wall to be removed.

The general opinion was that there would be no cricket at The Oval for two or three years, but Lock and his crew believed otherwise. He sought the permission of the committee to turf rather than seed the ground, then walked for miles over the marshes at Gravesend until he found areas of weed-free turf. Some 11,000 square yards of The

Soldiers dismantling the fences of the prisoner-of-war camp at The Oval in 1945.

Oval were levelled, and 35,000 turves were laid. Lock succeeded in his mission and on 27 April 1946 a trial match took place at the ground. Then on Saturday 18 May, the first county game for seven years at The Oval began. There have been many great achievements in the annals of Surrey cricket history but none of them betters the achievement of Bert Lock and his crew in making The Oval ready for first-class cricket in the six months after the ravages it had received during the war.

The club noted its centenary by launching an appeal for £100,000 in order to carry out the necessary reconstruction of the ground, and the club's patron, HM King George VI, made one of the first donations, of £100.

To celebrate the centenary, a special one-day game was arranged in 1946 between Surrey and Old England, which provided a great occasion with a large touch of nostalgia. The Old England side was: H. Sutcliffe, P.G.H. Fender, A. Sandham, D.J. Knight, F.E. Woolley, E.R.T. Holmes, E. Hendren, M.J.C. Allom, D.R. Jardine, E.W. Brooks, M.W. Tate and A.P. Freeman. J.B. Hobbs and H. Strudwick umpired the match. Runs from Woolley (62), Hendren (94) and Jardine (54) provided some lovely memories of the day. The match attracted some 15,000 spectators and was attended by His Majesty the King. The game inspired tremendous enthusiasm; one spectator, an old man shedding a tear, remarked: 'I was here for the 1880 Test match and to me the King is honouring all those fine players we have seen down the years.'

A similar match was staged in 1947, but without quite the same impact. Errol Holmes, having become captain of Surrey, led the county against Old England, and owing to the indisposition of Maurice Tate, Gover changed sides and played against Surrey for the only time in his career. Bill Hitch, returning at the age of sixty-one to the scene of his many triumphs, delighted everyone by bowling well and then scoring an excellent 51. Jack O'Connor of Essex was top scorer with a gem of an innings of 100 and the 'Old England' total of 305 for eight wickets was only 10 runs behind Surrey's score of 315 for 6 declared. The restoration fund received very good support, and nothing was more gratifying than the message from the South African Cricket Association that they would devote half their share of the net gate against Surrey during the 1947 tour as a donation to The Oval Centenary Appeal Fund. The appeal did not raise as much money as the club had hoped, despite being enthusiastically organised by Errol Holmes and later by Louis Palgrave. The problem was that it was a time of great austerity, and £100,000 was too optimistic a target.

The history of the club during its first century from 1845 to 1945 has been well documented, particularly in David Lemmon's book *The History of Surrey County Cricket Club*, published in 1989 by Christopher Helm Ltd. More insights can be found in *The Story of the Oval and the History of Surrey Cricket 1902 to 1948* by Louis Palgrave, published by Cornish Brothers in 1949 and *The Surrey Story* by Gordon Ross, published by Stanley Paul in 1957.

Formed in 1845, Surrey County Cricket Club is the oldest of the county clubs in that it has undergone no significant reformation since that date. Surrey can claim to be the first unofficial champions in 1864 and the first official champions in 1890. For most county clubs, the record of Surrey in the County Championship would be acceptable but

King George VI shaking hands with Alf Gover at the centenary match in 1946.

the ambitions at Kennington Oval have always been very high. The Championship has only been officially recognised since 1890 and Surrey were declared champions for the first three years, 1890 to 1892, under the captaincy of John Shuter. After finishing fifth in 1893, they were champions again in 1894, 1895 and 1899, when led by K.J. Key.

E.B.V. Christian wrote in the book *Surrey Cricket*, commonly known in Surrey circles as 'The Old Testament', published in 1902, that

> ...the comparative failure of the [Surrey] team was often due to lack of finishing power. The side would place itself in a position apparently free from the risk of defeat, yet fail to secure a victory. The batsmen would place many runs to their credit, but the bowlers fail to get the opponents out in time.

Keen supporters of Surrey were to suffer this phenomenon throughout the first half of the twentieth century. It was not until the 1950s that Surrey were to dominate the County Championship, later falling back again until the last few years from 1996 onwards. So, where do Surrey stand in comparison with other counties? Breaking down the list of champions into the two centuries of the County's history we find

County Champions

1890 to 1945

COUNTY	WINS
Yorkshire	21
Lancashire	7
Surrey	7
Kent	4
Middlesex	3
Nottinghamshire	2
Derbyshire	1
Warwickshire	1

1946 to 2003

COUNTY	WINS
Surrey	12
Yorkshire	10
Middlesex	9
Essex	6
Worcestershire	5
Warwickshire	4
Glamorgan	3
Kent	3
Leicestershire	3
Hampshire	2
Nottinghamshire	2
Lancashire	1
Sussex	1

N.B. The title was shared between two counties in three seasons

1890 to 2003

COUNTY	WINS
Yorkshire	31
Surrey	19
Middlesex	12
Lancashire	8
Kent	7
Essex	6
Warwickshire	5
Worcestershire	5
Nottinghamshire	4
Glamorgan	3
Leicestershire	3
Hampshire	2
Derbyshire	1
Sussex	1
Durham	0
Gloucestershire	0
Northamptonshire	0
Somerset	0

These tables show the predominance of Surrey since 1946, but it must be emphasised that this is due to only two periods of success within the club, these being in the 1950s when they won seven titles in a row and the recent team with their record of three Championships in four years from 1999 to 2002. The most glaring statistic in the above tables is that Gloucestershire have never been crowned champions despite being considered as one of the premier counties in the days of W.G. Grace. The title of Champion County is unreliable before 1890. Most sources accept the list of champions as researched by Rowland Bowen (See *Wisden* 1959, pp.91-98). In the years 1864 to 1889, Surrey were considered as champions in 1864, 1887, 1888 and 1889, the last year being shared with Lancashire and Nottinghamshire.

There was only one other win for the County in the first hundred years of the club, this being in 1914. Even this raised some controversy as Surrey did not play their last 2 matches of the season due to the outbreak of the First World War. Between 1919 and 1939, Surrey finished in second place twice and third place once in four seasons, despite the apparent strength of the squad of players and inspiring captaincy from the likes of Percy Fender and Errol Holmes. In the early 1920s they were winning many matches but the number of drawn matches affected their eventual position. There were shirt front wickets at The Oval and bowling sides out twice became a very big problem.

An analysis of where Surrey finished in the Championship over the years shows that the average position of the county was:

From 1890 to 1939:	4.82
From 1946 to 2003:	5.67
From 1890 to 2003:	5.29

On 8 January 1835, the Duchy of Cornwall granted a 99-year lease, dating from 27 January 1834, to the Otter family on a 'nursery and garden ground in extent about 10 acres, called the Oval, with buildings thereon'. The Oval became a market garden before it became famous throughout the world as a cricket ground. In March 1845 it is recorded that the Duchy of Cornwall was most happy to agree to a lease negotiated by William Baker for The Oval to be used for cricket. The ground was made by laying 10,000 turves that came from Tooting Common.

On 22 August 1845 approximately 100 members from different Surrey clubs gathered at The Horns Tavern for a meeting, and after dinner the Surrey County Cricket Club was formed amid scenes of great excitement. The formal inauguration of the club did not take place until a second dinner, held at the same venue on 18 October 1845, when William Denison became the first secretary. Charles Hugh Hoare was the first captain of the club. Born in Mitcham and educated at Rugby, Hoare had been elected honorary treasurer of the new club and had captained the Gentlemen of Surrey against the Players of Surrey. It was a natural progression for him to assume the captaincy, although it is probable that he was the choice of the team rather than a formal appointment of the Committee.

In a previous history of the club it was written that a famous landmark at The Oval, the gasholders adjacent to the ground, preceded the cricketers. Diligent research has established that in 1845 the site in question was occupied by the South London Water Company. In 1846 the Phoenix (Gas Light and Coke) Company agreed to purchase the land and it is generally agreed that the first gasholder was built in 1848 when a nearby gas works was commissioned. The second gasholder was constructed in the early 1850s.

There were very few fixtures in the first six years under Hoare's captaincy and only sixteen first-class games. The most famous victory was at The Oval in 1848 when Surrey beat All England by eight wickets.

By 1856 membership of the club had risen to nearly 1,000. In 1858 Surrey again beat England under the captaincy of Fred Burbidge, who held that position until 1865. By 1859, Surrey were considered the major team in the land. The matches between Gentlemen and Players were now staged at The Oval as well as at Lord's and inter-county matches were attracting interest. The season of 1864 formed a watershed in the game, not only for the legalisation of overarm bowling but also as the year in which the County Championship, albeit unofficially, came into being and *Wisden's Cricketers' Almanack* was published for the first time. Regarded as the most historic event in the Oval's history, Edgar Willsher, bowling for England against Surrey in August 1862, was no-balled six times for 'high', above the shoulder, bowling. He stalked off the pitch, accompanied by his fellow-professionals, and this incident led directly to the legalisation of overarm bowling.

Over the next few years, the press could not always agree on who was the leading county, but, in 1864, there was no disagreement. Of the 8 county matches they played, Surrey won 6 and drew 2, a record unapproached by any other county. John Shuter first captained Surrey against Nottinghamshire at Trent Bridge in July 1878, when neither Strachan nor Lucas was able to play. It was not until 1882 that he became sole captain of Surrey. At this time teams were not able to declare their innings closed and it was Shuter's approach to the game which showed up the absurdity of the laws and the need for them to be changed.

Following a meeting of all the first-class counties in December 1889, the 'official' County Championship was inaugurated in the season of 1890, when Surrey became the undisputed Champions.

Sir Kingsmill James Key succeeded John Shuter and was captain for six seasons, during which Surrey were County Champions in 1894, 1895 and 1899. In the period from 1900 to 1913, sometimes referred to as the 'Golden Age of Cricket', Surrey were blessed with many outstanding cricketers, but did not win the Championship.

Cyril Wilkinson captained the County when they did win in 1914 and captained again in the first two seasons after the First World War. Percy Fender first played for the County in 1914 and was the Surrey captain from 1921 to 1931. Errol Holmes was one of the most gifted amateur batsmen of his day and captained Surrey from 1934 to 1938.

Throughout its history an amateur had always captained the County. There was always a great divide between the amateurs and professionals. Amateurs often came into the side at the expense of a professional at short notice. In the period from 1845 to 1962, when the distinction between amateurs and professionals was abolished, 503 cricketers played in first-class matches for Surrey. Of these, 268 (some 53.6%) were amateurs. Many played only a few games for the County and were predominately batsmen. As bowlers only twenty-three amateurs have taken more than fifty wickets for Surrey, the highest being Percy Fender with 1,586, then Stuart Surridge with 464.

Surrey v. Derbyshire, 7 August 1936. Sandy Tait (trainer), E.W.J. Brooks, T. McMurray and L.B. Fishlock take advantage of a coal fire in the Oval dressing room during inclement weather.

The amateurs ('Gentlemen') used a separate dressing room from the professionals ('Players') and entered the field of play by a different gate. Travel to away games was nearly always by public transport, with the amateurs using first-class rail carriages and the professionals third-class. They also stayed in different hotels, partly because the professional had to find the cost of accommodation from his game fee. It is worth considering the status of the professional cricketer immediately before the Second World War: in his autobiography, *A Cricket Pro's Lot*, Fred Root commented:

> I once had occasion to complain about having had to bowl too long at the nets on a county ground, just prior to playing in a first-class match, and my answer came from the lips of a well-known official holding high office at Lord's. I am surprised at you, Root, he said. You are lucky to be playing in the match at all. Please realise that professional bowlers are nothing more nor less than the hired labourers of the game.
>
> In those days one had to be circumspect and take such outbursts as part and parcel of the ruling spirit; but I am delighted to say that things have altered since then in practically all aspects of the game, and the professional is treated not as a 'hired labourer', but as the very backbone of English first-class cricket. At the same time, I am willing to admit that the poor old bowler is expected to perform a tremendous lot of hard laborious work. His is undoubtedly the most important, as well as the most strenuous, department of the game. Coaches are practically unanimous in their opinion that whereas a good bowler can be taught to become proficient in batting and fielding, it is seldom indeed that batsmen learn the art of really good bowling.

It is fair to say that some of this attitude continued into the post-war period and it was a slow process for the lot of the professional cricketer to improve. This culminated in the abandonment of the distinction between amateurs and professionals in 1962, whereupon all players were classified as cricketers.

TWO

1946-1951

As cricket resumed after the Second World War the game was still firmly being run by amateurs, with the captain of every county being an amateur. The problem Surrey faced was that H.M. Garland Wells, captain in 1939, was badly wounded in the war and had decided to retire. His predecessor, Errol Holmes, had taken on the task of raising money for the restoration fund and that took up all of his time, so now there were no amateur players left in the club. This was not the first time that the County had been left in this predicament. In 1904 no captain was appointed for the season, but an amateur was asked to lead the side in each game on a match-by-match basis.

What happened next has gone down in history as one of the most intriguing stories in Surrey cricket. Nigel Bennett had played five innings for the Surrey Second XI in 1936 and then spent the remaining years before the Second World War in New Zealand. The folk tale is that the appointment of Nigel Harvie Bennett was a clerical error and that the man destined for the job was A.C.L. 'Leo' Bennett, a proficient club cricketer with the BBC, who had been educated at Dulwich and lived in Surrey. Leo Bennett played 16 matches for Northamptonshire from 1947 to 1949 and captained them on several occasions. It had been decided to ask Leo Bennett to lead Surrey when Nigel Bennett walked into the offices and asked if he could be offered some second-team matches as he was now back in England. In a case of mistaken identity, he was offered the captaincy, which he accepted. The tale may not necessarily be true, but the appointment of Nigel Bennett as captain remains one of the great mysteries of the club.

Nigel Bennett, when interviewed in 2004 at the age of ninety-one, recalled that he certainly only went into the office to ask if he could play for the Second XI, but was then offered the captaincy. Interestingly, he has never heard of A.C.L. Bennett. He was under strict instructions from the Committee not to mix with the professionals. On match days Bennett wanted to meet the players on the steps as they left their respective dressing rooms but was told that under no circumstances was this acceptable. He was informed that he must walk out on to the field of play and that the professionals should then join him there. He vividly recalls the loneliness and solitude of the amateurs' dressing room. One can only admire his courage in accepting the post, although he cannot have anticipated how difficult the task would be. It was soon apparent that Bennett had little knowledge of the county game and that he had hardly any control over the senior professionals. To a certain extent one must sympathise with Bennett but it was perceived that he neither

Nigel Bennett.

sought nor took advice from those more experienced in the game. His one year in first-class cricket was not a happy one, but he scored some useful runs towards the end of the season.

1946

County Championship: 26 matches, 12 points for win, 4 points for a draw, no bonus points, pitches not covered

Surrey played a total of 32 first-class games in the 1946 season. In a wet summer Surrey suffered several bad spells, culminating in consecutive defeats in the last six Championship matches. The county that had finished eighth in 1939 fell to twelfth in 1946. This was obviously very unsatisfactory for a side that had enough talent to be challenging in the top three, yet the season was by no means one of unending gloom.

As the 1946 side relied on the pre-war players who had returned to The Oval the average age of the side was nearly thirty-six. These players were Gover (thirty-eight years old), Fishlock (thirty-nine), Barling (forty), Gregory (forty-four), Squires (thirty-seven), Parker (thirty-three), Mobey (forty-two), Watts (thirty-five), the Bedser twins (twenty-eight) and McIntyre (twenty-eight). Bennett himself was thirty-four years old. Five of these were comparatively inexperienced cricketers, with the Bedsers having only played against the Universities in 1939. There was no strength in depth and the only other players used in the Championship were Whittaker, Constable and Pierpoint, with Lock and Yeatman playing in a single game.

Professional cricketers, lacking a union or association, discussed pay and conditions with their respective counties. Surrey were considered one of the most generous of the counties. For 1946 the playing staff was divided into three groups and their salaries were:

GRADE OF PLAYER	WEEKLY WAGE	ANNUAL INCOME
First grade, comprising nine capped First XI players	£6.50	Guarantee of £450
Second grade, predominately members of the Second XI	£5.50	Guarantee of £350
Third grade, that is the rest of the playing staff	£4.50	No guarantee

Match fees were £5.00 for a home match and £10.00 for an away match from which the players had to find their rail fares and living accommodation. The win bonus was £2.00 and a fund of £200 was set aside for talent money to be distributed by the captain at the end of the season.

AVERAGE NATIONAL EARNINGS		
Men 21 and over	£6.06	£315

Annual Abstract of Statistics, The Stationery Office.

Being a capped player brought you into the first grade, so caps were most prized. On being capped a player received from the club a cap, a blazer, a long-sleeved sweater and a short-sleeved sweater.

Bob Gregory.

As the season started only Watts and Squires failed to reproduce their pre-war form. Gover passed 100 wickets and played in The Oval Test against India. Fishlock, too, played in this Test and was picked for the MCC side that went to Australia, but there he played in only one Test, the last, at Sydney, and it was not a happy tour for him. In the match against Leicestershire at Leicester he scored a century in each innings and scored well throughout the year. Barling and Gregory scored heavily and Parker, though frequently indisposed, had an excellent all-round season.

Barling and Gregory shared a 3rd-wicket partnership of 267 against Nottinghamshire at The Oval. Gregory hit 164 and Barling was 233 not out. At Guildford, Tom Barling hit 172 against Oxford University, at that time the highest score hit by a Surrey batsman on that ground. It was not only Surrey batsmen who thrived, and one of the most remarkable events of the season came on 11 May, the day that first-class cricket returned to The Oval. The visitors were the Indian tourists, and with Alec Bedser in good form they were reduced to 205 for 9. The Indian nos 10 and 11 were Sarwate and Banerjee. They added 249, the highest last-wicket partnership to be recorded in England, with both batsmen hitting centuries, a unique achievement. Gregory hit a second-innings century for Surrey, but the tourists won by nine wickets.

Alec Bedser was the outstanding bowler of the year and began his Test career with 7 for 49 and 4 for 96 at Lord's. In May, he was in the Surrey side that beat MCC, also at Lord's. Jack Parker hit the County's first post-war century in that match and Alec Bedser,

Tom Barling (left) and Alec Bedser.

wicketless in the first innings when Alf Gover had taken 6 for 52, returned figures of 6 for 14 in 9.1 overs in the second. He bowled above medium pace, but Mobey stood up to him as he always liked his wicketkeepers to do. Alec finished the season with 128 wickets at 20.13 runs each, won his first Test caps and was chosen to go to Australia.

His brother Eric was less successful but he hit a maiden century, 101 against Hampshire in a non-Championship game at Kingston, where a week's cricket was arranged to augment the appeal fund. He took 25 wickets in all matches and showed signs of becoming a very useful all-rounder. Arthur McIntyre, a fine outfielder at this time, and Geoff Whittaker added 201 for Surrey's 5th wicket against Kent at The Oval, both men hitting maiden first-class centuries.

In the following match, against Combined Services at The Oval, Jim Laker and David Fletcher made their first-class debuts. Laker took 3 for 78 and 3 for 43, and Barling hit 134 not out, but the hero of the match was Bernard Constable who, batting at no.8 in a strong Services side, hit 107 before becoming one of Laker's victims.

1947

No declaration allowed for 60 minutes of innings

In 1947 Errol Holmes, at the age of forty-one, took over the captaincy and Surrey showed a welcome improvement, finishing sixth in the Championship. Yet those who

David Fletcher (left) and Errol Holmes.

regularly watched the side felt they should have done better. Too often Surrey gained a good position over their opponents and then failed to press home the advantage. Things went so badly early in the season that by the beginning of July Surrey stood third from bottom. Going to Bradford, they gained a handsome win over Yorkshire, and for a month they produced such excellent form that 5 of their 6 matches ended in victory. There followed another slump, culminating in two heavy defeats by Middlesex. When in May Fishlock was struck down with appendicitis, which kept him away for two months, Surrey gave a chance to Fletcher, who was then only twenty-two. Beginning with 65 and 46 against Somerset at The Oval, Fletcher hit 194 against Nottinghamshire in the Whitsuntide match at Trent Bridge, and at Bradford in July carried his bat through an innings against Yorkshire, scoring 127.

His innings at Trent Bridge was his highest score of the season and, as it transpired, his career. Replying to Nottinghamshire's 401, Surrey hit the highest score ever made against that county and the highest total ever made by Surrey away from The Oval, 706 for 4 declared. Fletcher shared stands of 155 for the 2nd wicket with Gregory, who scored 87, and 263 with Squires (154) for the 3rd. On the last morning, Surrey added 263 in two hours, Parker and Holmes putting on 247 in 110 minutes. Holmes reached his century in 90 minutes, finishing on 122 not out; Parker took 100 minutes to reach three figures on his way to 108 not out.

David Fletcher was never quite to live up to the role in which the press had cast him, but he was a fine player of sound judgement, common sense and a delightful range of

Jack Parker.

shots, particularly on the off. He revealed a neat style including a splendid off-drive, fielded well as he gained his experience of work in the deep, and was to prove a great asset to his county. He appeared for Players against Gentlemen at Lord's and Scarborough and finished a brilliant first season with an aggregate of 1,857.

Nine players hit hundreds during the season and twelve averaged over 25, but too often a breakdown occurred early in the innings.

Laker, a Yorkshireman, was found by Andy Sandham playing for Catford in London club cricket. Specialising in off-breaks, he headed the Surrey bowling averages as well as fielding smartly in the gully, and showing promise as a batsman. Sir Pelham Warner gave him a chance in the Hastings Festival and he was chosen for the MCC tour to the West Indies. He was one of England's few successes in a series in which they were outclassed.

The slow Oval wickets seldom encouraged bowlers, and again a tremendous amount of work fell upon Gover and Alec Bedser; Gover worked as tirelessly as ever and captured 109 wickets in Championship matches alone. Gregory hit 73 in a friendly match against Essex and 104 against MCC at Lord's. It was his 38th and last first-class century. Knee trouble worried Gregory and Watts, who underwent operations, and before the season ended both Gregory and Gover, after many years of splendid service, decided to retire. Alfred Gover's career statistics read thus:

Alf Gover.

SURREY

336 matches	2,170 runs at 9.35	1,437 wickets at 23.73

87 times he took 5 wickets in an innings and 15 times 10 wickets in a match

TESTS

4 matches	8 wickets at 44.87

ALL FIRST-CLASS MATCHES

362 matches	2,312 runs at 9.36	1,555 wickets at 23.63

95 times he took 5 wickets in an innings and 15 times 10 wickets in a match

He took 100 wickets in a season eight times, going on to 200 wickets twice

Squires and Parker were as good as ever, and Eric Bedser, being asked to bat in different places in the batting line-up quietly reached 1,000 runs for the first time. Arthur McIntyre took over from Mobey behind the stumps and not only proved himself a highly competent and exciting wicketkeeper but also gave a substance and panache to the lower-middle batting order which was the envy of other counties.

For Surrey, batting had never really been a problem, but at last a balanced attack began to take shape. Jim Laker grabbed the opportunity given to him and took 66 Championship wickets at 16.65 runs each. He took 79 wickets in all matches and was seventh in the national averages. Alec Bedser showed no falling off in form after the rigours of the series in Australia, and Eric Bedser's off-breaks began to bring reward. Squires' mixture of off-breaks and leg-breaks was also used to advantage at times. There was promise from the slow left-arm bowler Tony Lock, who was having considerable success in the Second XI, but then he had to leave to begin his national service.

The disappointments of the season were sharpened by the success of arch-rivals Middlesex from north of the Thames. When the sides met at The Oval in August, 47,000 paid for admission out of a total 54,000 spectators, and the gates were closed on a crowd of 30,000 on the Saturday. In this match Denis Compton scored 137 not out and took 12 wickets for 174 as Middlesex won by an innings and 11 runs.

As an appendix to the 1947 season, a trawl through the minutes of the club brought the following item to light:

> Burglars at The Oval were stripping lead from the roofs of the lower buildings on the ground. Due to the vigilance of the night-watchman the police caught the burglars. The Committee agreed to send a letter of thanks to the night-watchman, A.W. Spring, with a gift of £2. The lead that was recovered was sold for the sum of £368.

Was the night-watchman, A.W. Spring, the same as W.A. Spring who played 68 matches for Surrey from 1906 to 1913? He would have been sixty-seven years old at the time of the burglaries.

1948

Surrey suffered a setback at the beginning of 1948 when Tom Barling, after nine games, dropped out of the side and retired from first-class cricket. Matters were complicated further by David Fletcher's illness, which probably explained his loss of form, and by the inability of Errol Holmes to play in more than nine matches because of calls of business. Watts, too, had virtually dropped out of the side following an operation.

On top of these factors was an injury to McIntyre, which kept him out for five county matches, and Test calls that deprived the side of Alec Bedser and Jim Laker for long periods. Yet, in spite of all this, Surrey came very close to winning the Championship. The season began with defeat at the hands of MCC at Lord's, but the game had encouraging signs for Surrey: Stuart Surridge formed an impressive opening attack with Alec Bedser, Arthur McIntyre hit a delightful century in the first innings and Michael Barton scored an equally delightful 124 in the second.

This was Barton's first game for Surrey. He was a tall, elegant forceful batsman who had won his blue at Oxford in 1936 and had played for Norfolk with considerable success on a few occasions. His exciting debut for Surrey was followed by 4 and 15 against the Australians, 132 and 29 against Nottinghamshire, and 103 and 15 against Leicestershire.

Three centuries in his first 4 matches for the County naturally caused much excitement. It was always unlikely that Barton would be able to keep up such spectacular form, but he proved a valuable member of the side and reached his 1,000 runs for the season in all matches. This was a considerable achievement considering that the burden of captaincy was also thrust upon him when Holmes was out of the side, which was often. His natural charm and courteousness won him many friends; his willingness to seek and listen to advice from senior professionals won him many more. Barton's record was remarkable when one considers that his first-class experience before 1948 had been restricted to just three seasons with Oxford University more than ten years earlier from 1935 to 1937. However, he settled into the captaincy and carried out the job with ease, dignity and considerable success.

All-round strength provided the basis of Surrey's success in finishing runners-up, four points behind Glamorgan, in the County Championship, their highest position since 1925, when they had been second to Yorkshire. Between the Wars, from 1919 to 1925, Surrey finished no lower than fourth but from 1926 to 1939 they only finished above sixth once, being third in 1938. Although never heading the table, Surrey, after a moderate start, kept well within reach of the leaders. Attractive, enterprising cricket brought Surrey their excellent reward: 13 matches were won and 9 lost.

Eric Bedser's advance as a bowler was a tremendous boost to Surrey, particularly as his brother and Laker were missing for so many matches. It was McMahon, with 85 Championship wickets, who made the greatest advance of any of the Surrey players during the season and he was awarded his county cap. If at times his length was a little erratic, he spun the ball appreciably and was always testing batsmen. Surrey had discovered him playing club cricket for Southgate, and there were high hopes of him, but he struggled to repeat his good form in subsequent seasons and later moved to Somerset. In 1948 he easily headed the Surrey averages, and Laker excelled with both bat and ball. The amateur Stuart Surridge bowled with great zest and considerable profit. Another stalwart was Jack Parker. Stan Squires, in his benefit season, and Eric Bedser provided valuable all-round work, but there was no question that the team missed Gover. Happily, Fishlock returned to brilliant batting form. He scored a masterly 81 not out against the all-conquering Australians, carrying his bat through an innings of 141. At Leicester, when Surrey gained their first victory of the season, he shared a 4th-wicket partnership of 244 with Barton and went on to make 253 in six hours and twenty minutes. It was the highest score of his career.

Surrey's first real run of success did not come until the beginning of June. Rain restricted the match against Gloucestershire at The Oval to one day, and Surrey fell to the combined wiles of Cook and Goddard to be dismissed for 133. Crapp hit splendidly for Gloucestershire, and when he was sixth out with the visitors on 98 there were still thirty-three minutes remaining. The target was reduced to three runs in the last over with two wickets standing, but Laker bowled both Lambert and Cook as they attempted to make the winning hit, and Surrey won by 2 runs with 1 ball to spare. Laker finished with 8 for 55. There was victory at Ilford by four wickets, and then Lancashire came to The Oval. Surrey batted rather laboriously to reach 300 and, on a rain-affected pitch against McMahon and Eric Bedser, the visitors only just avoided the follow-on. Cranston, with

7 for 43, bowled Surrey out for 123 in their second innings so that Lancashire were left to make 248 to win. They were 119 for 5, but Winston Place was batting with complete composure, and he was now joined by Wharton in a stand of 97. With five wickets in hand, Lancashire needed only 32 to win. Eric Bedser then bowled Wharton and dismissed Nigel Howard and Cranston with the score on 232. Squires captured Roberts, and with Lancashire needing 2 runs to win, Hilton hit Eric Bedser high to long-off where Fishlock held a magnificent running catch. Eric Bedser had taken 5 for 75, and Surrey had won by 1 run.

The County could not string together a consistent run, but in August the Championship was very open. Most people would point to the innings defeat at Cardiff as being the reason that Surrey did not take the title, for Glamorgan were the eventual Champions, finishing four points ahead of Surrey. One more victory would have taken Surrey well clear, and Stuart Surridge maintained that one more win should have come in Stan Squires' benefit match against Middlesex. It was Surrey's penultimate match at The Oval, and the pitch was affected by rain. Surrey fell to Jack Young for 156, but they still gained a first innings lead of 38. Young then took seven wickets for the second time in the match as Surrey were bowled out for 103, although they were handicapped by the absence of Eric Bedser, who had been taken ill and could not bat. Middlesex needed 142 to win in as many minutes, but they lost half their side for 39 and looked beaten. Mann and Robins added an enterprising 62 and then Jim Sims came in at no.8 and hit 36 of the last 41 runs. He was twice dropped, and he and Laurie Gray, not noted for his batting, were allowed to score the last 10 runs. Surridge was very frustrated by the memory of the occasion:

> I didn't bowl a ball at them. I stood fuming at mid-off while Errol ignored me and it was too late when Alec was brought back. We should have won that game and the Championship. Surrey should have won the Championship every year after the war. They had the players. It was the close-to-the-wicket fielding that was the problem. It needs good fielding to turn good bowlers into great bowlers.

1949
Declaration rule rescinded

Holmes retired for the second and last time and was succeeded by Michael Barton, who had held the reins for much of 1948. Barton inherited a side that was changing in character. Of the pre-war stalwarts only Fishlock, Squires, Parker and Watts were left. Watts played just 5 games in 1949 before retiring, and the season was also to be the last for Stan Squires. Michael Barton acknowledged the immense debt that he owed to Stan Squires in his first season. Squires was a patient and kindly man who was so delighted he had been able to earn his living by playing the game for which he had the greatest passion that he set himself never to sully or demean his profession. He was liked and respected by all who played with or against him, and for young players he was a role model in style and attitude. His father had wanted him to follow a career in a City stockbrokers, but

Above: *Michael Barton.*

Right: *Stan Squires.*

Squires leapt at the chance Surrey offered him to leave the office for the cricket field. As a batsman he never appeared to hit the ball with any ferocity, for his technique was founded on the sureness of his timing and the suppleness of his wrists. With the exception of one post-war season he was a consistent scorer, and a useful wicket-taker with his variety of spin. In 1949, he scored 1,785 runs including 5 centuries, one of them, against Derbyshire, an innings of 210. Squires was a familiar and popular figure at The Oval and elsewhere, with his thick glasses (which for a period he forsook for contact lenses) making him instantly recognisable. There were those who believed that it was only the weakness of his eyesight which prevented him from becoming an England player, but his eyesight did not prevent him from scoring over 19,000 runs and hitting 37 centuries, nor from being a fine golfer and squash player. That he should be such a help to Barton and play so well in 1949 was a comfort to all who knew him, for in January 1950 he died of leukaemia at the age of forty-one. His death was much lamented, and he was greatly missed, but he is still remembered at The Oval with the greatest affection.

There were days when Surrey looked the best team in the County Championship and at one time they threatened to carry off the honours. Instead they fell from second place to fifth. Yet Surrey were the only side to beat each of the joint-Champions: they overcame Middlesex twice, and Yorkshire once. After taking twelve points from Hampshire, Warwickshire and Derbyshire in May, Surrey did not win another county engagement until July. Then they gained 7 victories in 10 matches, so that the middle of August found them third in the table, only sixteen points behind leaders Middlesex with 2 matches in hand. Afterwards they won only 1 of the 6 remaining games – that being at Lord's – a run which virtually deprived Middlesex of becoming outright Champions. Several factors contributed towards Surrey failing to realise their ambition. Generally they fared best when pitches helped bowlers and in this respect The Oval was not always the paradise the batsmen expected. Also, like other teams, Surrey were handicapped through injuries. One was to Alec Bedser, who strained a hip joint but still managed to take 110 wickets in 1005.2 overs. Another handicap was the lumbago that troubled Parker and made him, as Barton discovered, a reluctant bowler. Worst of all was the falling away of Fletcher and an injury to Whittaker. The latter was not an automatic choice at the beginning of the season, but he replaced Fletcher for the game at Northampton in May. Eric Bedser and Fishlock were out cheaply, but Whittaker launched a violent assault on the bowling. His innings of 148 included 9 sixes, 3 off successive balls from Broderick, and 8 fours, and in the second innings when he hit another 2 sixes he scored 89 not out. He had no success against Warwickshire or Derbyshire when Alec Bedser and Jack Parker bowled unchanged through Derbyshire's first innings and shot the visitors out for 52. Then, just as he was running into top form again, a knee injury kept him out of the side for what was the best part of half a season. Geoff Whittaker was destined always to be something of a fringe player dogged by wretched luck. This gave Bernard Constable a belated chance for a run in the County side. He hit his first 100 for Surrey in Watts's benefit match against Middlesex.

Constable and Squires added 191 for the 3rd wicket, and with Surridge taking 6 for 49 in the first Middlesex innings, Surrey gained their first victory over their close rivals since the war. It ended a run of 6 defeats. Again Fishlock was the leading run-maker.

Laurie Fishlock.

Despite being dismissed five times when in the nineties, he scored 2,426 runs in all matches. He hit 7 centuries, including 2 in the match against Nottinghamshire at Trent Bridge, and was the leading left-handed batsman in the country. Squires gave some excellent displays and Parker often excelled when forcing the pace. His 255 in the second New Zealand match was a gem of an innings. When Fishlock was going well and Squires was in form Surrey looked the best side in the Championship. Laker was gaining in maturity and was on the threshold of becoming one of the greatest off-break bowlers the world had known.

According to *Wisden*, 'Surrey owed much to Surridge, an amateur brimful with enthusiasm'. If one man leapt ahead more than any other, however, it was Eric Bedser. He had developed into one of the best offspinners in the country, with 88 wickets to prove it, and he hit 1,740 runs in all matches. This was all-round cricket of a quality that Surrey had not known since the days of Fender. Laker enjoyed spells when his off-breaks bewildered the best batsman and he regained his place in the England team. At the age of twenty, Lock showed considerable promise as a left-arm slow bowler and consequently McMahon, the Australian, who did so well the previous year, could not retain his place. Another all-round cricketer of the highest quality was Arthur McIntyre. Restored to full fitness, he scored 1,200 runs, and with 94 dismissals – 71 caught and 23 stumped – he came close to the very elusive and rarely performed wicketkeeper's 'double'. Only Yarnold of Worcestershire had more victims, and, as Barton pointed out,

McIntyre was still learning his trade in 1949. Barton, in his first full season as captain, did not do himself justice with the bat.

1950

County Championship increased to 28 matches

Squires was sorely missed in 1950, when his steadiness at no.3 would have been invaluable. Fishlock began in poor form, but soon found his touch and yet again passed 2,000 runs including 6 centuries to top the County averages. Parker, too, was forceful and the ever-reliable all-rounder. Constable held a regular place in the side and played some useful innings while McIntyre was good enough behind the stumps; he again finished second to Yarnold with 78 dismissals, and by scoring 1,105 runs won a Test cap and a trip to Australia. However, Whittaker, Fletcher, Eric Bedser, whose bowling deserted him totally, and Barton all found it hard to muster runs.

Weakness in the batting is apparent when it is pointed out that in 12 Championship innings the side failed to reach 200, with 53 in the disastrous first innings collapse against Kent at Blackheath their lowest total of the summer. Yet, in spite of these obvious flaws in the batting, Surrey finished level at the top of the Championship table, sharing top honours with Lancashire after an exciting struggle that lasted to the very end of the season. Between them Lancashire, with a negative approach at The Oval in August, and the weather tried hard to rob Surrey, but the success was fully deserved. Surrey nearly always played enterprising cricket, and they increased their championship victories from 11 in 1949 to 17, also halving the number of defeats. Moreover, 2 of the 4 reverses were suffered by very narrow margins, and 2 when the batsmen failed on turf that afforded marked assistance to bowlers. Had it not been for some unfortunate experiences during the month of July, Surrey might well have held undisputed sway at the head of affairs.

Whatever criticisms could be levelled against the batting, none could be aimed at an admirably varied attack. Alec Bedser and Surridge were potent with the new ball, and Parker did excellent work as first change. Laker was not yet fully recognised by the England selectors for the considerable bowler he was, despite his performance in the Test trial at Bradford. Playing for England against The Rest, he returned the amazing figures of 14 overs, 12 maidens, 2 runs, 8 wickets. He played in only one Test match against the West Indies and was not picked to go with Freddie Brown's side to Australia. Two of Laker's victims in the Test trial were Eric Bedser and Peter May. Lock was by now emerging as an exciting talent to create a formidable spin attack for the County. Eric Bedser had a poor season, taking only 13 very expensive wickets in all matches and scoring only 731 Championship runs, but 2 centuries outside the Championship took him past the 1,000 runs mark and lifted his average.

Laker bowled his off-breaks with skill and immaculate length. He included among his chief performances 12 wickets for 86 against Gloucestershire at Bristol and 10 for 98 in the corresponding match at The Oval; 11 for 97 against Worcestershire at Worcester and 10 for 89 against Essex at Chelmsford. He easily headed the Surrey averages. Alec Bedser, despite Test match calls, still took 90 wickets in Championship games and on rain-damaged turf proved a real menace, as when he dismissed six Glamorgan batsmen for 18 runs at The Oval. Lock supplemented his excellent bowling with first-class fielding close to the wicket, and McMahon, of similar style, found few chances of gaining a place in the side. Parker, too, did some good things, his 7 wickets for 54 in the Kent match at Blackheath saving Surrey from being even more overshadowed. Stuart Surridge bowled with fire and effect after a moderate start to the season, also bringing off a number of splendid slip catches which meant a great deal to the side. Two victories and two draws in the first wet weeks of the season gave little indication of what was to come and defeat at The Oval by Essex seemed to hint at a familiar pattern.

Surrey suffered another defeat at the beginning of July when they lost to Yorkshire at Sheffield by 5 runs. Their defeats, like many of their victories, tended to be by the narrowest of margins, and the game at Sheffield underlined Surrey's perversity. This win took Yorkshire to the top of the table above Lancashire and Warwickshire with Surrey, who had played one game less, in fourth place. Victories over Warwickshire, Kent, Gloucestershire twice, and Worcestershire maintained Surrey's challenge, but they also suffered 2 more defeats, by Kent at Blackheath and Yorkshire at The Oval. Then came victory over Middlesex at The Oval in Fishlock's benefit match, and Surrey were joint second with Yorkshire, twenty points behind Lancashire, although Surrey had now played 1 game more than their rivals.

The victory over Middlesex had been a wonderful benefit for the faithful and consistent Fishlock. The beneficiary himself hit 111, McIntyre hit 85, and Surrey made 401. The match had added interest because it marked the return of Denis Compton to first-class cricket after an absence of two months because of a knee injury. He did not disappoint and made 115 not out, but Middlesex were all out for 229 and had to follow on. In their second innings, with Laker taking 8 for 57, they were all out for 199 and Surrey won by ten wickets. Appropriately, Fishlock made the winning hit. A crowd of 48,530 people watched the three days' cricket. These were still heady days, but for many counties these were drawing to a close.

Peter May was in his first year at Cambridge and an innings of 227 not out for the university against Hampshire and several other stylish knocks had quickly earned him a good reputation. Although born in Berkshire, he had a residential qualification for Surrey having been at school at Charterhouse. Barton was aware of this and invited May to play for the County after the varsity match. He was still short of his twenty-first birthday. He first joined the Surrey side in July for the match at Bristol. Fishlock and Constable were the batting heroes, and Laker, with 8 for 45 in the first innings, the bowling hero as Surrey won by five wickets. May scored 1 and 1, but his presence in the next few weeks was to be decisive in bringing a share of the Championship to The Oval. At Worcester he hit 118, and it was this game which started Surrey's late run of good results. Lancashire arrived at The Oval on 26 August needing only to lead on the first innings and claim the four points to win the title. It should have been an exciting encounter, but it turned out to be a dour affair, often negative. Lancashire lost two quick wickets which determined their policy for the rest of the match.

The Red Rose County ground their way to 221 at less than 2 runs per over. Surrey took a first innings lead of 66 and the four vital points. Their hero was unquestionably

Action from Surrey v. Lancashire, 1950. Above: *Cyril Washbrook is bowled by Stuart Surridge.* Below: *Michael Barton appeals from the slips as Arthur McIntyre attempts to catch Jack Ikin.*

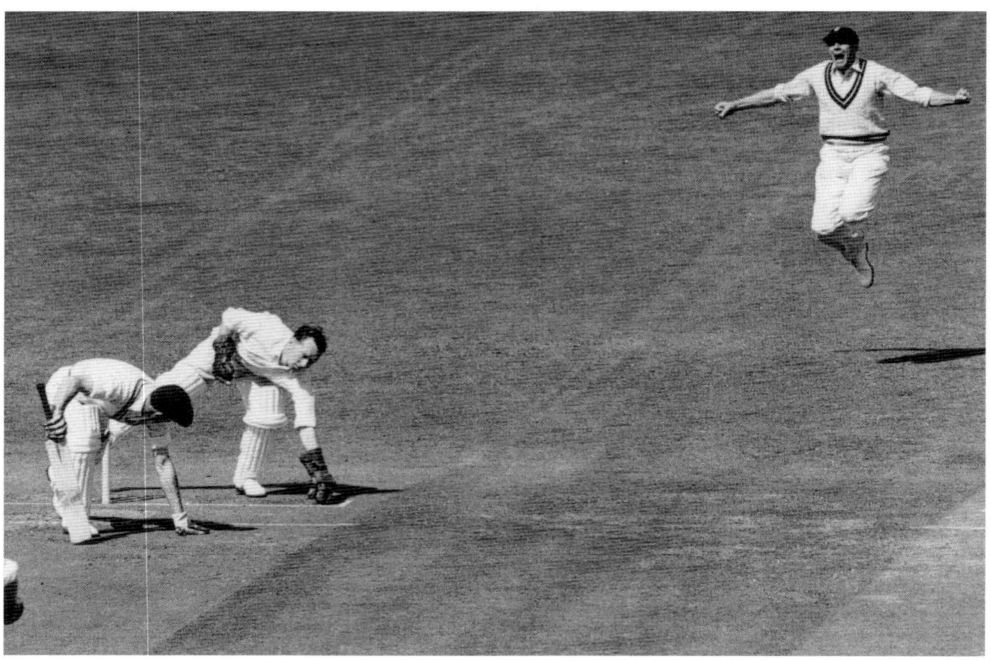

Peter May, and his innings of 92 in five hours was rewarded with a County cap. To be awarded one's cap after only 11 matches was quite unusual, but May's was a mature talent, and the part that he played in the successful closing matches of the season was recognised by all. He himself said how much he owed to Laurie Fishlock and Jack Parker. They advised him and guided him through partnerships and were a constant source of help and inspiration. To their shame, Lancashire made no attempt to win the match. They concentrated solely on preventing Surrey from winning, and, ultimately paid the price. Lancashire had now completed their programme, and Surrey could now earn a share of the title by beating Leicestershire at The Oval in their last game. The great fear was the weather, and it was a fear that was justified. The opening days saw two interruptions for rain and play ended eighty minutes early. The start was delayed for three-and-a-half hours on the second day so it was necessary for Surrey to waste no time in the field or at the crease. Alec Bedser bowled magnificently: at a little above medium pace, he bowled inswingers to a leg trap and the Leicestershire batsmen floundered. Nine wickets were down for 68. Walsh adopted the bold approach and hit 41 and the last wicket realised 45.

Fishlock was quickly on the offensive, and although Walsh accounted for Fletcher and May, Surrey took the lead with only two wickets down. Fishlock and Constable put on 101, and Fishlock hit 11 fours in his 108, which was made in under three hours. With the weather always a threat, the later batsmen went for quick runs and lost their wickets in the fray. On a worn wicket, made more difficult by rain, Leicestershire had little hope

The 1950 Surrey team. From left to right, back row: G.A.R. Lock, A.J. McIntyre, J.W. McMahon, J.C. Laker, E.A. Bedser, G.J. Whittaker, D.G.W. Fletcher, B. Constable. Front row: J.F. Parker, W.S. Surridge, M.R. Barton, L.B. Fishlock, A.V. Bedser.

of survival against a Surrey attack which was capable of exploiting such conditions. By just avoiding an innings defeat Surrey had to bat again to score 2 runs and Barton hit the boundary, which gave his side a share of the County Championship.

There was a large and enthusiastic crowd, and there were scenes of much delight at the end of the game. As Peter May said many years later:

> To a county which had not known such success for thirty-six years, half a Championship was glory indeed. For most of the next decade a halved Championship would have been something of a disappointment but none of us in 1950 could have guessed what was to follow and we were far from blasé then.

1951

Surrey fielded almost the same side in 1951 but the continuing frailties in batting cost them dearly. A poor start to the season could not be rectified, and the County were never in contention for the title. *The Cricketer* reported:

> At the beginning of the season Surrey beat a good MCC side by an innings, Laker having a match analysis of 10 for 34. After losing on the first innings to Lancashire they went to Nottingham and won by ten wickets, and then came a slump, 4 matches being lost in succession, to Lancashire at Old Trafford then at Glamorgan, Somerset and Essex at The Oval. This setback was too big a handicap to overcome and in the end the county dropped from equal first place to sixth. In a disastrous spell in May at The Oval, Alec Bedser was unable to play owing to ill health, and then the Test matches claimed him, so that he played in only 15 Championship games. As Bedser had probably never bowled better in his live than last season this was a tremendous handicap.

In the 'Notes by the Editor' in the 1952 *Wisden* Norman Preston wrote:

> If we could look ahead say ten or twenty years I wonder where Alec Bedser would stand in a list of great bowlers. All his first-class cricket has been played since the war and already his total number of wickets in Test matches, 162, have been surpassed by only two men. C.V. Grimmett 216, and S.F. Barnes 189. In the course of one year, September 1950 to August 1951, Bedser claimed 62 Test victims in twelve matches. In Australia his haul was 30, then he took two in New Zealand and returning to England again he took 30 wickets in the Tests against South Africa. Bedser has the gift of rising to the occasion because of the care and seriousness which he attaches to the importance of playing for England. Not even the most tempting invitation would induce him to break his self-appointed rule of bed by ten o'clock throughout a Test match.

This was in a time before central contracts for international players had ever been thought of and Test match players were required to return and play for their counties the day after each Test match. The counties did not operate a squad system and the calls by the national side seriously affected the county teams. In 1951 Peter May played 2 matches, Jim Laker 2 and Alec Bedser 5.

At The Oval, in the final Test match against South Africa, Laker took 10 wickets for 119 and virtually won the game for England after they had trailed by 8 on the first innings. Throughout the season Peter May was in magnificent form, hitting 2,339 runs in all matches. Topping the national averages, he won his first Test caps and hit his first Test century, but his advance to the highest level meant that he could play in only 7 Championship matches. The fact that he hit 614 runs in those games with a century in each innings against Essex at Southend and a century against Middlesex at Lord's emphasises how much his vital late-season contributions were missed. He averaged 76.75 in 10 innings for Surrey, and second to him was Whittaker with 37.27.

Whittaker regained a regular place in the side and became a renowned six-hitter. He hit 185 not out against Kent at The Oval, 'yet', as *Wisden* said, 'one felt, despite his thirty-two 6s he could do better with only a little discretion and become one of the big personalities that modern cricket badly needs'.

Brazier, Clark and Fletcher could not command regular places in the side, but Eric Bedser rediscovered his bowling form, taking 61 wickets, and also scored over 1,000 runs. When one considers that he was rarely given the chance to bowl on a pitch that would have given him great assistance (for Laker, naturally, and the ever-improving Lock had first call) Eric Bedser's quality as an off-break bowler can be measured. He was also pressed into service as an opener, for Surrey struggled to find a regular pair as Fishlock, after the first weeks of the season, dropped to no.4 in the order.

Fishlock showed little loss of skill even if he did not score so prolifically as in the past, but Parker fell away a little and was more reluctant than ever to bowl. Perhaps one of the problems that beset Surrey and upset the rhythm of the side was the constant rearrangement of the batting order. Constable was luckier than most, finding himself regularly at no.3 until he lost form late in the season. He responded well and scored consistently early on. However, there was no reliable run-getter until May joined the side in July.

In July a special event happened at The Oval when Len Hutton scored his 100th century playing for his native Yorkshire against Surrey. It was an appropriate venue as his highest-ever score of 364 was made at The Oval for England against Australia in 1938 and is now commemorated by a unique feature, a brick sculpture just inside the Hobbs Gates. (It should be said, however, that members and onlookers have commented that this sculpture tends to overshadow the Hobbs Gates, erected to commemorate the career of Surrey's greatest player, 'The Master', whose life is celebrated each year on his birthday, 16 December at 'The Master's Lunch' held in The Oval pavilion.) Hutton remained a good friend to the club when he retired to live in Surrey at the end of his career.

Michael Barton scored more than 1,000 runs in the season and always led the side with a quiet efficiency, but he decided that the time had come for him to stand down as captain. He could look back on his three-year term with pride and satisfaction. He left Surrey a tidier and more efficient side than he found it, and he won many friends with his attitude to the game and to those who played under him. The Committee named Stuart Surridge as Barton's successor.

The Len Hutton Wall overshadowing the Hobbs Gates.

THREE
1952-1956

In 1937 Stuart Surridge, the grandson of the Stuart Surridge who made cricket bats and violins and who had set up his own business in the 1870s, first played for the County Second XI. He made his debut for the full County side in June 1947 when Alec Bedser was on Test match duty. In 1948 he took the new ball when Bedser was away and his performances were good enough to secure him a permanent place in the side.

When Michael Barton retired at the end of the 1951 season Surridge was invited to take control of the side, which at the time had an abundance of talent yet seemed unable to produce consistent results. When the captaincy was confirmed it is said he wrote in his diary: 'Surrey will win the Championship within the next five years.' In the event they won it in each of the next seven years, though only five were under his leadership.

It is for his captaincy that he will always be remembered, even though as a cricketer he was demonstrably more than an average performer, especially as a close-to-the-wicket fielder. Like an earlier Surrey captain, Percy Fender, he controlled every game and several of his decisions seemed eccentric at the time but when proved correct only added to his reputation as a forceful and inspirational leader. It must be said that for much of the time he was captain Surrey were not the most popular side in the County Championship but then how many winning teams are? At times the aggression of the field placing of the close fielders was greater than many felt to be acceptable. Perhaps this was one reason why he was never chosen to captain any representative sides when he had so much to offer.

To win the County Championship for the five seasons of his captaincy is an achievement that is never likely to be equalled. He was fortunate in having around him bowlers of the calibre of Alec Bedser, Laker, Lock and Loader and batsmen such as May and Barrington, so technical ability was always available. The bowling was beyond reproach, and it is worth considering the figures of the leading bowlers over this five-year period in all Surrey matches:

	OVERS	MAIDENS	RUNS	WICKETS	AVERAGE	STRIKE RATE
G.A.R. Lock	4,513.5	1,766	8,746	649	13.47	6.95
J.C. Laker	4,425.5	1,476	9,124	557	16.38	7.94
A.V. Bedser	4,391.2	1,221	9,195	541	16.99	8.11
P.J. Loader	2,878.5	691	6,592	410	16.07	7.02
E.A. Bedser	2,483.4	780	5,292	240	22.05	10.34
W.S. Surridge	2,266.1	479	5,867	209	28.07	10.84
TOTAL	**20,959.4**	**6,413**	**44,816**	**2,606**	**17.19**	**8.04**

Surridge leads out Surrey.

These are impressive figures when one realises that they represent the work of six men playing in the same team at the same time. They accounted for 92.1% of the wickets and conceded 88.1% of the runs. During this period Surrey used only 17 bowlers with McMahon taking 63 wickets in the two seasons of 1952 and 1953, Clark taking 65 wickets and Cox 50 wickets in the five-year period.

The team record of Surrey during the years of Surridge's reign should also be studied:

YEAR	P	W	L	D	PTS	WINNING MARGIN
1952	28	20	3	5	256	32 pts
1953	28	13	4	10	184	16 pts
1954	28	15	3	8	208	22 pts
1955	28	23	5	0	284	16 pts
1956	28	15	5	6	200	20 pts

The system of scoring during this period was twelve points for a win and four points for a first-innings lead in a match drawn or lost. Surrey had one match in 1953, two in 1954 and two in 1956 in which no result was reached because of bad weather. Surridge's approach to a match was simple. He went for victory from the very first ball that was bowled. The side engaged in constant fielding practice before the season, and everyone adopted the attitude from the start of the season that every game was a vital one.

As has been shown so often, mere ability is not enough and a leader is needed to direct such undoubted talents. This was Stuart Surridge's achievement and in those five years

Surrey won 86 and lost only 20 of the 139 Championship matches they played. Always one of the team, he travelled with his players and stayed at the same hotel, a style that was none too popular with the County Committee. If he was hard on his players on the field, all was forgotten at the close of play. The ability to fashion Surrey's diverse and flowing abilities into one effective force proved to be the rare gift of a natural leader. The Surridge approach was dynamic. Others have achieved this for a season but Surridge did it for five years in a row and, what is more, the side he left behind was as strong, if not stronger, than when he started.

Surridge asserts that he learned an early lesson from Brian Sellers when Surrey were playing against Yorkshire and had been on top for most of the match only to lose in the end. He spoke to Sellers after the match and said, with some despair and naivety, 'We were winning but you turned it round on us.' Sellers looked at him and replied, 'Remember one thing, lad. It's no bloody good being second.' It was a lesson he never forgot when he became captain, and he retained the greatest admiration for Sellers: 'He was tough, he was hard, he stood no nonsense, and he led by example.'

Fielding was the greatest attribute that Surridge brought to the side as a player. The standards became almost unreal. Modern fielding is accepted as the last word in competence and athleticism but Surrey under Surridge must still be the ultimate yardstick in respect of the close positions. Without a helmet in sight Surrey supported their unmatched attack with zeal and efficiency and many an unfortunate batsman, knowing

Surrey in the field, Surrey v. *Worcestershire, 30 June 1955.*

his first half-mistake would be his last, must have thought the natural laws of justice were being roughly overthrown. Surridge had hands like buckets, a fearless disposition and he would never ask any fielder to do what he was not prepared to do himself. *Wisden* said of him after his first season in charge: 'His ability in this direction resulting in the acceptance of some catches which might be regarded by many cricketers as bordering upon the impossible, at times exerted an unnerving effect upon opposing batsmen and paved the way to more than one of the twenty victories.' But it was not just his own fielding which became supercharged, for he infected and demanded more of those around him. Critics had described the Surrey fielding in the early 1950s as efficient or satisfactory; Surridge thought it was awful, and that there was a lack of enthusiasm. He insisted on practice and concentration in this aspect of the game, and suddenly players found they were enjoying their cricket more. For the rest of the decade sides felt that they were being attacked by Surrey in the field, and many succumbed to the pressure.

If there was any question about Surridge when he took over, it was that some of his players felt he had too little experience. Did he have any problems? 'Not after the first two matches', he says. It did not take people long to know who was in charge at Surrey. He had undertaken the job only on the understanding that he had complete control of the team. Sandham was coach and dealt with the Second XI. Surridge respected Sandham's experience and perception; when he needed replacements in the first team he would simply say to Sandham that he wanted a batsman or a seam bowler and would know that Sandham would send the right men for the job.

In concentrating on his captaincy and his fielding, one runs the risk of neglecting Surridge's fine qualities as a player. He stood nearly 6ft 2in and used his height to great advantage in his fast medium bowling. He took 78 wickets in 1952 and he would have taken more in the next four years had he bowled more himself. He kept the side happy by always giving his main bowlers a chance to bowl when the wickets were giving them help or there was a chance of easy victims. When the wicket was good and the going was hard Surridge would bowl and often throw up a few long hops or full tosses in an effort to break the stand. He never claimed anything cheap for himself.

As a batsman, his appearance coming down the pavilion steps always brought cheers of delight and anticipation. The highest score he ever made was 87 against Glamorgan in 1951, but he frightened a few bowlers and fielders over the years with the violence of his batting and he could turn the course of a game. When Surrey were making their challenge for the title in August 1950, they travelled to Hastings and faced a total of 404, which Sussex had made in good time. Surrey were 141 for 8 and looked doomed for the follow-on when Surridge joined Constable. They added 86, of which Surridge made 55 with some ferocious hits. The follow-on was saved, and Surrey went on to win the match.

As a captain Surridge established a record which, one suspects, is likely to last for a very long time, even forever. Lancashire had won the title in the three years when Leonard Green was captain in the 1920s, and Alfred Shaw led Nottinghamshire to four titles in his four years as captain in the 1880s, when the Championship was not on an official basis, but none had a record that challenged that of Stuart Surridge.

When Surrey took the title in 1952, Roy Webber in the old *Playfair Cricket Annual* welcomed the achievement with a succinct judgement:

> By common consent, the best side won the Championship. Surrey had probably the strongest and almost certainly the best balanced attack in the history of the club; the close fielding was brilliant; and the virile batting was equal to all demands. Apart from these things, there was that intangible factor, a true team spirit, which sprang from the inspiration and boisterous precept of Surridge in his first year of command.

The comment on the 'virile batting' is particularly interesting in that it was Surrey's batting which was to be most often criticised over the next four years. It was not possible to be kind about Surrey's batting, as it was so remarkably fallible for a Championship-winning side, and it changed little in the five years of Surridge's leadership except that May was able to play more often. Barrington, Stewart and, for a time, Subba Row took over from Fishlock, Parker and Whittaker, which hardly suggests a weakening. Surridge's attitude was straightforward and he said: 'If you get 200, the other side has got to get 201. We didn't get a lot of runs. We didn't need to. We got enough. Besides, if we had got many more, I wouldn't have known when to declare.'

In 1952, the early season running was made by Middlesex, although Surrey quickly showed their promise by beating the Indian tourists and Gloucestershire in low-scoring matches. Then came a victory of quality against Sussex at The Oval. John Langridge and Jim Parks hit centuries, and Sussex declared at 365 for 9. Fletcher and Eric Bedser began Surrey's reply with a partnership of 162. Bedser made 73, and Fletcher hit 116 in two-and-three-quarter hours. Constable, McIntyre and Whittaker all hit briskly, and Surridge declared at 432 for 7. At lunchtime on the last day a draw looked certain, but in the afternoon, Lock had a spell of 4 for 8, the last 6 Sussex wickets fell for 18 runs, and, needing 70 to win, Surrey hit off the runs in under 20 overs. These early-season victories caused no great surprise, but what did draw attention was the quality of the Surrey fielding and catching. A draw at Ilford was followed by victory at Rushden, an uncommon venue for a Northamptonshire home match. The victory was founded on another splendid opening partnership of 94 between Fletcher and Eric Bedser, after which the pitch crumbled. Clark, at no.4, was left stranded on 26 not out, and Surrey were out for 182. Freddie Brown took 6 for 42 against his old county, but it proved to be insufficient. Alec Bedser took eight wickets and Laker nine in the match, and Surrey won by 132 runs. The outstanding batting performance came from Tom Clark, who, on a wicket giving the bowlers every assistance, hit 92 in the second innings. He was a polished player, especially strong on the on-side, but by no means limited in his repertoire of shots. He had worked as a labourer in the winter in order to lose weight and to get himself fit for the season. He was broad-shouldered and dependable, and he epitomised the Surrey spirit and attitude. Surridge rated him very highly, and the pity was that Clark was so often hampered by hip trouble.

Wins over Warwickshire at The Oval, Nottinghamshire at Trent Bridge and a draw in a rain-marred match with Leicestershire at The Oval were followed by an innings victory over Gloucestershire inside two days at Bristol. This win brought Surrey's record to 6 wins and 2 draws in 8 matches and took them eight points clear of Middlesex at the top of the table. Middlesex were now to fade from the scene, and the main challenge was to come from Yorkshire. The win at Trent Bridge in the first days of June was significant in that Clark and Parker added 165 for the 5th wicket, and Parker hit his last century for the County. Equally significant was the fact that, in an effort to find the ideal preparation for the Trent Bridge pitch, the Nottinghamshire committee had ordered that the heavy roller should not be used on the strip for a week before the match. The result was that Alec Bedser was able to bowl, in the second innings, on a wicket that suited his fast medium pace to perfection, and he took 6 for 23 as Nottinghamshire were dismissed for 52 in 90 minutes, their last five wickets falling for the addition of 2 runs.

In the drawn game against Leicestershire, Eric Bedser and Laurie Fishlock both hit centuries in the second innings and added 186 in under three hours for the 3rd wicket. It was Fishlock's fiftieth and last hundred for Surrey. By 24 June, still unbeaten, Surrey had increased their lead to twenty points. They had beaten Essex at The Oval for the first time since 1938, drawn at Llanelli and won at Blackheath as well as beating Cambridge University by an innings at The Oval. In the match against Glamorgan, Surrey were bowled out for 248, and the home side made 257. This was the first time in the season that a side had taken any points off Surrey, and it was the only time in the season when a full-strength Surrey side surrendered points to the opposition. Even without Laker and Alec Bedser, they overwhelmed Kent at Blackheath. Their close catching was exhilarating, and Jack Parker established a County record which was to last five years when he held seven catches at slip.

Clark and Fletcher hit centuries in the match against Cambridge University, but in the absence of Laker and Alec Bedser, Dennis Cox, fast right-arm medium, took 7 for 22, the best performance of his career. 'Cox', says Surridge, 'was a fine cricketer, but we were so strong that he spent his time in the Second XI and grew old with the rest of the team.' Fletcher had played one of his finest innings when, trailing by fourteen on the first innings, Surrey had been asked to make 275 to beat Hampshire at Guildford. They had five hours in which to get the runs, and they won with thirty-five minutes to spare and five wickets in hand, Fletcher hitting 123. Against Somerset at The Oval at the beginning of July, Bernard Constable hit 205 not out, the highest of the 27 centuries in his first-class career, and Surrey won by an innings and 180 runs.

When considering Surrey cricket, studded with great names such as Hobbs, Hayward, Hitch, Sandham, Laker, Lock and May, the name of Bernard Constable is rarely mentioned. But in the opinion of Stuart Surridge, and for many that watched those years of glory, he was the great unsung hero of Surrey cricket. He was a neat, compact, nimble batsman who could use his feet well to move down the wicket to either attack or defend. He was slightly built, and he moved so lightly on his feet as to suggest a dancer. It was his grace of movement that made his cover fielding a delight to watch. 'He knew', says Surridge, 'exactly where to position himself. He had studied batsmen and knew their strokes so that he positioned himself at just the spot where he knew that they would hit the ball. He was a marvellous fielder.'

The match against Yorkshire at The Oval in July naturally drew much attention, and there was even some angry crowd reaction. In the first innings Yorkshire made 137 and Surrey 285. When Yorkshire batted again Len Hutton hit a century, but on the last morning, intent only on saving the game, they batted dourly, and there was some barracking from the crowd. Umpire Price reacted by sitting down and refusing to allow the match to continue until the barracking stopped. Eventually, Surrey were left to make

Bernard Constable.

102 in 100 minutes, and Fishlock and Eric Bedser gave the side a rollicking start, lashing the ball to all parts of the field. Gordon Ross told how Fishlock had arrived late in the morning, believing the game started at 11.30 a.m. and not 11.00 a.m. He batted splendidly as Surrey sought victory, but appeared to throw his wicket away unnecessarily. He came panting into the dressing room and offered the view that Surrey could still get the runs even though there were only ten minutes left. There were, in fact, forty minutes remaining – again, his timing was half an hour adrift. Surrey won in fine style.

There was a comfortable win at Kidderminster and then a quite stunning victory over Kent at The Oval. Peter May was now in the side, and he hit 124 as Surrey took a first innings lead of 133. Godfrey Evans, in swashbuckling form, and a more sedate O'Linn brought Kent back into the game and Murray-Wood's declaration left Surrey the task of scoring 188 to win in 92 minutes. It was a declaration which at least gave Kent an equal chance of victory if Surrey accepted the challenge. All knew by now, of course, that Surrey would accept any challenge. *Wisden* told how: 'Although wickets fell frequently, Surrey pursued their aggression to the end without regard to the risk of defeat. They required 128 in the last hour, 50 with seventeen minutes to go, and 26 when the eighth wicket went eight minutes from time. Surridge, the next man in, scored from 8 of the 9 balls bowled to him before he slashed Dovey over extra cover for the final stroke. Both he and Clark were missed in the deep. With less than a minute left and the game still open, Kent raced into position and Dovey hurriedly bowled the first ball to ensure another over. So marked was the tension in the final minutes that the crowd rose to their feet and a burst of cheering broke out as Surridge made the winning hit with the clock pointing to a shade after half-past six. This was in the days when matches were played to specific time limits with no consideration of the number of overs to be bowled.

This famous victory was followed by the first defeat of the season as Surrey, without May, Lock, Laker and Alec Bedser, went down to Lancashire. Four players were called up for the Gentlemen *v.* Players match at Lord's. Betty Surridge recalls that Stuart made a request to the MCC that fewer players be taken from Surrey for this match only to be informed that it was a great honour to be selected for this match. His response was: 'Rubbish, it is just a bun fight. Anyway, the fixture will have disappeared from the calendar within ten years.' The last Gentleman *v.* Players match was played in 1962. Although Stuart Surridge lost this argument it was of no consequence as Surrey beat Sussex at Horsham by 64 runs. When the Surrey players returned from Lord's and subsequent Test match duty, Nottinghamshire were routed in poor weather. They were bowled out for 84 and 51, and Surrey made 215 for 4. It was an historic match in that Alec Bedser took his 1,000th first-class wicket and took 8 for 18 in the second innings, which was to remain the best bowling performance of his career. After beating Middlesex at The Oval, Surrey lost twice in a week, to Warwickshire and to Yorkshire, and there were suddenly suspicions that they might crack, although they still held a lead of twenty-eight points. There was no loss of nerve. In August, Derbyshire visited The Oval for the deciding game. Rain delayed the start until 3.00 p.m. and then Eric Bedser and Fletcher, a fine opening pair throughout the summer, began Surrey's innings with an invaluable partnership of 42. After that wickets began to tumble on the damp turf and Surrey were out for 156. Then came Lock. He caught Hamer off Surridge before a run was scored, took two more stunning catches and produced a bowling spell which gave him 6 for 16 in 10.3 overs. Surrey made 258 for 4 in their second innings, and Surridge gave his bowlers the last day in which to bowl out Derbyshire. They needed only one session. When Alec Bedser bowled Smith to claim his fourth wicket Derbyshire were out for 95, and Surrey were Champions.

A large crowd gathered in front of the pavilion and called for Surridge and his team. Surridge's acceptance speech was typically modest and honest. He pointed to his teammates below and said to the crowd: 'There are the boys. What more can I say?'

The season saw the end of the careers of Parker and Fishlock. Surridge tried to persuade them to stay on: 'They were wonderful pros', he said. But they were both delighted and thrilled by what had happened and felt it was best to leave the game then and there. They were probably right to end on such a high note. Fishlock's career statistics read thus:

SURREY		
347 matches	22,138 runs at 40.47	50 centuries
TESTS		
4 matches	47 runs at 11.75	
ALL FIRST-CLASS MATCHES		
417 matches	25,376 runs at 39.34	56 centuries

Surrey had amassed more points than any side since the war. For eight Championship matches they had been deprived of their leading players, yet they had gained fifty-two points from those matches, and they had not lost a match when they were at full strength.

At the beginning of the year, at a dinner given by the Cricket Writers' Club for the Indian tourists, Lord Cobham had urged people to remember that cricket was a game to be played for fun. Surrey had answered him by bringing joy back into cricket. The Oval was an exciting and bubbling place to be.

1953

Parker and Fishlock were missed at the start of 1953 when, on occasions, an old head would have been an advantage. May, now regularly available, was slow to find his form. The Australians gave him a hard time when they beat Surrey at The Oval in two days at the beginning of May and, unwisely in the view of many, he was left out of the England side after the First Test. He reasserted himself later in the season and was recalled for the deciding Test at The Oval and played an important part in England regaining the Ashes for the first time in twenty years.

There was no indication in the opening county game of the season that Surrey would have any difficulty holding on to the title. On Saturday 16 May, Warwickshire came to The Oval to begin their county programme. They had won the Championship in 1951 and were still a talented side. The match was all over in a day and the Surrey members rose as one when the triumphant Surrey side walked off the field. It was the first time since 1857 that a first-class game at The Oval had been completed in one day. In fairness the conditions were treacherous for batsmen, but Warwickshire were subjected to unrelentingly aggressive bowling of the highest quality, supported by dynamic fielding. Alec Bedser bowled unchanged throughout the match and his first innings return of 8 for 18 equalled his best in first-class cricket. Intelligently adapting to the conditions because he could not gain a foothold on the damp turf, he reduced his pace and attacked the leg stump. The hawks in the leg trap did the rest. It was a wonderful way for Alec Bedser to start his benefit year.

Surrey lost only two wickets in passing Warwickshire's meagre score of 45, but they slipped to 81 for 7, and it was the aggression of Surridge, Laker and Lock that raised them to 146. Surridge's 19 included 3 sixes in 4 balls off Hollies, and Lock was hitting fiercely when he was hit above the eye by a ball from Grove and taken to hospital. Laker joined Alec Bedser in the attack when Warwickshire batted again, and after tea he performed a hat-trick. It was the first of three hat-tricks to be performed by Surrey in 1953. The game had not started until midday, but with Warwickshire dismissed in seventy minutes, it was all over ten minutes into the extra half-hour. The day saw 29 wickets fall and 243 runs scored, and Surrey won by an innings and 49 runs. For Alec Bedser this match, like so many others, was a triumph. He was a giant among bowlers, and for the first six or seven years after the Second World War, until the arrival of Statham, Trueman and Tyson, he was the beginning, middle and end of the England attack. A large and heavy man, yet quick and agile, he moved in smoothly off a run that was never exaggeratedly long and

Alec Bedser.

hustled the ball on to the batsman with an action which was precise and economic. He was in the great tradition of S.F. Barnes and Maurice Tate, fast-medium, relentlessly accurate with an ability to move the ball sharply both ways and with a capacity for work which would shame many who play the game today. In all that he did, and has done, there is a workmanlike honesty. He was blunt, straightforward, a jealous respecter of tradition and conservative by habit and nature. He was never a man who needed encouragement or inducement to be loyal or to give of his best, for such qualities and characteristics were natural to him. The problem is that because he gave of himself so naturally and unstintingly it was possible for spectators and commentators to take him for granted, for it appeared that he could go on bowling for ever. Sometimes he did! But to accept him as a bowling machine, grinding out over after over, smoothly and precisely, and amassing hundreds of wickets year after year is to overlook the man's inventiveness, variety and subtle command of his art. Bedser took 1,924 wickets in first-class cricket and he bowled for much of his time on wickets that were death to most bowlers. He troubled Bradman and he troubled Compton and Hutton, and there are not too many who did that.

It was not likely that such form as was shown in the sensational one-day win over Warwickshire could be sustained, but Surrey led the tables at the end of May in spite of injuries and representative calls. Reserves like wicketkeeper Kirby, who played in glasses, and left-arm spinner McMahon, who had lost his place to Lock, did well when given the chance, as did Ron Pratt, a left-handed batsman and off-break bowler who was also a brilliant fielder in the Surrey mode of the time. Another to sparkle on a few occasions was Alan Brazier, a forceful right-handed batsman whom Sandham recommended to Surridge as worthy of a regular first-team place. He scored prolifically in the Second XI but as a first-team player he never really found his touch and he later moved to Kent.

Luckier were two other reserves, Ken Barrington and Peter Loader. Barrington made a quietly impressive entry into first-class cricket, playing in 9 matches, scoring over 200 runs and hitting 81 in the innings victory over Worcestershire at The Oval in mid-July. He was a young man very eager to hit the ball hard. Loader's appearances as understudy to Alec Bedser were of a more dramatic nature. At Edgbaston he took 8 for 72 and 4 for 45, but Surrey lost, and in the next match, at Blackheath, he took 9 for 28 and 4 for 85, and the game was drawn. He bowled magnificently in these games, accuracy in length and direction complementing a lively pace. He was desperately unlucky not to take all ten wickets at Blackheath, for Doug Wright, the last man, ran himself out. The defeat at Edgbaston was the third that Surrey had suffered in a period of three weeks, and with Sussex in top form and leading the table convincingly, it seemed that Surrey were not to retain their title, particularly as Middlesex had run into fine form as well. Indeed, a fourth defeat, at the hands of Gloucestershire at the end of July, left Surrey fourteen points behind Middlesex and Sussex.

The Surrey batting had been strengthened in late July by the arrival of Subba Row, who had completed a highly successful season at Cambridge. May too was now in scintillating form and as their nearest rivals wavered, Surrey prospered. Nottinghamshire and Hampshire were beaten at The Oval. May hit 159 at Lord's where Surrey had the better of a draw, and in the return match at The Oval, with Lock taking nine wickets, they won convincingly and Middlesex's interest in affairs was over. In the last match at The Oval, Fletcher and Clark hit centuries, and Surrey beat Glamorgan by 172 runs. Surrey now travelled to Hove for a decisive game. To retain any chance of winning the title, Sussex had to beat Surrey, and they began well by claiming Clark, May and Constable for 49 runs on a damp pitch after a delayed start. Fletcher batted 285 minutes for 81. In contrast, Surridge clouted 38 and Surrey reached 220. The Sussex batting was incomprehensibly subdued. Needing to score briskly, they managed a rate of less than two an over and lost eight wickets in taking first-innings points. The match was destined to be drawn and Surrey batted out time, May scoring 136 not out against some occasional bowling, and Surrey were Champions for the second year in succession.

They beat Hampshire at Bournemouth in the final match of the season to bring their total number of points to 184. Only Glamorgan in 1948 had won the title with fewer points since the war. Of the five Championships won under Surridge, this was probably the least satisfying in that it depended much upon the mistakes of others, but the County Championship tests the quality of the side because it is determined in all weathers throughout four months of the year, and none had the staying power nor the ability to cope with setbacks or absences in the way that Surrey had.

1954

Their capacity to succeed when everyone about them doubted was never more in evidence than in the wet summer of 1954. Yorkshire won 6 of their first 7 matches to set a furious pace in the Championship. Middlesex and Warwickshire also began well, and Derbyshire moved into menacing form in June. It seemed that Surrey were out of the hunt. When they began their game against Essex at The Oval on 28 July they stood eighth in the table, forty-six points adrift of the leaders, Yorkshire. Surrey had 10 matches to play and victory over Essex by ten wickets heralded the start of one of the most remarkable runs in the history of the County Championship. Surrey failed to win only 1 of those last 10 matches, and paradoxically the 'failure' saw them at their finest. Nottinghamshire were crushed by ten wickets inside two days. The match against Northamptonshire at Kettering also ended in two days, but it was a much closer affair: Laker, 6 for 58, was prominent as the home side were bowled out for 125, but Surrey collapsed against Broderick and were all out for 121. Laker took 5 for 31 when Northants batted again and they were all out for 133. Needing 138 to win, Surrey were 119 for 8 when Lock joined Laker. With Lock defending doggedly on a pitch that was treacherous, twelve were added. Loader came to the wicket with seven wanted. He hit two, and Laker clumped Starkie for four to win the match. His 33 not out on top of his eleven wickets showed the man's all-round value to the team. As well as being one of the best off-break bowlers in the world, he scored over 5,000 runs for Surrey in his career, including two centuries.

In early August Middlesex were the visitors to The Oval. This was the only match of the last ten that Surrey failed to win, but it was the one that showed them at their most dynamic. Norman Preston, the editor of *Wisden*, drew special attention to Surridge (who often did a couple of hours work at the business in the Borough before coming to The Oval) and to this match in particular in his appraisal of Surrey's achievement during the season:

> Above all the retention of the title came about through the supremacy of the attack, supported by fielding of uncommon excellence, together with the initiative and imagination of the captain, Surridge, who so accurately assessed the tactical risks and possibilities of each situation. Of few players would it be more true to say that his batting and bowling averages completely misrepresented the full value of Surridge to the side. Surridge thought and acted in terms of attack from the first ball and once again the force of his own drive infected his men. A typical example of his initiative occurred in the match with Middlesex early in August. Surrey needed every point possible to keep alive what appeared to be a faint chance of winning the Championship and, when rain limited play to three-quarters of an hour on the first two days and prevented a start before lunch on the last, their hopes of taking any points from the match looked remote. Surridge was not prepared to regard the position as hopeless. Surrey responded to his call for aggressive batting and following a declaration, they bowled out Middlesex for 51 in two hours ten minutes, with a quarter-of-an-hour of extra time remaining.

Leicestershire, Gloucestershire, Worcestershire and Middlesex at Lord's, were all beaten within the next fortnight. No other county could match such form and when Worcestershire came to The Oval on 25 August, Surrey needed only to win the match to retain the title. Rain had affected the pitch and play could not begin until 2.00 p.m. Surridge won the toss and asked Worcestershire to bat. In 100 minutes they were bowled out for 25, which was the lowest score in first-class cricket since 1947 and the lowest score hit against Surrey that century. The last eight Worcestershire wickets went down for 5 runs, Lock taking 5 for 2 in 33 balls. Surrey moved into a solid lead and with May and Barrington going well they seemed set for a good score. Peter May remembers the occasion:

> Worcestershire were short of spin in those days, the pitch seemed easier and I was enjoying myself when to my astonishment I saw Stuart appear on the balcony and declare. It was not yet half past five on the first evening. Our score was 92 for three. In those days the amateurs still used the upstairs dressing room. Downstairs among the rest of the side the general verdict was that the captain must have lost his senses. His explanation as he led us out was that it was going to rain, which did not entirely clear up the misgivings.

Most of the Surrey members and supporters were also of the opinion that the captain was acting irrationally, and the capture of two wickets for 13 runs before the close did little to persuade them otherwise. The dismissal of Peter Richardson should have given some warning of what was to come. Richardson offered no stroke at a ball from Laker and lifted his bat high above his shoulders, but the ball turned and rose so steeply that it still took the edge of the bat for him to be caught at the wicket. Within an hour the next morning, Surrey had won. At one time, Worcestershire were 18 for 6 in their second innings and it was only a few shots by Yarnold as the fielders clustered round the wicket that boosted the score to 40. Having scored only 92 themselves, Surrey had won by an innings and 27 runs in little more than five hours of cricket. Surridge was now looked upon in awe as one who saw further and deeper than other men. The 157-run aggregate of the Worcestershire game remains the lowest for a completed match in the County Championship.

Surrey were Champions for the third year in succession. They confirmed their superiority with victory over Lancashire in the last game, which meant that from their last 10 games they had taken 112 points out of a possible 120 and only rain, one suspects, had robbed them of the other eight. In the last month of the season Laker took 48 wickets at 9.39 runs each and Lock 43 at 9.45, yet neither of these two bowlers was in the side to tour Australia, a fact which left people astonished. Both took more than 100 wickets in all matches, as did Alec Bedser and Peter Loader; the strength of the attack was indeed Surrey's chief reason for success. In many quarters it was thought that Alec Bedser did not have a good season by his standards but most bowlers would have been well pleased with 89 Championship wickets at 13.30 in a 'bad' season. Loader's advance was considerable, and he found his way into the MCC side that went to Australia, but of the three Surrey players in the party, only May played a significant part in the Test series.

Micky Stewart and Tom Clark coming out to bat.

Michael Stewart made an impressive start to his first-class career, hitting 134 against Essex at Colchester in his second match. He did not maintain that form and was criticised for his tendency to hook too early in an innings, but he opened with a certain flamboyance and his fielding was of the highest quality in a team of outstanding fielders. May was the outstanding batsman, and Subba Row contributed many valuable runs in the lower order, but in a side in which everybody was invariably contributing something with the bat, it was the form of Ken Barrington in August that played a decisive part in that memorable surge toward the Championship. The success of Barrington and the arrival of Stewart and Loader emphasised the strength in depth of the Surrey team. From the side that beat Worcestershire at The Oval, for example, Eric Bedser, Fletcher and Subba Row were all missing, yet all three made vital contributions and played in three-quarters of the matches during the season. Swetman, too, had deputised most ably for McIntyre on occasions and had been a member of a Second XI side which went through the season unbeaten and won the Minor Counties Championship to complete a Surrey double.

1955

This quality of reserve strength became apparent in 1955 when, with Subba Row having moved to Northamptonshire and Clark troubled by injury, Surrey were still able to sweep all before them. The County played 34 first-class matches in 1955, winning 27 and losing the other 7. Draws did not interest them. Their number of Championship wins, 23, and points, 284, were records. If one must point to one season in the Surridge era which stands supreme above all others, it is the season of 1955.

It began with 12 wins in succession, 9 of which were Championship matches. The most remarkable of these victories was at Leicester in the third week in May. Lock, Laker and Clark bowled Leicestershire out for 114 but Charles Palmer, the Leicestershire skipper, a medium-pace bowler of average ability, took 8 wickets for 7 runs in 14 overs and Surrey were dismissed for 77. It is generally accepted that Palmer brought himself on for one over because he wanted Munden and Jackson to change ends, but he bowled Peter May with his third ball. He had found a spot which he exploited to the full, and he took eight wickets before conceding a run, and it was Laker who broke the sequence when he hit Palmer for four. In spite of this debacle, Surrey won by seven wickets.

The only side which kept pace with Surrey at the start of the season was Yorkshire, and Arthur McIntyre had chosen the game with them in early June for his benefit. The excitement was great and 45,000 people paid for admission on the first two days. Yardley won the toss for Yorkshire and asked Surrey to bat first on a pitch which had been saturated. It was a wise decision. With Appleyard's brisk off-breaks rearing awkwardly to give him 7 for 29 Surrey were bowled out for 85 in two-and-a-half hours. By the close Yorkshire were 108 for 7. That Surrey were in such close contention was due mainly to Lock, who not only bowled magnificently but also took a memorable return catch to

The 1955 Surrey team. From left to right, back row: H. Strudwick (scorer), B. Constable, P.J. Loader, T.H. Clark, G.A.R. Lock, E.A. Bedser, D.G.W. Fletcher, J.C. Laker, R.C.E. Pratt, J. Tait (masseur), A. Sandham (coach). Front row: M.J. Stewart, A.J.W. McIntyre, P.B.H. May, W.S. Surridge, A.V. Bedser, K.F. Barrington.

Arthur McIntyre.

dismiss Lowson. He held the ball inches from the ground with his right hand as he flung himself across the pitch. The Yorkshire innings ended on 131 on the Monday morning and, batting a second time, Surrey were indebted to Fletcher, who took four-and-a-half hours to score 84. May batted with more enterprise and there were valuable contributions from Clark and Constable. More rain made the pitch difficult again and play could not begin until a delay of half-an-hour on the last day. Surridge declared and set Yorkshire the task of scoring 216 to win. Loader bowled Hutton for 1, and Bedser had Lowson for 0. Billy Sutcliffe played what Surridge considers one of the finest innings he ever saw played on a bad wicket. He made 40 in two hours and twenty minutes before Alec Bedser took a brilliant left-handed catch off his own bowling to dismiss him. Surrey went on to win by 41 runs. They now had maximum points from 8 games and led Yorkshire by twenty points.

Arthur McIntyre, born within a quarter of a mile of The Oval, had joined the staff as a leg-spin bowler and as the lad in charge of the bicycle shed. He played cricket in North Africa and Italy during the war and it was on the suggestion of the Bedsers and of Errol Holmes that he turned to wicketkeeping, but he won his County cap purely as a batsman. Herbert Strudwick helped him enormously in his early days and McIntyre was soon recognised as one of the two premier 'keepers in England. His aggressive batting and above all his keeping to an attack of such variety and vitality as Surrey's established him as one of the outstanding players of his time. Alec Bedser always maintained that McIntyre behind the stumps made him a better bowler.

Surrey suffered their first defeat at Headingley on 21 June. More than 60,000 people saw the three days of this match, and the gates were closed on a crowd of 35,000 on the Saturday. It was reported that 'The atmosphere resembled that of a Test match.' Surrey led by 102 on the first innings, but Trueman and Cowan bowled them out for 75 at the second attempt in very poor light and Yorkshire went on to win by six wickets. It was Surrey's first defeat for eleven months. However, they still led Yorkshire by twelve points and had a game in hand.

Briefly, in July, when Surrey surprisingly lost to lowly Kent, they surrendered the lead to Yorkshire, but even then they had games in hand. On 24-26 August they entertained Sussex at The Oval and, recovering from 26 for 4, won by an innings. The victory assured them of the Championship. They lost their next match away to Hampshire and Surridge admits now that it was the only time in his five-year reign that the team was not in the right frame of mind: 'We'd done well, and we had a little party and a few drinks before the Hampshire game. It showed.'

The superlatives had been exhausted. What more could people write about Surrey? Alec Bedser took more than 100 wickets, and Lock and Laker took over 250 between them in Championship matches alone. Seven Surrey men had played for England in the course of the season: Barrington, Alec Bedser, Laker, Lock, Loader, May and McIntyre. Peter May was now captain of his country and Ken Barrington had won his first 2 Test caps. Like May and the Bedsers, he was born in Reading. He was a genial man of great good humour who was to become immensely popular with all who met him. Initially a rather carefree attacking batsman, his early experiences in Test cricket saw him make 0 on his debut. The competition for places both in the England and Surrey sides made him reassess his game. He decided to eliminate risky shots from his batting, to develop his powers of concentration and to become the sheet anchor of the side. The transformation made him the backbone of Surrey and England. As well as his smartly groomed appearance, his gear would be in perfect condition. His bats, normally a light 2lb 4oz or 2lb 5oz size, were carefully chosen, clearly marked and lovingly tended. The application that Barrington showed in shaping his career was, perhaps, no more than every member of the great Surrey side of the 1950s did in one way or another.

1956

In 1956, McIntyre was to miss more than half the season with a hand injury. His presence was much missed but Surrey still won the Championship for the fifth year in succession. Swetman was a capable deputy behind the stumps, although he was not in the same class as a batsman. Stewart and Clark scored heavily and, as ever, there was always somebody who would produce the runs when needed.

Clark hit the two highest scores of his career in successive matches in July. The higher, 191, was made at Blackheath where Kent were beaten by an innings and 173 runs. This was a memorable match for in Kent's second innings Tony Lock took all ten wickets for 54 runs, and his figures for the match, 16 for 83, remain a record for the County. It was also the match in which Peter May hit his second century of the season.

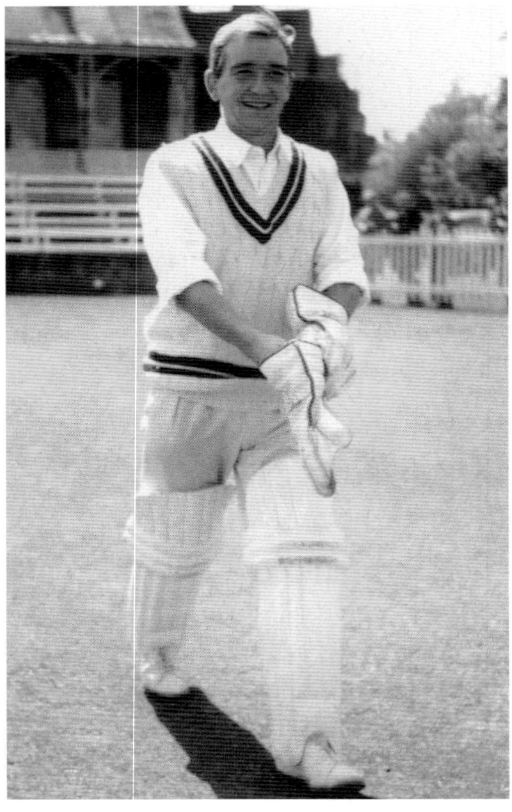

Roy Swetman.

The first had come at The Oval a few days earlier when Kent were also the opponents. May had been having a very lean time, and although he was captain of England and vice-captain of Surrey, Surridge said to him, 'Look, Peter, there's a lot of good players in the Second XI. I can't go on ignoring them.' May was a deceptively gentle man, for beneath the courtesy and the reticence there was a steely determination. He would not have been the great cricketer he was without it. His reply to his friend Surridge was: 'Don't worry, skipper, I'll get you a hundred today!' And he did.

Lock's ten-wicket performance at Blackheath was the second time that a Surrey player had taken all ten wickets in 1956. The first was against the Australian tourists in the middle of May. Ian Johnson won the toss, and the Australians appeared to have gained considerable advantage from this as Burke and McDonald put on 62 in ninety-five minutes. McDonald batted freely to score 89, and when he was caught at the wicket the Australians were 151 for 4. Laker now caused such devastation in the Australian batting that five wickets fell for 48 runs, and 12 of these were hit in one over by Davidson. The last wicket added 42 but Wilson finally fell to Laker to give the off-spinner all ten wickets. It was the first time since 1878 that a bowler had taken all ten Australian wickets, and in that year too the bowler had been a Surrey man, Barratt. A patient innings by Constable and some fierce hitting by Laker took Surrey into the lead, and Surridge and Loader

Tony Lock.

Jim Laker.

plundered 34 for the last wicket. When they batted again the Australian vulnerability to the turning ball became apparent and a significant chapter in English cricket history was written. Surrey won by ten wickets, so becoming the first county for forty-four years to triumph over an Australian team. Later in the year, Laker took 46 Test wickets in the series, including 19 at Old Trafford. It was the crowning achievement for one of the greatest off-spinners the world has known.

Laker was a Yorkshireman by birth but played most of his cricket for Surrey. He was a passive, phlegmatic player in that he would look the same whether he had just taken a wicket or been hit for six, but the passivity hid a burning passion. He was a master of his art. Line and length were under complete control all the time, and the control was founded on the perfection of his action. He bowled his off-breaks not by rolling the ball out of his hand as some latter-day off-break bowlers have done, but by spinning the ball with his fingers, sometimes to the extent that fingers became raw and sore or that calluses formed. He was not, as has been asserted, a bad-wicket bowler. 'He could turn the ball on anything', said Stuart Surridge. 'When I stood at short leg to him I could hear the ball zipping through the air. He needed a little cajoling at times, but he always gave his best, and he could spin them out whatever the wicket.' Surridge's admiration for Laker did not prevent him from dropping the great man in his benefit year. Surrey had arrived at Lord's, and as Middlesex was one of the leading sides in the Championship, the game had an added importance. 'Jim was worried about his finger', said Surridge, 'and I felt that if he went into the match worried about himself he wouldn't give one hundred per cent, which was probably wrong of me because he always did. It was a spur of the moment decision, and I brought in Eric Bedser.'

Surrey were bowled out for 113 but they still won by 71 runs. Lock had 12 for 75, and Eric Bedser 4 for 49. Eric Bedser again proved his worth as an all-round cricketer in 1956, scoring 804 runs and taking 92 wickets in all matches. He would bat anywhere and there was a solid grandeur in his batting. If it had not been such a wretched summer he might well have done the 'double' but rain robbed him. Surridge valued Eric Bedser's contribution highly and is adamant that if he had left Surrey for another county Eric would have played for England. He was a very fine off-spinner, but his chances at The Oval were reduced because of the presence of Laker and Lock, and to the England selectors he was always in the shadow of Laker. Like his brother, Eric's cricket was founded not only on unquestionable ability and endeavour but on the qualities of faith and loyalty. He had started out as a medium-pacer but had changed to off-breaks on the advice of their coach Alan Peach so that he and Alec would have more chance of playing together in the same team. They were, and are, inseparable, and when in 1988 a lunch was held to celebrate their fifty years at The Oval, the warmth of the affection in which they are held was obvious to all.

Although Surrey were always in a challenging position in 1956, the County did not head the table until the first week of July, and then only briefly. It was 2 victories over Essex, 2 over Middlesex and 1 over Sussex that took them clear in August. Lancashire were the only county with a slender hope of overtaking them, so the meeting between the two counties at The Oval at the end of August was eagerly awaited. Lancashire had to win this match to retain any chance. They did well: Tattersall and Hilton bowled

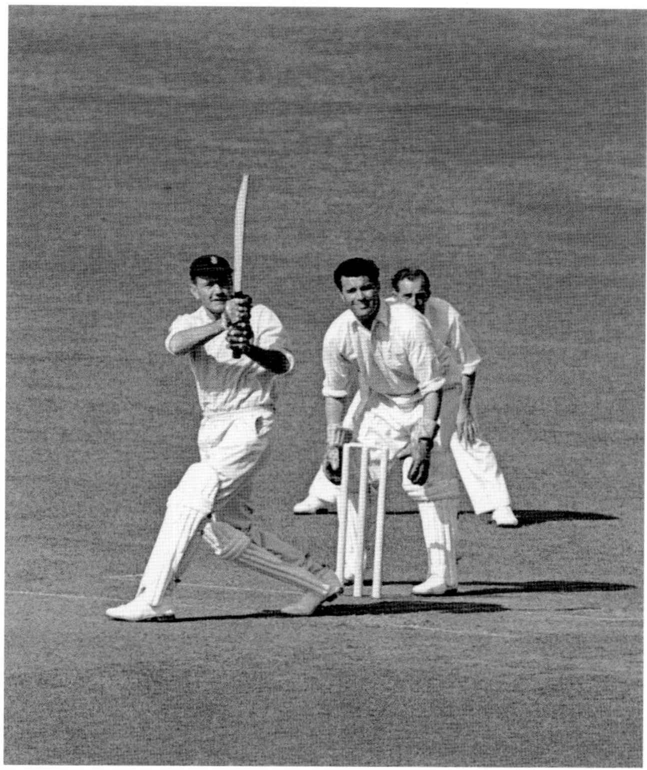

Eric Bedser.

Surrey out for 96, Lancashire ending the day at 40 for 2. Then it rained for two days and Surrey were Champions for the fifth year in succession, a record that remains unapproached.

They had 2 matches to play but the game at Worcester was badly affected by rain with Surrey leading on the first innings, and the match with Warwickshire at The Oval was abandoned without a ball being bowled. Surrey lost to the Rest of England at The Oval, and the only real moments of enthusiasm occurred when Surridge, the Surrey captain, appeared for his final innings. He was applauded all the way to the crease and again after Milton caught him superbly in the leg-trap where Surridge himself had been such a fearless fielder during five successful years as leader.

In those five years, Surridge had held 220 catches lurking close to the wicket. Moreover, he had not only fulfilled his promise that Surrey would win the Championship within five years but had led them to five wins in succession. He looked back with pride and pleasure: 'It was a most enjoyable experience. They were great men.' Indeed they were. 'There were giants on the earth in those days.'

After he retired he continued to serve the club for many years on the Committee, being President in 1982. He died in April 1992 whilst visiting one of his factories in Glossop in Derbyshire. His widow, Betty, became the first and only lady to hold the office of President of the club, in 1997. Walter Stuart Surridge's career statistics read thus:

SURREY

254 matches	3697 runs at 13.01	464 wickets at 29.64	361 catches

ALL FIRST-CLASS MATCHES

267 matches	3,882 runs at 12.94	506 wickets at 28.89	375 catches

So how were the players rewarded in these heady days?

The sustained brilliance of the Surrey professionals was relatively well rewarded by the Committee. In 1948 the basic weekly wage of a capped Surrey professional had been increased by £1 to £7.50, and it stayed at that level until November 1951. The previous year the best-paid Surrey player received total earnings of £760, including match fees, talent money and win bonuses.

The Surrey professionals had two problems however. First, retail prices were rising sharply, by almost ten per cent in 1951 and roughly the same again in 1952. Secondly, they complained of a 'very fluctuating income' due to the relative importance of match fees in their total earnings. As a consequence the players experienced a 'very real anxiety in balancing their budgets'. The Committee's response was that large match fees 'engendered keenness, prevented scrim-sharking and gave disciplinary control'. The last-mentioned point was clearly important to the Committee, but they did also recognise that discipline could be maintained by 'withholding of talent money and win money' or suspension on half-pay.

The compromise reached in November 1951 and 'welcomed' by Fishlock and Parker, the players' representatives, recognised the principle of 'a much increased weekly wage with a corresponding decline in match money'. Capped First XI players were to be paid £10.50 per week and match fees were to be £8.00 for an away match, instead of £12.00, and £4.00 for a home match instead of £5.00. As an incentive, the Committee raised the win bonus to £5.00. Two years later the win bonus reverted to £2.00 as part of a package that saw the away fee rise to £10.50 and the home rate to £7.00. By then the senior staff at The Oval had achieved the important goal of making their income more dependent on a regular weekly wage and less determined by a payments-by-results system.

In 1953 and 1954 the Committee allocated £800 as talent money for the Championship-winning sides, which meant that a leading professional received an additional £60 to £100. From 1955 to 1959 the sum to be dispensed rose to £900 and star players like Jim Laker benefited by more than £100 at the end of the season. Towards the end of the 1955 season the club secretary, B.K. Castor, met the professionals' representatives Alec Bedser and Arthur McIntyre to hear the players' case for a better pay deal. Bedser and McIntyre argued that not only was it three years since there had been a pay adjustment but that also, in that time, the cost of an away trip had increased. They cited the case of a visit to Weston-Super-Mare to play Somerset for which the fee was £10.50 but the hotel bill £6.00. However the most novel proposal advanced by the two players was that talent money should be calculated on the number of appearances, not match performances.

In January 1956 the Committee rejected the Bedser-McIntyre talent money proposal on the grounds that it was vital to 'distinguish the great and successful player'. Further, they noted, Jim Laker opposed any idea of talent money being based solely on appearances. A five per cent pay increase was granted while at the same time the Committee minuted that the professionals at the Oval earned £100 per annum more than at any other county. Nonetheless the following July the players again raised the question of away expenses and stated that it had become 'extremely difficult to make ends meet'. Clearly the Committee agreed because the fee for a mid-week away fixture was increased to £13.50, with an additional £2.50 for a weekend away match.

By the end of the 1950s a leading Surrey player, the best-paid professional cricketer in England, could expect to earn between £900 and £1,000 from the County. From that he would have to deduct his away expenses, maintain and renew his equipment and, of course, pay income tax. The average male earnings in the manufacturing sector were about £750 gross. The professional's life may have included some fame but it did not produce much of a fortune. After his retirement Alec Bedser wrote an article for the 1961 edition of *Wisden* in which he commented that:

> Fewer people are taking up cricket professionally these days. The rewards are not great and, with advanced education and higher wages, there are safer and definitely more attractive prospects for the average youngster outside the game.

FOUR
1957-1962

1957

Boundaries standardised to 75 yards

Stuart Surridge stood down for a number of reasons. He felt that the Second XI were growing old together without being given enough opportunities to display their talents at first-class level, and above all, he felt that Peter May, as captain of England, must be allowed to lead his county. Surridge had achieved what he had promised, and when he handed over to May he told him that he thought he was passing on a side that would win the Championship for another three years. He was one year out.

There are those who feel that May's task was an easy one, that all he had to do was to carry on where Surridge left off. In fact, he had the most difficult of tasks. Surrey had won the title five years in succession under his predecessor, putting May in the position where anything less than the Championship would be seen as failure. His philosophy was that of Surridge, persistent aggression from the first ball to the last, but his way was his own. He had learned much from Surridge, but he had inherited much too from Len Hutton, formerly his captain in the England side, and with these two influences he blended his own positive, intelligent and highly personal approach. He was a gentle man, but he had a very hard streak, and he was uncompromising in his demands. He was also ably served by his vice-captain, Alec Bedser.

The most talented English batsman of his generation, May first came to the public eye whilst at Charterhouse, where he was in the Eleven for four years, heading the school's batting averages at the age of 14. His career with Surrey started with two poor matches but then he scored 1 century and 3 fifties in the 11 Championship matches to the end of the 1950 season. He was considered by many critics and his contemporary players as the finest batsman of his era and had an outstanding international career with 66 appearances, 41 as captain.

What were his strengths as a player? He possessed intense, watchful concentration, which made him one of the best bad-wicket players ever seen. He invariably took the fight to the bowlers, always ready to attack and ready to drive the fast bowlers down the ground. He was a master of all strokes using a bat no heavier than 2lb 6oz, but his glory was the on-drive, perhaps technically the most difficult to execute.

It was feared that the pressures of captaining England and Surrey as well as being his country's leading batsman would affect him. However, he led both sides to triumph,

Right: *Peter May.*

Below: *Micky Stewart.*

topped the Surrey averages and the national averages and scored more runs than anybody else on either side in the Test series.

Surrey had lost none of their dynamism and the tone was set in the first Championship match of the season. After wins over Cambridge University and MCC, Surrey hit 259 against Glamorgan at The Oval and bowled out their opponents for 62 and 31. Lock had match figures of 12 for 34. The only mishap in the first two months of the season came when Northamptonshire were victorious at The Oval at the end of May. They were the closest challengers to Surrey but they were emphatically beaten in the return game at Northampton five days later. This was a milestone match as Micky Stewart established a world record by taking 7 catches in the second innings. Six were taken at backward short leg and one in the gully. Suprisingly, none of these catches were considered difficult, but this could not be said of many of the 77 catches that Stewart held during the season. To stand at Stewart's 'pocket picking' distance at short leg needed more than a safe pair of hands, quick reflexes and a stout heart; it demanded complete faith in his bowlers to maintain an accurate length. They never failed him. Barrington, in his first season at slip, shared with Stewart and Lock the outstanding performance of exceeding 60 catches. Whereas in the past the older members of the side used to field close to the wicket, Surrey placed their youngest players there, and demonstrated that this method was the soundest.

By mid-July, Surrey were 52 points clear in the Championship, and although they lost to Gloucestershire at the end of the month, there was never any likelihood that they would be caught. Nottinghamshire and Hampshire were brushed aside and Fletcher's benefit match was ruined by rain when Surrey were within fifteen runs of taking a first-innings lead over Middlesex. Stephenson, the Somerset wicketkeeper, had chosen the Surrey match at Weston-Super-Mare for his benefit, for he was assured of a big crowd. Somerset made 250 and Surrey 286 in their first innings. When the home side batted again Tremlett played a fine innings of 83 and Wight batted solidly, but Laker took 6 for 66 to leave Surrey requiring 153 to win. The asking rate was close to 4 an over and Surrey found themselves struggling against a determined attack and the clock. May played well, and Barrington hit briskly to ease the worries. The 7th wicket fell with the scores level, and when Laker hit Langford for the winning single there were just eight minutes of extra time remaining. The final margin of Surrey's superiority over the team in second place was enormous:

	P	W	L	D	NR	BONUS	PTS
Surrey	28	21	3	3	1	48	312
Northamptonshire	28	15	2	10	1	22	218

Throughout the season Surrey were the dominant side, attracting large crowds wherever they appeared. They played, acted, thought and looked like the magnificent champions they were. Surrey's achievements undoubtedly entitle them to be considered the greatest county combination of all time.

Generally Surrey could hope for runs down to no.9. Their batsmen cheerfully took risks in the interests of their side; their true worth lay in their determination to give the team's bowlers time and runs in which to dismiss the opposition twice. The batting was

Peter Loader.

exhilarating. May, Stewart and Barrington all passed 1,000 runs in Championship matches. The bowling, with young Gibson impressive in his few outings, was of a class unapproached by any other county. The following Championship figures emphasise this:

Lock	153 wickets at 11.58
Laker	85 wickets at 12.41
E.A. Bedser	60 wickets at 13.40
Loader	101 wickets at 14.73
A.V. Bedser	109 wickets at 15.57

Alec Bedser had suffered an attack of shingles in Australia in 1954/55, and had not fully recovered his form after that illness. He played his last Test match in 1955 and ended with 236 Test wickets, which was then a record. Considering how many matches he may have played but for the loss of six years for the war his record could well have been quite outstanding even compared with those who have subsequently taken more than 300 Test wickets. In 1957, although not regaining his England place, he was back to his best for Surrey. May had wanted him as his vice-captain, and it proved a wise choice, for Bedser had to lead the side in a third of the Championship matches: Bedser was a brilliant deputy. His wide experience, deep technical knowledge, shrewdness and willingness to encourage the new members earned him a new status in English cricket.

McIntyre lost none of his wicketkeeping ability. Throughout the Test series he stood by as reserve to Godfrey Evans and there was little doubt that he was England's second-best 'keeper. Keeping to Surrey's varied attack, especially on a pitch helpful to the bowlers, called for the highest skill and McIntyre was seldom lacking.

At the end of the year Surrey parted company with B.K. Castor, who retired having been secretary since 1946. He was succeeded by the assistant-secretary, Commander B.O. Babb.

1958

Surrey won the Championship for the seventh season in succession in 1958. In a wet summer, they won more games, 14, and lost fewer, 5, than their nearest challengers, Hampshire, who finished 26 points behind the Champions.

Alec Bedser went down with pneumonia on the eve of the season and could not play until July. With May also absent on international duty, McIntyre led the side most capably on several occasions. Lock's knee and Laker's finger injuries meant that they missed occasional matches, but Gibson and Sydenham took their chances well. David Gibson, a fast medium bowler and useful batsman, benefited from a fine physique, as befitted a county rugby player and schoolboy international, and David Sydenham's left-arm fast medium gave the attack an extra dimension on occasions.

Batting stuttered a little in the damp conditions, but May rose head and shoulders above everybody else in the country. Not only did he score more runs than any other batsman, but his average, 63.74, was more than 17 runs better than his nearest rival in the national averages, Willie Watson, 46.62. For Surrey, May averaged 64.23, scoring his runs briskly and invariably putting his side in a strong position. Constable and Fletcher also gave consistent service and shared in a partnership of 137 in the opening Championship match against Gloucestershire, who were beaten by nine wickets. This was the first of five consecutive victories which culminated with Lancashire being outplayed at Old Trafford. In their second innings, with Gibson taking 4 for 8, Lancashire were bowled out for 27, their lowest score of the century, and this on a pitch where May hit an imperious 174.

Such form was not sustained, and, at the end of July, having suffered four defeats, Surrey were 18 points behind Hampshire and in third place. Nottinghamshire were entertained at The Oval in early August and Surrey led by 11 on the first innings. In a low-scoring match they were set 96 to win and May arrived at the wicket with the score 25 for 2. He hit the first ball he received from Jepson straight back over his head for six in an astonishing display of confidence which left Nottinghamshire stunned and defeated. After a draw against Leicestershire and a two-day win over Middlesex, by 12 August Surrey stood in second place, just four points behind Hampshire. Wins over Middlesex and Worcestershire and a draw with Northamptonshire preceded the visit of Somerset to The Oval at the end of the month. After Surrey scored over 300 Somerset were bowled out for 66. Rain did not allow any more play but the first-innings lead had given Surrey sufficient points to assure them of the Championship.

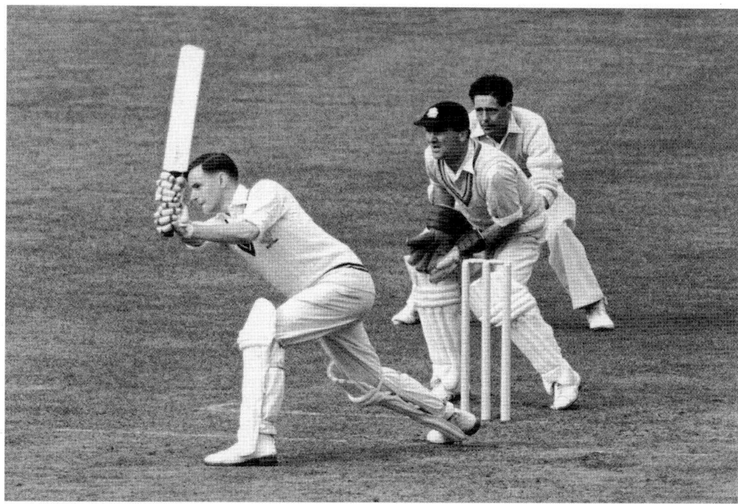

Peter May.

During Surrey's fine run at the beginning of the season Peter Loader took 9 for 17 against Warwickshire at The Oval. These were the best figures of his career. In 1957 Peter Loader had earned fame by performing a hat-trick in the Fourth Test with the West Indies, a feat never previously accomplished by an England player in a home Test. His pace, ability to make the ball move late in its flight and skill in disguising the occasional slower delivery placed him at the forefront of fast bowlers.

Loader was one of five Surrey players who went with the MCC side to Australia in 1958/59, the others being May (captain), Laker, Lock and Swetman. It was considered to be one of the strongest teams to go to Australia, but things did not go well and the tour marked the point at which the fortunes of England and Surrey began to decline. At the end of the season Arthur McIntyre retired, a top class wicketkeeper to the last, and succeeded Andy Sandham as coach. In turn, Sandham took over as scorer from Strudwick, who went into retirement after serving the club for over sixty years.

1959

Peter May did not make a full return to cricket in England after the Australian tour. His marriage made him an absentee until the end of May, and then in the third week in July he had to undergo an operation which brought his season to a premature end. He played in only 7 Championship matches, and Alec Bedser led the side for most of 1959. He did admirably, but May's brilliant batting was sorely missed. Barrington, Stewart, Clark and Fletcher enjoyed good seasons, but the outstanding contribution came from John Edrich, a 22-year-old left-hander who had played in 5 first-class matches in the previous 3 seasons, 1 of them a Championship match in 1958. Injuries to Clark and Fletcher caused Edrich to be drafted into the Surrey side for the game at Trent Bridge in May 1959. He was asked to open the innings and scored 112 and 124. He added 5 more centuries in the season and in total scored 1,799 runs at 52.91 despite twice breaking a finger, being idle for four weeks in mid-season and having to retire in the last match. Barrington scored 1,498 runs at 53.50 in the Championship with 5 centuries, Stewart 1,549 runs at 33.67, Clark 1,073 runs at 33.53 and Fletcher 790 at 28.21.

The real difference in their matchwinning power was the falling off of the attack, which to some extent was only to be expected in a dry summer. Alec Bedser, Laker, Lock and Loader all took their wickets but at much greater cost. In the Championship Loader took 100 at an average of 19.51, Lock 92 at 21.89, Laker 72 at 23.91 and Bedser 78 at 24.93. Having won at Bath and Gloucester, Surrey needed victory in their last 2 matches to be sure of retaining the Championship. In fact, they won neither. Whilst scraping a draw against Middlesex, Yorkshire had won in sensational manner at Hove and were the new Champions. Surrey finished third.

James Charles Laker's career statistics are as follows:

SURREY

309 matches	5,531 runs at 17.44	2 Centuries	1,395 wickets at 17.37

93 times he took 5 wickets in an innings and 24 times 10 wickets in a match

TESTS

46 matches	676 runs at 14.08		193 wickets at 21.24

9 times he took 5 wickets in an innings and 3 times 10 wickets in a match

ALL FIRST-CLASS MATCHES

450 matches	7,304 runs at 16.60	2 Centuries	1,944 wickets at 18.41

127 times he took 5 wickets in an innings and 32 times 10 wickets in a match

1960

Counties were given the option of playing either 28 or 32 matches with the Championship being decided on average points. Surrey opted to play 28 games

In another dry summer, none of the Surrey bowlers was as successful as in previous seasons. Lock was in the process of remodelling his action to remove any suspicion of a kink and although no-balled once, taken day by day it appeared to be scrupulously fair. Laker had lost the edge to his bowling and he retired before the start of the season. The Bedsers were nearing the end of their careers as they celebrated their 42nd birthday in July. This was the time that the great side of the fifties was breaking up. Peter May took no part in the 1960 season, as he was recuperating from his operation. Constable had a kneecap removed and Clark was troubled by arthritis that ended his career.

Edrich confirmed his promise of the previous season and Stewart, Barrington, Fletcher and Parsons scored consistently. Edrich and Stewart began the season with an opening partnership of 204 against Northamptonshire in a drawn match. Four of the first 5 matches were drawn and Surrey were never in a position to challenge for the title, eventually finishing in seventh place in the Championship.

Brian Parsons.

Brian Parsons was a mature player before he claimed a regular place in the side, so strong had been the competition. Born in Guildford, he gained his blue at Cambridge in 1954 and 1955, but national service prevented him joining the staff at The Oval until 1958. He was a cultured-looking right-handed batsman who, for a few seasons, was consistent rather than brilliant. Willett, Tindall, Storey and Long were other younger players whose names began to appear on the team sheet. Arnold Long deputised for Swetman in three matches. Swetman played in 11 Test matches for England between 1959 and 1960, without ever suggesting that he was the real successor to Evans or McIntyre. Neat and compact, he kept creditably for Surrey until 1961, and later played for Nottinghamshire and Gloucestershire. Gibson showed a considerable advance in 1960 but the attack, Lock apart, was a shadow of what it had been three or four years earlier. Lock took 139 first-class wickets and his Test career was far from over. Eric Bedser remained the only effective right-arm spinner.

Alec Bedser captained in all but 3 Championship matches and took 67 first-class wickets. He led Surrey out against Glamorgan in the last three days in August, shared an unbroken 8th-wicket stand of 48 with Swetman and took 5 first-innings wickets for 25 runs. Surrey won by an innings. It was the 72nd time that he had taken 5 wickets in an innings for Surrey, and when he had Don Shepherd lbw it was his 1,459th and last wicket for the County. He announced his retirement from first-class cricket, and we had seen the last of one of the greatest of medium-paced bowlers. His career statistics read thus:

SURREY		
370 matches	4,108 runs at 14.61	1459 wickets at 19.13

72 times he took 5 wickets in an innings and 15 times 10 wickets in a match

TESTS		
51 matches	714 runs at 12.75	236 wickets at 24.89

15 times he took 5 wickets in an innings and 5 times 10 wickets in a match

ALL FIRST-CLASS MATCHES		
455 matches	5,735 runs at 14.51	1,924 wickets at 20.41

96 times he took 5 wickets in an innings and 16 times 10 wickets in a match

1961

The follow-on abolished in Championship matches. New ball taken after 85 overs

Little went right for the County in 1961 and they finished in the lowly position of fifteenth in the Championship. Of their 5 victories only 1 was achieved at The Oval, against Nottinghamshire. This turned out to be the last season for both Eric Bedser and Fletcher. Clark, suffering from hip trouble that compelled him to retire, was not to reappear in what was his benefit year. Swetman, who did not miss a match, decided to retire from professional cricket at the end of the season at the age of twenty-eight. Peter May had returned but England duty claimed much of his time, and Stewart, who had been appointed vice-captain, led the side for most of the season. He did not have a happy year with the bat, but still managed 1,000 runs for Surrey, as did Barrington, Edrich, Willett and Parsons. Barrington played in 5 Test matches and Lock 3. Constable, who made a wonderful return to the side after his knee operation, scored 1,799 runs in all matches.

1962

Amateur status abolished. Last Gentlemen v. *Players match*

Willett and Tindall had brought fresh aggression to the middle order, but it was the attack, so long the strength of the side, that began to look thinner and found it harder to bowl out sides at The Oval, where batsmen began to dominate again. Fifteenth in the table was a shattering drop and confirmation that the golden days were finally at an end. Not even the resurgence in 1962 could really hide this fact. Surrey climbed back to fifth in the table and, suffering only 3 defeats, were outside contenders for the Championship until the last weeks of the season, but eventually finished fifth. The batting was strong, with four players scoring over 1,000 runs in the Championship: Edrich with 1,674, Stewart 1,450, Barrington 1,310 and May 1,180. Both Sydenham and Loader took 107 wickets, with Lock capturing 73.

May had retired from Test cricket and played in 21 Championship matches, the most he had played for the County in five years. With Stewart and Edrich opening, Barrington

David Sydenham.

at no.3, May at no.4, Constable at no.5 and Parsons, Willett and Tindall also scoring well, Surrey possessed a batting side as strong as any in the country.

The main problem remained in attack because Gibson, in whom many hopes rested, again broke down with injury. Sydenham responded magnificently, with both he and Loader taking more than 100 wickets. Lock, recalled to the England side for 3 Tests against Pakistan, was back to his best form. Ron Tindall, like Willett a soccer player of note, was encouraged with his off-breaks and performed well, although it was apparent that he would never become a spinner in the top flight. Richard Jefferson came down from Cambridge to bowl his medium pace to good effect, and he also strengthened the tail, for he could be a very hard-hitting batsman.

On the brighter side there was the form of Arnold Long in his first full season as Surrey's wicketkeeper. He accounted for 90 batsmen in all matches, 73 caught, 17 stumped, and so established a Surrey record at his first attempt. It was not to be his last. Arnold Long had attended Wallington Grammar School where he was spotted by Surrey at a young age. A complete team player, an outstanding keeper and a more than useful bat, he was a quiet man and would never appeal unless he was convinced the batsman was out. He would have stood a good chance of playing for England had the gloves not been so firmly in the hands of Alan Knott. He had an enviable ability to switch off the minute he left the field and would be found in a corner immersed in a textbook as soon as the pads were off.

Arnold Long.

At the end of the season, May went home and reviewed his life. He felt that he was not enjoying the game as much as he once did: 'Perhaps it was the anticlimax after the glorious years of the 1950s, beer after champagne, as it were. I was not playing up to the high standards which I set myself.'

He did indeed set himself the very highest of standards, and there was no dissuading him. He resigned the captaincy, but said that he would be pleased to play when on holiday from his work in the City or when the County felt they particularly needed him. He never played one-day cricket and played only 3 more games for Surrey in 1963. Peter May did not enjoy the idea of letting anybody down and quietly left the game. His career statistics are as follows:

SURREY		
208 matches	14,168 runs at 50.41	39 Centuries
TESTS		
66 matches	4,537 runs at 46.77	13 Centuries
ALL FIRST-CLASS MATCHES		
389 matches	27,592 runs at 51.00	85 Centuries

He captained England in 41 Test matches, of which 20 were won

FIVE

1963-1970

1963

All counties played 28 matches in the Championship. Points system changed to 10 points for a win and 5 points for a tied match. Follow-on rule re-introduced. Start of Gillette Cup

Micky Stewart took over as captain at a difficult time and held the side together most ably in a transitional period. The 1963 season saw the last of Loader and Lock, both of whom went to settle in Australia, and of Parsons who decided to follow a business career. The season also saw the County establish a record when in the First Test against the West Indies at Old Trafford they supplied the first three England batsmen, Stewart, Edrich and Barrington. This was the first time in a Test match in England that one county had provided the first three batsmen for an England side. Their absences during the season, while they took part in between 3 and 5 Tests, and Lock's while he took part in 3, put extra pressure on a developing side which had other problems, notably the loss of Arnold Long with appendicitis halfway through the season. Three men were called upon to deputise for him, one of them being coach Arthur McIntyre, at the age of 45. The other two were Owen Kember and Nicholas Majendie, neither of whom appeared for Surrey again after 1963.

Bernard Constable, the last of the pre-war staff still playing for the First XI, captained the side for several matches but was now less likely to play an extensive innings. With leading batsmen absent for much of the season, Willett and Tindall shouldered responsibility well, although Tindall's off-breaks showed little improvement. Indeed, the Surrey attack, until recently so strong in spin, was now more reliant on medium-pace bowling. Gibson enjoyed a better season, Storey showed promise as an all-rounder and Geoff Arnold, eighteen years old, made the first of his 218 appearances for the County.

His career began in the second Championship match of the season when Surrey beat Derbyshire by an innings. He conceded only 40 runs in 16 overs and finished the year with a creditable 18 wickets in his 6 matches. Of the pace bowlers, the one to enjoy the most successful season was David Sydenham, who was the only one to take 100 Championship wickets. He also contributed a useful batting performance in an astonishing game at Northampton. The home side hit 301 for 3 in their first innings and bowled Surrey out for 106. Enforcing the follow-on, Sydenham joined Jefferson with the score at 262 for 9. Jefferson attacked the bowling and showing remarkable control scored his first Championship century, and in an amazing stand of 138 which occupied only an hour and three-quarters Sydenham gave fine support. His contribution was 15 not out.

Richard Jefferson was a medium-pace bowler and hard-hitting batsman who got his blue at Cambridge in 1961. He was an enterprising player who hit 100 not out in 100 minutes against Derbyshire at Buxton in 1964. However, he could not hold a regular place in the side, so rich were Surrey in seam bowlers, and it was generally felt that the County did not make the best use of his services.

The career statistics of Peter James Loader are as follows:

SURREY

298 matches	1,827 runs at 8.95	1,108 wickets at 18.66

65 times he took 5 wickets in an innings and 13 times 10 wickets in a match

TESTS

13 matches		39 wickets at 22.51

Once he took 5 wickets in an innings

ALL FIRST-CLASS MATCHES

371 matches	2,314 runs at 8.50	1,326 wickets at 19.04

70 times he took 5 wickets in an innings and 13 times 10 wickets in a match

Micky Stewart.

Ron Tindall.

Successors to Lock and Laker were unsurprisingly difficult to find. There were some encouraging signs from Roger Harman, a twenty-one-year-old left-arm spinner who, in 1963 against Kent at Blackheath, performed a hat-trick whilst taking four wickets in 5 balls. These were isolated individual performances in a season which saw Surrey finish eleventh in the Championship, also being comprehensively beaten by Worcestershire in the first round of the Gillette Cup in the first year of one-day cricket. In all, twenty-three players represented the County in Championship matches.

The career statistics of Graham Anthony Richard Lock are as follows:

SURREY

385 matches	5,391 runs at 15.35	1,713 wickets at 17.41

123 times he took 5 wickets in an innings and 31 times 10 wickets in a match

TESTS

49 matches	742 runs at 13.74	174 wickets at 25.58

9 times he took 5 wickets in an innings and 3 times 10 wickets in a match

ALL FIRST-CLASS MATCHES

654 matches	10,342 runs at 15.88	2,844 wickets at 19.23

196 times he took 5 wickets in an innings and 50 times 10 wickets in a match

1964

Far better luck attended Surrey in the second year of the Gillette Cup competition, when they beat Cheshire at Hoylake, Sydenham taking 4 for 6 and the individual award. They beat Gloucestershire at The Oval, with Edrich hitting 96, and Middlesex at The Oval before going down to Sussex at Hove in the semi-final. The improved form was not restricted to the one-day knockout tournament, for in 1964 a young and eager Surrey side finished fourth in the Championship, although it would be true to say that they never seriously threatened the leaders. They suffered only 3 defeats, losing by just 6 runs away to Northamptonshire and going down heavily to Somerset at Weston-Super-Mare and Warwickshire at Edgbaston.

Harman had a magnificent year, taking 136 wickets at 21.01 in all matches. He had a high action, flighted the ball intelligently and spun it considerably. Twice in the season he took eight wickets in an innings. His spell at Trent Bridge turned a probable defeat into victory. Surrey trailed by 68 runs on the first innings and Nottinghamshire were 63 for 1 in their second when Harman joined the attack and produced figures of 17.1-10-12-8. Against Kent at The Oval, he took 8 for 32 and Surrey again won a match in which they had been trailing.

So much was expected of Harman. It seemed to those close to the game that he had every chance of becoming an England player, but the second season is always more

Ken Barrington.

difficult than the first. When batsmen began to read him he seemed to lack the spark of aggression that had characterised Lock and Laker and, delightful man that he was, he became dispirited. Never again was he to produce the form of 1964, eventually leaving Surrey at the end of the 1968 season. Before the end of the 1964 season he had been joined in the Surrey attack by Pat Pocock, a seventeen-year-old off-spinner. Pocock took six wickets against Cambridge University, and in his first Championship match, against Nottinghamshire at The Oval, took three wickets in each innings. He was recognised as an off-spinner of exceptional ability, an opinion he was to confirm over the next twenty-two years. Sydenham, although missing many matches through injury, was always threatening and he began the season with 9 for 70 against Gloucestershire at The Oval. It was the best performance of his career and Surrey won by eight wickets. A balanced and aggressive attack was forming, and the batting was as strong as ever.

Ken Barrington, 'The Colonel', in his benefit year, topped club, national and Test averages. Stewart had a splendid season, scoring a career best of 227 not out against Middlesex at The Oval. This was an unusual match. Surrey were bowled out for 119 in their first innings with Willett scoring 73 not out. Middlesex replied with 365, which looked a winning score. Bill Smith and Stewart began Surrey's second innings with a partnership of 219. Three wickets fell quickly and Willett joined Stewart in a stand of 149 in eighty minutes. In this stand Willett scored 102 to record the fastest century of the season. The match was drawn. Meanwhile, Ken Barrington was hitting 256 for England against Australia at Old Trafford.

Willett, always a forceful player, had his best season for the club in 1964, but a cartilage operation was to cause him to miss much of the following season. Stewart, who led the side skilfully, enjoyed one of his best seasons, scoring 1,980 runs. Edrich was as resolute as ever, and Storey's advance as a batsman was most marked. A young man named Roope made his first appearance for the County, but his great deeds lay in the future, just as those of Bernard Constable lay behind him. Constable, now 43 and the only survivor from before the war, played his last innings for Surrey in September, when he took a delightful 61 not out off the Warwickshire bowling. It was his 434th match for the County on whose history he had printed his name indelibly. In his career he scored 18,849 runs at 30.45 of which 18,224 were for Surrey at 30.37. He accumulated more than 1,000 runs in 12 seasons and scored 27 centuries.

Arnold Long, having recovered from an appendicitis operation, and with his career still in its infancy, equalled the then world record when against Sussex at Hove he caught seven batsmen in the first innings and four in the second. Over the years Long was to give remarkably fine service to Surrey.

1965

Gibson had blossomed into a fine all-rounder by this time, and Storey was not far behind him, but a slight falling away by Sydenham, and Harman's loss of form and confidence, saw Surrey fall to eighth in the Championship. Their first Championship success did not come until they mastered Gloucestershire at The Oval at the end of July. Consequently, they had the strange experience for them of occupying the bottom place in the table midway through the season. But as they finished with 7 wins and only 4 defeats they rose to eighth position by the end of the season. In the Gillette Cup, however, they carried all before them until the final in September.

They started their campaign beating Glamorgan by five wickets with 18 overs to spare, having bowled them out for 146 Arnold taking 4 for 26. Northamptonshire were the visitors in the quarter-final. Surrey batted first, with Tindall scoring 73 out of 222 for 8, but the visitors were then dismissed for 97 with Storey taking 4 for 14. The semi-final against Middlesex was at The Oval and in front of 8,000 paying spectators Middlesex set a daunting target by scoring 250 for 8 in their 60 overs. After a solid start by Stewart and Edrich 92 runs were added in 10 overs by Barrington and Edwards to see Surrey home with 3 overs to spare.

Surrey were the favourites for the final against Yorkshire at Lord's. Stewart won the toss and asked Yorkshire to bat first. Taylor was dismissed early as Yorkshire made a slow start. Then, Close joined Boycott in a partnership of 192. During the season Boycott had failed to score a first-class century, but in this final played what many consider to be the best innings of his career. He hit 3 sixes and 15 fours as the Surrey bowling and fielding wilted. Boycott's 146 remains the highest score in a 60-over final. Facing a total of 317 for 4, Surrey looked to be without heart and in 40.4 overs were bowled out for 142.

There had been a change in the administration at The Oval in 1965 for Brian Babb had retired as secretary and been succeeded by Geoffrey Howard, formerly with Lancashire and previously assistant secretary at The Oval. Surrey gave trials to two left-handed batsmen in the match against the South African tourists, Ian Finlay and Younis Ahmed. Younis hit 21 and 66, so beginning a rather turbulent career. He had to be content with Second XI cricket in 1966 whilst qualifying for the County. His performances in the Second XI, scoring more than 1,000 runs, must have made Surrey wish they could play him, for the batting of the first team seemed to lose confidence.

1966

A major experiment was made in the Championship for 1966 where in 102 of the 238 scheduled matches the first innings of each side was restricted to 65 overs. This experiment was dropped after two seasons.

There were niggling injuries and illnesses to Gibson, Barrington and Arnold, and the team as a whole played with an uncharacteristic lack of flair. There were exceptions: John Edrich was now a power in the land. He had hit 310 not out for England against New Zealand the previous summer and his batting had a resolution that was awesome. Michael Edwards, born in Balham and educated at Alleyns and Cambridge, where surprisingly he had failed to get a blue, was moved up the order to open with Edrich, Stewart dropping down. The move was an instant success and Edwards responded with a maiden century against Gloucestershire at The Oval and 1,000 runs in a season for the first time.

Just as encouraging was the form of Stewart Storey, who became the first Surrey player since Freddie Brown in 1932 to do the 'double', i.e. 1,000 runs and 100 wickets in the

All hands to the roller – helping out at The Oval, 2 May 1966. From left to right: M.J. Stewart, A.J.W. McIntyre, R.I. Jefferson, W.A. Smith, I.W. Finlay, K.F. Barrington, R. Harman, K.B. McEntyre, G.R.J. Roope, G.G. Arnold, M.J. Edwards, D.J.S. Taylor, M.D. Willett, P.I. Pocock, R.D. Jackman, J.M.M. Hooper, D.A. Marriot.

same season. Yet, in a sense, Storey's achievement was symptomatic of so much of Surrey's cricket in the mid-1960s, in that it promised more than it ever really fulfilled. In 1963, John Arlott had written:

> Stuart Storey had, to some extent, curbed his earlier impetuosity, to come into the team and win himself a place. He plays his strokes smoothly and easily, with time to spare; and when his selection of the ball to hit improves a little further, 1,000 runs per season, perhaps far more, should be within his scope. His ability to bowl at medium pace could simplify the whole question of team balance.

This prophesy was quite accurate as Storey reached 1,000 runs in a season in five of the fifteen years he played for the County and took five wickets in an innings eleven times in first-class matches and twice in one-day matches. He rarely took part in a match without making some important contribution with either bat or ball, and sometimes as a slip fielder. When in full cry, he could be a spectacular batsman. His progress for Surrey built up slowly from 1960 to 1963 and he then became a stalwart member of the side until his retirement in 1974.

The side, which had looked excitingly young, eager and balanced, fell apart before it ever came to maturity. Sydenham had retired, and Gibson, Tindall, Jefferson, Willett and Harman all left the game in the space of a couple of years, plagued by injury or unrealised potential. There were, of course, compensations. Geoff Arnold had developed into

Above: *Stuart Storey.*

Left: *Geoff Arnold.*

a potential Test match bowler. Whilst many a fast bowler flags after the exertion of four or 5 balls of an over, Geoff Arnold gave the impression of boundless stamina and endless willingness to go on attacking batsmen. That knees-high approach culminated in a side-on delivery with a healthy circular sweep of the arm. The ball usually took anything but a direct course on to the bat, or the edge, or into the 'keeper's gloves. The sportsman's scourge, cartilage trouble, upset his progress and for a few years he was regarded as physically suspect. Typically, he faced up to the problem, toughening himself by rigorous training and so becoming a dependable opening Test bowler for his country.

In his first season, Robin Jackman took 22 Championship wickets. Pat Pocock had made a tremendous advance as an off-spinner, to the extent that in 1968 he made his Test debut at the age of twenty-one. Roope, too, was maturing into a very capable all-round cricketer, but, as yet, it seemed that Surrey was like a jigsaw puzzle that was tantalisingly incomplete.

1967

The points for a win were changed to 8 with 4 points awarded for leading on the first innings

With Pocock, Arnold and Storey bowling well and the batting boosted by the arrival of Younis, looking more adventurous and exciting, hopes were raised when Surrey finished fourth in the Championship. However, the side needed an opening bowler to partner Arnold. Both Gibson and Willett suffered knee trouble and at the end of the season felt compelled to retire. Pocock and Arnold each took 100 wickets in the season for the first time. Edrich hit his highest score for Surrey, 226 not out against Middlesex at The Oval when he and Barrington shared a 4th-wicket stand of 297. Edrich (1,658), Edwards (1,155), Stewart (1,133) and Barrington (1,058) batted well and Edwards distinguished himself as a catcher at forward short-leg. However, a bad start to the season had really destroyed any chance the County had of making a serious challenge for the title.

1968

Ten points for a win plus bonus points in the first 85 overs

In 1968 Surrey played some of the worst cricket in their history. They were dull and unenterprising, and throughout the club, both on and off the field, there was an unhealthy feeling of depression. Only Edrich hit a century in the Championship. Arnold missed practically the whole season with injury and Storey underperformed. Jim Cumbes, lively and cheerful with a good high action, used the new ball well when he was released from his soccer commitments. Jackman bowled, as he was to do his entire career, with tireless energy and enthusiasm. Pocock consistently displayed his precocious talent. Roope, and occasionally Knight, showed encouraging all-round form, but the batting was both listless and disappointing. Most alarming was the decline of Barrington. Only some months later, when he collapsed in Australia with heart trouble, did the reason for his decline become apparent. He was forced to retire and this came as a shattering blow to both Surrey and

England. A man of wit and cheerful charm, he taught many of those around him the meaning of professional application, and his influence on a side was enormous and always for the good. As a batsman he seemed to be hewn out of granite, his nose and chin defiantly projecting his immovability. In 82 Test matches he was the backbone of the England side, scoring 6,806 runs at 58.67, and was much feared by the opposition.

The loss of Barrington, together with a season in which things had gone so badly that Surrey plunged to fifteenth in the Championship, hit the County hard. They made no impact in the Gillette Cup and this caused some reassessment of staff and attitudes at The Oval. An examination was made of whether the County was coming to terms with the game as it was now ordered. In 1968 the rule allowing immediate registration of an overseas player had been introduced but some counties, including Surrey, had not grasped the significance of the impact that this would have on the game. While Procter, Barry Richards and Sobers paraded their talents elsewhere Surrey offered no new fare. There were also the increasing demands of the one-day game and, with the arrival of the John Player Sunday League in 1969, its growing popularity.

The career statistics of Kenneth Frank Barrington read thus:

SURREY			
362 matches	19,197 runs at 41.28	43 centuries	133 wickets at 35.55
TESTS			
82 matches	6,306 runs at 58.67	20 centuries	29 wickets at 44.82
ALL FIRST-CLASS MATCHES			
533 matches	31,714 runs at 45.63	76 centuries	273 wickets at 32.61

1969

To accommodate the Sunday League, the number of championship matches was reduced to 24.

Surrey woke up to the recent changes in the game and for the 1969 season they enlisted the aid of Intikhab Alam, the Pakistani leg-spinner and hard-hitting batsman. It was something of an anachronism to sign a leg-spinner in an age when they had all but ceased to exist, but it was an inspired move, for here was a cricketer of modesty and lavish talent, adaptable to all forms of cricket, who became loved by friend and foe alike. Surrey cricket had received the blood transfusion that it needed. In an era when there was so much adverse criticism in relation to the employment of too many overseas cricketers, Surrey will always look back with pleasure on their first such appointment. Possibly one may say that Intikhab did not make the same impact on the county scene as several of his contemporaries, yet he brought to Surrey so many other ingredients and no other overseas player displayed more loyalty over twelve years.

Pakistan's leading cricketer did not push for an exorbitant contract but was merely content to be accepted on similar terms to his new-found colleagues. Within a matter of weeks his cheerfulness, his intense love of the game and his hard work had made him a

Intikhab Alam.

most popular member of the side. Being able to play cricket every day of the week he reached the highest echelon of leg break bowlers at a time when they were fast becoming a dying breed, and seldom did he ever find conditions suitable for him.

Intikhab was one of the four players to be capped by the County in 1969. The others were Younis, Roope and Derek Taylor, who would depart to become Somerset's wicket-keeper, and a very fine one, at the end of the season. A wonderful team effort brought victory over Hampshire at Southampton with 7 balls to spare and took Surrey into the

Michael Edwards.

quarter-final of the Gillette Cup, where they lost to Yorkshire at The Oval before a disappointingly small crowd. Some enterprising cricket was played in the John Player League and Surrey finished fifth, while in the Championship they were once again a team to be reckoned with.

Younis (1,449 Championship runs), Edrich (1,416), Edwards (1,114) Stewart (996) and Roope (934), all found their form with the bat, and they were ably supported by Intikhab and, when available, Roger Knight. An injured heel took Arnold out of the attack in the closing weeks of the season, and this cost the County dearly in the run-in to the Championship in spite of the pounding efforts of a raw, tearaway fast bowler named Bob Willis. On 20 June, with only 2 victories to their credit, Surrey were top of the County Championship, eight points ahead of Warwickshire, who had a game in hand and who, like Surrey, were unbeaten. However, by 2 July, with still only 2 victories and 0 defeats, Surrey had dropped to fourth. Their strength was easily discernible, with Younis and Edrich respectively first and fourth in the national averages. By the end of July, Edrich was first and Younis second. By this time Surrey were third in the Championship, still unbeaten and with 4 wins. The last 2 wins had come in a ten-day period towards the end of the month. The first was a thrilling victory over Leicestershire at The Oval. After Surrey had declared at 324 for 7 in their first innings, Leicestershire took a lead of 40 runs. Surrey declared their second innings, setting them to score 137 in 105 minutes. At 108 for 4, this did not seem an arduous task, but clever bowling by Intikhab changed the course of the match. He sent back four batsmen in quick succession, and when the last over began Leicestershire needed 5 to win with one wicket to fall. On the fifth ball, a fine throw by Pocock ran out Dudleston and gave Surrey victory by 2 runs.

Victories over Sussex and Essex kept up the challenge, but in late August, despite beating Yorkshire at Scarborough, they began to tire, and they suffered their only Championship defeat of the season when Essex won at The Oval. Pocock, with 65 Championship wickets, and Intikhab, with 62, had bowled well throughout the season, but now, without Arnold, 67 wickets, to act as strike bowler, the challenge faded, and Surrey finished third.

1970

The 1970 season followed an identical pattern. Five wins, 4 draws and 1 defeat in the first 10 Championship matches kept them well to the fore in mid-June. Six points from a draw with Gloucestershire at The Oval took them to the top of the table on 8 August, but defeats at Bradford and Blackheath heralded a falling away, and Surrey finished fifth. There was general frustration and criticism. It was now twelve years since Surrey had won anything, and many found this unacceptable, for it seemed the County possessed the best-balanced side in the country. They were so strong that Roger Knight had moved to Gloucestershire to get regular cricket, and Willis was to move on in 1972 for the same reason. Storey had rediscovered his form as a batsman and joined Edwards, Younis, Roope, Stewart and Edrich on 1,000 runs. There was a balanced and lively attack, with two potent spinners in Pocock and Intikhab, yet the County had nothing to show for all this talent.

There were allegations that Stewart was not getting the best out of his men, and that his tactics were unenterprising. The Oval pitches came in for severe criticisms, and there was general unrest.

SIX

1971-1972

1971

Micky Stewart was well aware of the frustration and criticism, much of which he felt was directed at himself. He announced early in the 1971 season that he would resign the captaincy at the end of the campaign. He felt that there was too big a gap between Committee and players, and he was critical of the sluggish pitches at The Oval and the lack of atmosphere at the old ground. Micky Stewart recalled that pitches were prepared by rolling in a mixture of marl and cow dung on a Monday for the match starting on the Wednesday, and on the Thursday for a Saturday match. He was voicing a view that many now felt. Gone, albeit only by fifteen years, were the days when 50,000 swarmed through the turnstiles in three days to see Surridge and his men take on Middlesex or Yorkshire. The world had changed and Surrey had not always kept pace with the fresh demands that now came from the game, its players and spectators. Social and environmental factors had taken their toll, too, and Kennington, blitzed by traffic and the intersection of main artery roads, was no longer the fashionable King's Town of the nineteenth century. It is easy to consider these points with some thirty years hindsight, harder to assess their effect when living through the changes themselves. To what amounted to a crisis of identity, Surrey responded in the best possible way.

They began the 1971 season in fine form, beating Lancashire and, as it transpired most importantly, Warwickshire in 2 of their first 3 matches. In the early stages of the season they were always in a challenging position but by the first week in August they had begun to fall apart, and it seemed that a familiar pattern was emerging. On 10 August, Surrey stood seventh in the table with 6 wins and 2 defeats in 17 matches. They were thirty-seven points behind Warwickshire, who were at the top of the table, but they had 2 games in hand. No one saw them as potential Champions. On Saturday 14 August, they began their three-day match with Middlesex at Lord's. Brearley declared at 242 for 7, and Stewart declared 12 runs in arrears, having settled for the three batting points that they had earned. In 1971, the system in operation gave one point for each 25 runs scored over 150 during the first 85 overs and one point for each two wickets taken in the same period. Batting again, Middlesex were routed by Pocock and Arnold and Surrey won by 5 wickets. A week later, with Arnold taking 9 wickets in the match, Surrey crushed Northamptonshire in two days at Kettering and followed this with an innings victory over Yorkshire in Arnold Long's benefit match.

Pat Pocock.

Graham Roope fielding at slip.

Surrey needed all the bonus points they could possibly get, and they got nine. The basis of their innings came in a 2nd-wicket stand of 132 between Stewart and Roope, Roope playing a magnificent innings of 171, the highest of his career. Roope was a lovely player to watch when in full flow, his driving free and eloquent. Like several Surrey players he was a fine footballer, and this no doubt contributed to his outstanding fielding. He became a close-to-the-wicket catcher on a par with the Locks, Stewarts and Surridges of the 1950s. Tim Lamb, of Middlesex and Northamptonshire, and later a respected administrator with Middlesex and TCCB, once proffered the remark that he wished he had spent all his career bowling with Roope at slip or close in on the leg side. Roope's century helped Surrey to 381 against Yorkshire, who were twice bowled out by Intikhab and Pocock. Intikhab had joined the side late in the season, for he had been captaining the Pakistan side against England, but Chris Waller, slow left-arm, had served Surrey well in the earlier part of the year.

Derbyshire provided stiffer opposition than Yorkshire, and Surrey were reeling at 70 for 5 before being rescued by a most impressive innings of 164, the highest of his career, by Stewart Storey. Since doing the 'double' in 1966, Storey had had a somewhat fluctuating career, and he was now more a bits and pieces player than a fully-fledged all-rounder, for his medium pace was used less in the first-class game than it had been. However, he was invaluable as an all-rounder in the one-day game. His high-scoring innings against Derbyshire came at a time when it was needed most, for Edrich was absent with a back injury, and Surrey needed all the runs they could muster. Derbyshire were eventually left with the task of scoring 205 in 165 minutes to win the match. They were never in with a chance. Willis, bowling very quickly, took two wickets in his second over, and Pocock and Intikhab came into the attack to destroy the lower order and give Surrey victory by 40 runs with ten minutes to spare.

This was Surrey's fifth win in succession, for Gloucestershire had been beaten at Bristol just before the triumph over Yorkshire, and they now stood second in the Championship. Warwickshire had finished their programme with 9 victories and 255 points. Surrey already had 11 victories, so they needed only to draw level on points with Warwickshire to take the title. With 2 matches to play, they had 244 points, already seven more than Kent had gained in winning the Championship the previous year.

The first of Surrey's 2 remaining games was against Glamorgan at The Oval. Glamorgan, runners-up in 1970, had plummeted to sixteenth in 1971, but they were never easy opposition. Stewart gave his side the ideal start with a chanceless century on the first day and Dudley Owen-Thomas, an attractive and aggressive batsman, scored well towards the close, but the pitch was sluggish and Surrey managed only 3 batting points. On the second day, Intikhab and Pocock troubled all the Glamorgan batsmen and bowled their side to an 82-run lead. Edrich and Roope added 107 in brisk time so that Stewart was able to declare and give his bowlers five hours in which to bowl out Glamorgan, who were set a target of 287. For much of the time, Glamorgan looked likely winners. They were 186 for 3, and Majid Khan and Roy Fredericks had made their task look a light one, but the Surrey bowlers persevered and when the last hour started Glamorgan required 55 runs from 20 overs with three wickets in hand. They could still have won but they preferred to stop Surrey from winning, which led to an hour of unbelievable frustration for Surrey. Long, behind the wicket, had a bad day. He had dropped Majid off Pocock when Majid was on 15 and now he dropped Roger Davis off Intikhab with 15 overs still to go. This was the same Roger Davis who was back in the side after suffering a terrible injury earlier in the year when he was hit on the head fielding at short leg. The 9th wicket fell with five minutes remaining, but Davis and Lawrence Williams held out as eight Surrey fieldsmen clustered round the bat watched by an excited but small crowd.

The failure to beat Glamorgan was a disappointment for it left Surrey still six points short of the Championship with one game to play in uncertain weather. Happily the sun shone at Southampton and Edrich and Stewart gave Surrey a rollicking start with a partnership of 109. Roope too, played well, but the middle order fell apart. Surrey were 240 for 3 and going well, but they crashed to 269 all out, so missing a fifth bonus point by 6 runs at a time when they had hopes of gaining six points. One of the big disasters came when Pocock ran out John Edrich, who had made 113 and on whom, naturally enough, hopes rested for the fifth and sixth points. As it was, Surrey did not even last the 85 overs.

They endured a worrying weekend, and when the game resumed the anxieties were not eased. Hampshire had a formidable batting line-up, Barry Richards, Gordon Greenidge, David Turner, Roy Marshall, Richard Gilliat, Peter Sainsbury and Trevor Jesty being the first seven. Arnold and Willis removed the first two for 1 run, but Turner and Marshall added 101 before Willis bowled Turner. There seemed, as Pat Pocock expressed years later in his autobiography:

The 1971 Surrey team. From left to right, back row: J. Hill (scorer), R.D. Jackman, Younis Ahmed, C.E. Waller, R.M. Lewis, R.G.D. Willis, J.M.M. Hooper, G.R.J. Roope, Intikhab Alam, D.R. Owen-Thomas. Front row: L.E. Skinner, G.G. Arnold, M.J. Edwards, S.J. Storey, M.J. Stewart, A.J.W. McIntyre (coach), J.H. Edrich, A. Long, P.I. Pocock, G.R. Howarth.

> … an agonising wait, and then Intikhab flicked the edge of Richard Gilliat's bat, Arnold Long held the catch at the wicket and as I ran in from fine leg I knew that this was the most marvellous moment I would ever know in county cricket. Micky's wife, Sheila, ran on to embrace him. Stuart Surridge, then the chairman of cricket, strode on to the field to congratulate the whole side.

The players drank champagne on the field and Surrey had come in from the cold. It was an outstanding success against considerable odds, with the placid Oval pitch not the least of their hindrances. At the beginning of the season the groundsman Ted Warn had striven to make faster pitches, but none could then be sure of the outcome of his endeavours, and in 1971 The Oval pitches proved to be as slow as ever. Evidence of this is seen in the figures of Geoff Arnold, who took 83 wickets in the season, less than a third of them at The Oval.

The quality of Stewart's achievement was that he welded together a side of disparate personalities into a competitive unit. Arnold and Roope were men who needed constant encouragement, surprising in two such dedicated and talented cricketers, while Younis required a firm hand. Thickset and strong, he was a dashing left-handed batsman with a large repertoire of strokes, including a magnificent off-drive. Occasionally he bowled either slow left-arm spin or medium pace. He was a glorious batsman, and when watching him late in his career playing for Glamorgan he was so technically and stylistically superior to the rest on view that it was almost an embarrassment, but he was a man with a fatal flaw: initially it seemed like an arrogance which could be harnessed into displays of contemptuous ease when batting, but later this manifested itself in acts of naïve misjudgement, like betting against his own side at Worcestershire, which led him to part company with three counties in less than happy circumstances.

The committee met Micky Stewart at Southampton and asked him to reconsider his decision to resign and remain as captain. He considered the position for two months and then agreed, on the understanding that the reasons for disquiet that he had forwarded should be investigated. Stewart was still critical of the Oval pitches, pointing out that Surrey had taken all twenty wickets to beat a county there only once in 1971, a remarkable feat in a championship season.

Bob Willis, having been in dispute with the Committee over his wages, could not be persuaded to change his mind, and he left the County to join Warwickshire. He had been flown out to Australia as a replacement for Derbyshire's Ward in 1970/71 and had played Test cricket without being a capped county player. He bowled very fast, but was wild in line and length, and Surrey could not agree to ensure him a regular first-team place against the competition of such superb professionals as Arnold, Jackman and Storey. Both England and Surrey were right. England selectors recognised him as a great Test fast bowler; Surrey had doubts about his strength and stamina for continuous county cricket. He did become one of the greatest of Test match fast bowlers; his county record was less impressive. His well-known thoughts on county cricket must date from this time, together with his views on protecting Test match bowlers to ensure they do not bowl too often.

1972

Benson and Hedges Cup initiated. Championship reduced to 20 matches

Perhaps it was a mistake that Stewart allowed himself to be persuaded to lead the side for one more year, for it was hard to sustain the momentum that had taken Surrey to a title at a time when cricket was in a state of flux. As Surrey did not win a Championship match until they beat Hampshire at Guildford in July, their final position of twelfth came as no surprise.

Jackman, Intikhab and Pocock carried the bowling, for Arnold had hamstring trouble. Edrich could play in only 11 matches because of Test calls, and of the other batsmen, only Roope and Younis hit reliable form, although Lewis was an able deputy for Edwards, once seen as unlucky not to be opening for England, now showing something of a decline.

When he came down from Cambridge University, Dudley Owen-Thomas batted with considerable panache, and was named Young Cricketer of the Year, but some rather exaggerated claims were made of him. One writer considered that, with his uncoached background and his complete lack of nerves, he was Bradmanesque and should be considered for England, but his brief career did not blossom to that extent. At this time Surrey gave debuts to two young players, Alan Butcher and New Zealander Geoff Howarth. Butcher was primarily a left-arm medium-pace bowler, and it was his 6 for 48 in the first innings against Hampshire at Guildford that set up Surrey's first victory. Ironically, it was to remain the best bowling performance of a career that was to be spent mostly in the plundering of runs.

The most memorable match of a season in which Surrey failed to make progress in any of the four competitions was at Eastbourne. Chasing a target of 205 in 135 minutes, Sussex seemed well set for victory at 187 for 1 with 3 overs remaining. Pocock then began one of the most remarkable bowling spells in cricket history. He bowled Gordon Greenidge with the first ball of what was his 15th over, having taken 0 for 58 in his first 14. Michael Buss played the second ball, but was bowled by the third. Jim Parks took 2 off the fourth ball, failed to score off the fifth and was caught and bowled off the sixth. The score was 189 for 4, meaning that Sussex needed 16 off the last 2 overs. Prideaux and Griffith took 11 runs off the penultimate over of the match, bowled by Jackman, so that 5 were needed off Pocock's last over. The off-spinner had Prideaux caught by Jackman with his first ball, Griffith caught by Lewis with the next and Morley stumped by Long with the third to make him the third Surrey bowler to take four wickets in four balls. The other two were Alan Peach in 1924 and Alf Gover in 1935. Spencer took a single off the fourth ball of the over, but Pocock bowled Tony Buss with the fifth. This meant that Joshi had to hit the last ball for four to win the match. He took a wild swipe and was run out going for a second run.

There were several records in this remarkable achievement. Sussex had lost five wickets in 1 over. Pocock had taken a world-record six wickets in 9 balls, seven wickets in 11 balls and a world-record-equalling five wickets in 6 balls. The last over had taken ten minutes to bowl, and Sussex, on the brink of victory, had lost eight wickets for 15 runs in 18 balls and drawn. Amazingly, this feat was not reported in the press at the time and did not come to light nationally until some time later.

It was sad that Stewart should end on a low note. Cheerful, honest, reliable and unquenchably enthusiastic, he had led Surrey with great integrity through a most difficult period that had witnessed many major changes in the game. He had tasted success in the great side of the 1950s and he knew the discipline and endeavour required to produce a Championship-winning team. He reached the pinnacle in 1971 after nine years of hard work, and he could never call on the wealth of talent that had been available to Surridge and May. After retiring from the game in 1972 he worked as UK sales manager for a sports company before being invited back by Surrey in 1979 to take up the position of cricket manager. This led to a similar position for the England team and he was subsequently awarded an OBE for his services to cricket. In 1998 he was appointed president of Surrey CCC. He remains closely involved with both Surrey and the ECB. His career statistics are as follows:

SURREY

498 matches	25,007 runs at 33.20	48 centuries	605 catches

TESTS

8 matches	385 runs at 35.00	0 centuries	6 catches

ALL FIRST-CLASS MATCHES

530 matches	26,491 runs at 45.63	49 centuries	634 catches

SEVEN

1973-1977

1973

In 1973 John Edrich was appointed captain of Surrey in succession to Micky Stewart. In the circumstances, it was the only logical appointment. He was thirty-five years old, the senior professional, and had first played for Surrey fifteen years earlier. Edrich was a genuinely great player with 83 first-class centuries to his credit, and 59 England caps, yet the qualities that made him an outstanding Test opening batsman with an average of 43.54 were not necessarily those that would equip him to lead a county side.

He was a chunky, strong left-hander whose success was founded on unwavering concentration, self-discipline and a phlegmatic temperament. Like the legendary Herbert Sutcliffe, he revealed no emotion if struck or beaten by a ball. He would simply take up stance again and quite likely nudge the next delivery for four as if nothing had happened. His innings did not always live in the memory as being full of beautifully executed shots, but they have endured in the record books and many a lost cause was won because of John Edrich. The problem was that the characteristics of his batting demanded almost a retreat into himself so that he remained undistracted by all else around him. This remoteness was what enabled him to accumulate so many runs, but it was not conducive to good leadership.

Edrich had every cause for satisfaction in his first season as captain, but, as Pocock revealed some years later, many of the players were not totally satisfied and asked that Edrich be relieved of the captaincy. This was not out of any dislike for him, but simply because they felt that he was not the right man for the job. The Committee chose to ignore their opinions. This decision caused no rift as the players had indicated at the outset that they would support whomever the County chose as captain, but they felt that their communication with Edrich was not what it should be. Edrich believed that he could do the job and responded in the way that he did when just beaten by a ball that shaved the off stump. He set about the next task.

After a woeful start to the 1973 season, Surrey ended on a high note. With a devastating late run they finished runners-up in the County Championship. This compensated for the disappointments earlier in the season of being eliminated from the Benson and Hedges Cup at the group stage for the second year running and being knocked out of the Gillette Cup in their first game by Gloucestershire, the eventual winners. In the Sunday League Surrey failed to impress, finishing in mid-table with only 6 victories.

John Edrich.

During the first two months of the season there was little indication of their eventual success. They opened with 2 successive defeats, both at The Oval, firstly by Essex in two days, and then Gloucestershire. In their next 7 matches they recorded 6 draws and 1 further defeat at the hands of Somerset at Bath.

In July the tide turned and they began an astonishing run of success with 3 wins in a row against Warwickshire and Yorkshire at The Oval, and Derbyshire at Chesterfield. In all, they won 9 of their last 11 matches, finishing with 6 successive victories. This was all the more praiseworthy because they were without Arnold for all England's 6 Test matches and without Roope for 4 of them. In fact Arnold, their leading bowler, played in fewer than half the Championship games, and Roope in only 12.

Surrey completed the double over both Sussex and Yorkshire. The latter suffered an innings defeat at The Oval for the third successive year. In the first innings they were dismissed for 60, Jackman taking 7 for 36, and in the second innings they made only 43, Pocock having the remarkable figures of 6 for 11. Their second innings total was the lowest first-class innings of the season and brought Stuart Storey's benefit match to a close on the second day. Although Edrich could feel well pleased with his first season as leader, his form with the bat was poor by his standards (although it should be noted that he was worried by an injury). His opening partner Edwards experienced another lean summer. The failure of the openers put the middle-order batsmen under considerable pressure, especially when Roope was on England duty. Fortunately, Younis Ahmed, the dashing left-handed Pakistani batsman, was in sparkling form and was easily the side's leading run-getter. He made 1,389 runs in the Championship, for an average of 53.42 – no other Surrey batsman reached 1,000 – and finished sixth in the national averages. He was a great inspiration and made his highest score, 155 not out, against Warwickshire at The Oval, followed by a century in each of the next 2 county matches against Yorkshire and Derbyshire.

Younis Ahmed had made his first-class debut as a fourteen-year-old in Pakistan for the Inter Board Schools XI in March 1962. He made 4 Test match appearances for Pakistan, playing twice in 1969/70 against New Zealand and returning seventeen years and 111 days later to play against India in 1986/87. Thickset and strong, he was a dashing left-handed batsman with a large repertoire of strokes, including a magnificent off-drive. Occasionally he bowled either slow left-arm spin or medium pace. His contribution for

Robin Jackman.

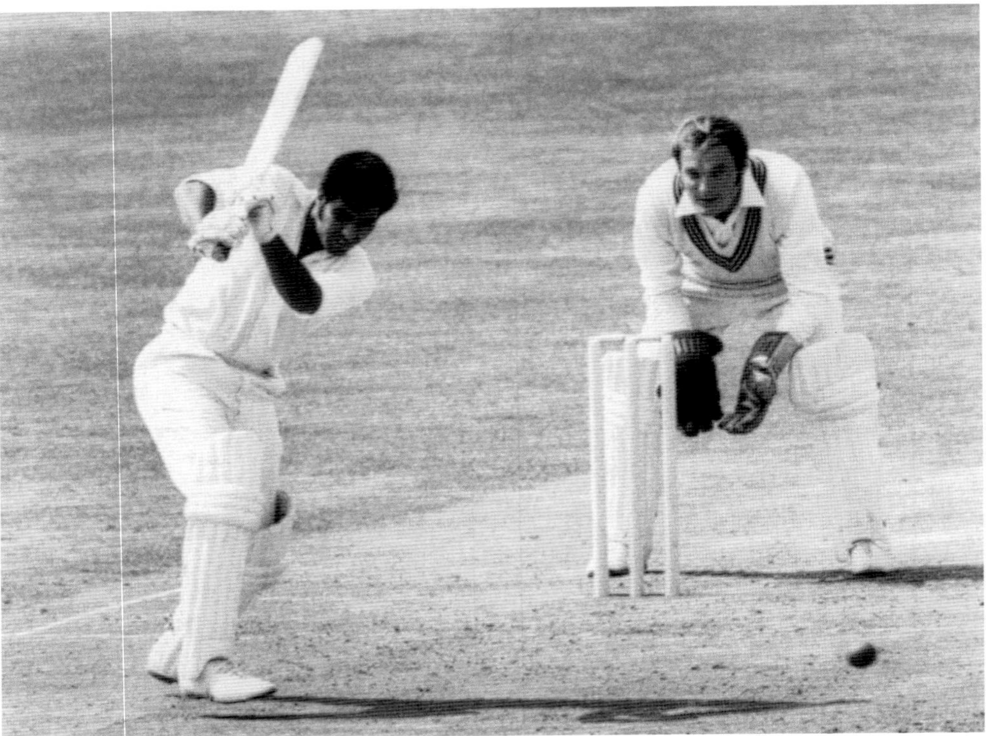

Younis Ahmed.

Surrey in one-day matches was substantial, playing in 194 matches with a batting average just below 30, scoring 2 centuries and 31 other scores over 50.

Geoff Howarth was given a chance to prove his worth and responded with some confident and aggressive batting. His innings of 159 against Kent at Maidstone was the highest score of any Surrey batsman in the season, and followed an earlier knock of 156 not out against Leicestershire at The Oval. Storey, who with Younis, Jackman and Long played in all 20 County matches, made some useful contributions with the bat, including a century off Glamorgan at Cardiff.

With the frequent absences of Arnold, Jackman manfully shouldered the responsibility for the opening attack and also emerged as a true all-rounder. His 92 wickets put him third in aggregate after Bedi and Lee in the national averages and he made great strides with the bat to finish third in the County averages with 509 runs, compared with only 203 in 1972. The spinners Pocock and Intikhab Alam took 157 wickets between them and Pocock earned a trip to the West Indies with the MCC. Intikhab also hit 2 centuries. Not the least of Surrey's qualities was their fielding, where Roope was outstanding. Attendances at The Oval were disappointing and the £2,000 Surrey won as runners-up in the championship must have been particularly welcome.

1974

Championship matches: limit of 100 overs on first innings, total of 200 overs both sides, balance taken up by side batting second if side dismissed in less than 100 overs

Surrey won their first limited-overs trophy in 1974, the Benson and Hedges Cup. It was the undoubted highlight of their season and a personal triumph for John Edrich. Surrey had not particularly distinguished themselves in one-day cricket previously and much credit must be given to Edrich for improving all aspects of their game. In the quarter-final, Surrey beat Yorkshire by 24 runs at The Oval, Geoff Howarth winning the Gold Award for his innings of 80 which formed the backbone of the Surrey innings. The semi-final was at Old Trafford, where Surrey batted first on a difficult pitch in uncertain conditions. Edrich batted through the morning session and with Jackman scoring freely Surrey reached 193 for 8. Alan Butcher bowled 11 overs conceding only 11 runs and Surrey won with remarkable ease by 63 runs.

In the final against Leicestershire, Edrich won the toss and elected to bat. No batsman was able to dominate and Surrey scored only 170. Defending such a moderate total Surrey needed an early strike, which was provided by Arnold who had Dudleston lbw with the first ball of the innings. Wickets fell at regular intervals and Surrey won with ease by 27 runs. Adjudicator Freddie Brown gave the Gold Award to John Edrich in recognition of both his solid innings and his inspired field settings. There were those in the press advocating Edrich as captain of England and his subsequent appointment as vice-captain on the tour to Australia was well deserved.

Surrey, at full strength one of the best-equipped sides in the country, were seriously depleted by Test calls. Again, they mounted a strong challenge for the County Championship but the losses of Edrich, Arnold and Intikhab Alam proved crucial. The reserves were not quite able to fill the gap and finally Surrey slipped down the table, eventually finishing seventh.

They began the season with a two-day victory over Nottinghamshire at Guildford and then won by an innings and 134 runs away to Leicestershire. They had convincing victories at Chesterfield, Northampton and Hove, but the loss of three senior players began to hit them hard. After a two-day win over Somerset at the start of August, they ended the month with losses, by ten wickets to Middlesex, and by an innings to Yorkshire. The defeat by Middlesex at Lord's finally meant they had no chance of finishing in the top three.

In the Gillette Cup, Surrey looked set for victory in their quarter-final match. Put in to bat in humid conditions, Surrey batted vigorously. Edrich, Younis and Storey all did well and 254 for 7 seemed to assure them of success but before a capacity crowd of 10,000, Somerset were inspired by Denning's 112 and won with 10 balls to spare. Their winning score, at the time, was the highest ever made in a competition batting second. In the Sunday League, Surrey failed to impress and again finished well down the table.

Although he played in fewer than half of the Championship matches, Edrich still managed to top the Surrey batting averages with 578 runs. His 152 not out against Sussex at Hove was the highest score of the season by any Surrey batsman. Younis Ahmed was again the side's leading batsman in terms of runs scored, but he was less consistent than in 1973. As usual he produced a large range of attacking strokes and was at his best when going after the bowling. He made one century against Leicestershire at Leicester.

Storey came to the rescue with hundreds against Derbyshire at Chesterfield and Essex at Ilford, and Surrey were able to save the match against Worcestershire at The Oval thanks to his brave defence. Storey was the only Surrey batsman to score more than one century. Both Storey and Edwards retired at the end of the season from first-class cricket with Surrey. Howarth continued to advance and was awarded his County cap during the match with Somerset at The Oval. Roope, who with Pocock and Long played in all 20 county matches, failed to advance his claims for further Test honours. Nonetheless he showed what a good attacking batsman he could be with his only century of the season against Middlesex at The Oval. He was a fine driver and a superb fielder.

The irrepressible Jackman, who made such great strides with the bat in the previous season, maintained his form. His 92 not out against Kent at The Oval was the highest innings of his career. Sadly, Owen-Thomas again failed to fulfil his potential. He was given his chance in 15 matches but scored only 298 runs. Jackman and Pocock shared the main burden of the attack, each of them bowling more than 600 overs. Jackman, with plenty of stamina and the ability to achieve a great deal of movement, bravely shouldered the responsibility of sharing the new ball. The spin department was in the capable hands of Pocock, who continued to be one of the most deceptive off-break bowlers in the country.

It seemed a curious decision by Surrey to allow the left-arm slow bowler Waller to go to Sussex when they knew that they would be without Intikhab for so many matches. If Pocock had also been chosen for Test duty they would have had an even more serious problem in balancing the attack. Intikhab was greatly missed. He played in only 6 matches, taking just 11 wickets and scoring only 126 runs, compared with 72 wickets and 600 runs in 1973. Although Arnold appeared only 8 times, he still topped the Surrey bowling averages with 51 wickets at only 10.09 apiece. He finished second in the national averages. In Surrey's Championship match at Leicester he performed his first and only hat-trick in first-class cricket. On the debit side, the Test and County Cricket Board suspended Arnold for 2 matches for showing public dissent against the decision of an umpire. Peter Wight had ruled a ball bowled by Arnold in the Sunday League match against Warwickshire at Edgbaston to be a wide. Arnold was forced to miss the Championship match at Lord's and the Sunday League match against Northamptonshire.

Roope was called on much more often to bowl his seamers and responded with 32 useful wickets. With so many seam bowlers in the side, Surrey were one of only four counties who failed to average 18.5 overs per hour during Championship matches. They were fined £1,000, a large slice of their prize money for winning the Benson and Hedges Cup. Geoffrey Howard, secretary of Surrey County Cricket Club since December 1964, retired in September, at the age of sixty-five.

1975

In 1975 May was a miserable month for Surrey. Not a single victory came in either the County Championship or the John Player League, and the 2 wins that transpired in the

Benson and Hedges competition were insufficient to bring progress towards the retention of the trophy. Somerset went forward instead because they took their wickets at a faster rate. The memory of this did not help the players to find Taunton cider any sweeter when in June, also at The Oval, they went out of the Gillette Cup at the hands of Somerset for the second year running.

Rain washed out the second day of Surrey's first Championship match against Yorkshire, then five of their batsmen were out for 'ducks' in an innings against Lancashire in the second match. As a final straw Warwickshire marched home with seven wickets in hand when Edrich left them what seemed to all a stiff task, 258 runs at 96 an hour. The return amounted to twenty-four points from the 4 matches, 3 of them at home.

So in the event there was something to be said for the gap which, partly because of the Prudential Cup, left Surrey without a match at The Oval from 28 May to 5 July. By the time they returned they had 2 wins to their credit, with a defeat at the hands of Warwickshire on the debit side. They stood twelfth in the table and it took victory by one wicket in a remarkable match against Leicestershire to hoist them up to seventh and in a position to make their presence felt.

By 19 August Surrey had risen to second, and they were still third a week later after an honourable draw against Kent. Then came a dismal showing at Bristol that definitely ended the bid to emerge with something tangible from a summer of almost unbroken sunshine. They lost by an innings and 112 runs to the side second from bottom at the time, and thoughts of £500 for the County finishing fourth in the table, let alone £3,000 for the one at the top, soon became wishful thinking. In the end five counties stood above them.

Paradoxically, Surrey's defeat at Bristol reflected their revival. A partnership which had contributed greatly towards the team's improved performances, that of Younis and Roope, was split by the recall of Roope to the England team. The inclusion of Edrich for all 4 Tests and Arnold for 1 gave considerable satisfaction to the County and it also helped to lessen the disappointment of their final position. Younis Ahmed made his highest score of 183 not out against Worcestershire at Worcester, sharing a blistering 7th-wicket partnership of 173 with Intikhab Alam. Edrich, Roope and Younis scored over 1,000 runs in the Championship.

Edrich found that 1975 had much to offer. Reaching the mature age of thirty-eight, he completed a year that confirmed his comeback to the international scene. During the English season Edrich scored 4 centuries to take his total number of three-figure innings to just 6 short of the 100 hundreds harvested by sixteen elite players, among them three famous Surrey 'ancestors', Jack Hobbs, Andy Sandham and Tom Hayward. One of Edrich's centuries was 175 in the Test at Lord's, and helped by an innings of 62 in the next at Headingley and then 96 on his home ground in the last, Edrich hit 428 runs, the most for England in the series. He progressed to within 7 of 5,000 runs in Test cricket, an aggregate obtained by only six Englishmen since international matches began nearly 100 years earlier. Yet many of the additional furrows in the creased forehead of Edrich appeared because of the inability of Surrey to make a satisfactory start to the innings, and as an opening batsman as well as captain this was very much a personal problem. His opening partners were Skinner, Howarth, Hansell and Butcher in Championship matches and Intikhab in one-day games. The problem seemed to resolve itself at the end of the

Alan Butcher.

university season. Aworth, the Cambridge captain, became available on leaving St Catherine's College for the last time and after entering the Surrey side with 115 against Middlesex while Edrich was away playing for England, he and Butcher, both left-handers, were with few exceptions the nos 1 and 2 for the remainder of the summer.

Butcher's success in changing from a bowler who bats to one with the onerous job of opening proved perhaps the most gratifying aspect of the year. This capable left-hander, born in Croydon and a member of the local Addiscombe Cricket Club, reached a standard that suggested he would enjoy a long and successful career. After playing for Beckenham Under-11s, Alan Butcher spent five years in southern Australia, where his family had emigrated. He made a considerable impression, being selected for the South Australia Under-15 side and later for an All-Australia representative team. Had Alan's family decided to reside permanently in Australia he would almost certainly have played for his state team and through qualification he would have been eligible for his adopted country. Skinner, who ousted a loyal servant, Long, from behind the stumps, similarly found a more suitable niche lower in the order. Although Howarth experienced an indifferent season and Owen-Thomas departed from county cricket in September there was proof from the young players that the season was one on which better things could be built. Arnold and Jackman still combined in an opening attack that was usually as effective as any in the country and Pocock and Intikhab continued to prosper even in one-day cricket with their differing spin. In the Benson and Hedges at Cardiff Intikhab returned figures of 11-6-5-2.

Lonsdale Skinner.

Lt-Col. W.H. Sillitoe took over as secretary. There were many delays in obtaining planning permission and the country's deteriorating financial climate led the Surrey Committee to believe that a planned redevelopment of The Oval was unlikely to take place.

1976

Surrey had more reason than most to look back in anguish on the year 1976. The ground development scheme had fallen through, the form of the players deteriorated, injuries and accidents increased and finally, for the first time since the MCC tour to India in 1951/52, the touring party announced in September did not contain a Surrey cricketer. That was no personal reflection on Edrich. He might have remained in the England side with an outstanding chance of going to India but for his courage, allied to that of Close, on the Saturday evening of the Manchester Test. The pair withstood a battering from the West Indies fast bowlers for eighty minutes, taking blows on the body when it was impossible to use the bat. By so doing they brought a weekend of condemnation from those who objected to the game being devalued and following that outburst the bowlers changed their tactics. On the Monday the bowlers aimed at the stumps and limited the bouncer. It was decided to dispense with Edrich and Close. They had done their job and younger and less seasoned players could be brought in without fear that the experience might stunt their development.

Edrich, having recovered from the battering, presented as broad a blade as ever but though he would never have declined to continue in the England side, there was a feeling that he did not want to return after going through the mill. Many still thought he would have been an excellent choice for India. At thirty-nine he still seemed still to be batting well when he recorded his 99th hundred against Middlesex on 1 September. On the second day The Oval became the scene of bubbling celebrations, not to mark any Surrey achievement, but to crown the visitors as County Champions.

So back to the beginning, when the ponderous working of the local authority and the Greater London Council killed the hopes of developing The Oval, not only into a ground comparable in comfort and amenities with others of Test status, but also an arena where the locals could enjoy their leisure. For ten years various schemes had been on the books, and in 1975 agreement was almost complete but the delays had been so protracted that by 1976 it was no longer an economic proposition. The bureaucrats had defeated the developers. The outcome meant that the Surrey club was left with the responsibility of improving a ground of about 9½ acres, including a square measuring 88 yards across and on which ninety-three days cricket were played in 1976. Every inch belonged to the Duchy of Cornwall, so nothing was saleable, and there was never any chance that a county club by its normal sources of income could even start to think about alterations on the scale of those envisaged by the developers. They entailed an estimated £7 million, and takings at The Oval were not to increase as the fortunes of the side dwindled.

Arnold went down with Achilles tendon trouble that at one time was thought to need an operation. He escaped that but later became the victim of the fast bowler's malady, a pulled hamstring, and his appearances in his benefit year were limited to 12 of the 20 Championship games. Then on 26 June a car carrying Jackman, Baker and Skinner from Old Trafford to Worcester for a Sunday League game was involved in an accident, which meant that when Arnold was back for his one protracted stay, Jackman was not always available to partner him. He injured ribs, resulting in him missing 3 Championship matches. Baker, who needed many stitches in facial wounds, missed 5. Meantime the career of Aworth came to a sudden end when he decided that seven-day cricket was not for him. Finally Edrich, in taking the run which gave him his century against Middlesex, pulled a muscle at the back of the leg.

With Edrich and Pocock, who played in 2 Tests for a meagre return of 4 for 173, out of the England side, Surrey's stock internationally sunk low even before the tour party was announced. Alan Butcher, who hit his maiden century against Warwickshire, made nothing of his opportunity in the Test trial because of injury. Jackman, the County's most successful bowler with 85 wickets in all, received rough handling when chosen for the second of the 3 one-day Prudential trophy internationals. In the end it was Howarth with his elegant style who left the biggest impression. He hit 1,554 runs in all first-class games, against his captain's 1,526. With Butcher he set up a 1st-wicket record of 218 against Gloucestershire in the Sunday League, in which the side finished midway in the table after heading the other sixteen for most of June. Progress to the semi-final of the Benson and Hedges was creditable, but exit came in the opening round of the Gillette Cup and after fluctuating from sixth to sixteenth in the Championship, the County finished in mid-table at ninth.

1977

22 Championship matches. 12 points for win plus bonus

Since the tactics of the bureaucrats in 1976 had delayed the reconstruction plans for The Oval, little had gone right for Surrey cricket. The standard of play deteriorated, disillusioned players did better elsewhere, the secretary handed in his resignation and the club went across the river into Middlesex to find a coach. This is not to imply any criticism of new coach Fred Titmus, but for more than 100 years there had been a chain of Surrey's own players willing and able to pass on the gospel. These included players like Arthur McIntyre, Andrew Sandham, Alan Peach, Ernie Hayes, 'Razor' Smith, Roger Thompson and Maurice Bird, to go back to the turn of the century.

Titmus was capable of unearthing the required talent. The wicketkeeper Richards, nineteen, and the off-spinner Needham, twenty, were two under his wing in 1977 who looked as though they could make the grade. Raised in Penzance, Cornwall, Jack Richards was as a child only interested in riding horses. At the age of thirteen a friend asked him up to the local cricket club and eight years later he was the regular wicketkeeper for Surrey. There was no history of cricket in the family but his promise was so apparent at the age of sixteen that his father suggested he write to Middlesex and Surrey. At Middlesex he attended pre-season nets, but Surrey gave him a week's trial, which was followed immediately by a six-month contract. On the tall side (5ft 10in) for a wicketkeeper, one of his strengths was his ability to stand up to medium-pace bowlers. He had made his debut in 1976, although he spent most of that year in the Second XI. In 1977 he played in 11 championship matches, sharing the wicketkeeping duties with Lonsdale Skinner.

Meantime the results were still miserable: fourteenth in the Championship, thirteenth in the John Player League, exit from the Benson and Hedges tournament in the qualifying stages and defeat in the Gillette Cup at the second hurdle. The captain, Edrich, produced a rare moment when he recorded his 100th hundred but even then an occasion which should have riveted the attention passed almost unnoticed. The Oval was almost deserted and the game a certain draw when the Derbyshire captain signalled his willingness to continue into the extra time so that Edrich could have the chance of getting from 97 into three figures to put himself out of some considerable misery. This he did at 5.32 p.m. on 12 July. He had been struggling mentally and physically for the century to add to his 99th, scored in the last match of 1976. Having succeeded, more were to follow, one in each innings of the game against Kent, whereupon Edrich went lame again, not to reappear until the last fixture. But at least Edrich had the memory of something well earned and well won to sustain him through this disappointing season. The award of the MBE in the Queen's birthday honours could not have been unconnected. Having played 945 innings in nineteen years, Edrich became only the seventeenth player to make a hundred centuries in the first-class game, which was proof enough of the magnitude of the achievement.

The century in each innings of the Kent match was the fourth such double recorded by Edrich, but even that match turned sour. The umpires cautioned the Surrey captain for 'unfair play' when his bowlers reduced their output to 8 overs in forty minutes soon after Kent set off for a winning target. Such a happening was indicative of the season. If one thing went right, two went wrong. There seemed neither the will nor the skill to escape.

By the end of four months, the services of two young players who had at one time showed considerable promise, David Smith and Andrew Mack, had been dispensed with. Bob Willis and Mike Selvey, and the much improved John Emburey, who played for Surrey Young Cricketers, had moved outside the County to make their respective marks while still in their mid-twenties. Aworth and Owen-Thomas, two other young players of talent, departed the scene altogether, and of the older school Knight and Long were doing good things for Sussex.

Of those who remained in the confines of Kennington, Roope with the bat and Jackman with the ball were most worthy of commendation in 1977. As Edrich played in only 13 of the 22 Championship matches and 2 of the 16 Sunday fixtures, Jackman shouldered the extra responsibility of captaincy well. He came out by far the best of the bowlers with 75 wickets in the Championship. The next best was a very indifferent 38 by Pocock.

Howarth hit 2 centuries but could do no better than average 23.92 for 646 runs. Younis did even less well at 23.51 from 682 and Alan Butcher, averaging 27.00 from 837, continued to be one of those younger players of obvious talent struggling to get further than the embryo stage. Only Roope did himself justice, hitting 5 centuries in all three-day games and winning back an England place at Headingley and The Oval. Scores of 34 and 38 in those Tests did not reflect any great contribution but they were enough to bring Roope a trip to Pakistan and New Zealand.

Another debutant in 1977 was Monte Lynch. Some batsmen are born to block, others to entertain the crowds. There is not the slightest doubt into which category Monte Lynch fitted. Over the years he added a discipline to temper the reckless moments that terminated early innings too often but the basic instincts did not change. Even in his most attentive knocks, Monte Lynch never foreswore his attacking shots or resorted to strokeless defence.

At the end of the season Edrich resigned the captaincy, played one more year and then left the game quietly with dignity while still a very good player. His career statistics are as follows:

SURREY		
410 matches	29,305 runs at 46.07	81 centuries
TESTS		
77 matches	5,138 runs at 43.54	12 centuries
ALL FIRST-CLASS MATCHES		
564 matches	39,790 runs at 45.47	103 centuries

EIGHT
1978-1983

1978

Following negotiations with Sussex, Geoff Arnold moved to Hove and Roger Knight was invited to rejoin Surrey as their captain in 1978. He was capped and led the side for six seasons, during which they won the NatWest trophy in 1982. In his first season as captain Surrey finished sixteenth in the County Championship and tenth in the Sunday League. However, there was great improvement in the following years when they finished third in 1979, second in 1980, sixth in 1981, fifth in 1982 and eighth in 1983. Knight scored 6,797 runs during these years and he said about this period:

> To be invited to return to The Oval as captain was a challenge not to be missed. Instead of being a schoolmaster who played county cricket, I needed to become a county cricket captain who taught in the winter. The years of my captaincy were a very stimulating period and an opportunity to work with some very talented cricketers.

He must be considered extremely unlucky never to have been selected for an England tour, let alone actually play for England. With an honest and open approach to the game of cricket and the model way in which he conducted himself both on and off the field, his peers held him in high esteem.

The season of 1978 is remembered with shudders of horror among those connected with Surrey cricket. It represents the nadir of the County's fortunes. They finished second from bottom in the County Championship, the lowest position in their history, and made no impact whatsoever on the three one-day competitions. Ian Scott-Browne took over from Sillitoe as secretary and Derek Newton succeeded Subba Row as chairman. Newton was able to bring shrewd business acumen to the job and free Raman Subba Row to concentrate on cricketing matters.

In their fourth match of the season Surrey recorded a victory over Essex, the first Championship win for Surrey since 5 July the previous year, but the change of fortune did not last. The County were propping up the table by the middle of August, and having handed over that unhappy position to Northamptonshire, they were not sorry to see the Midlanders' final game at Old Trafford washed out. Like others before them, Surrey found that bad luck hit them while they were down. Entry into the knockout phase of the Benson and Hedges Cup would have provided encouragement, but they lost in the group

Roger Knight.

stage to Nottinghamshire on the rate of taking wickets. Defeat by Essex after overcoming Shropshire meant an early exit from the Gillette Cup, and only a late burst which produced 3 victories brought a share of tenth place in the John Player League.

There was no consistency, particularly in the batting. With Howarth required by New Zealand once their tour of England began, Butcher returned and seemed to have benefited from his period out of the limelight. He put together his highest score, 188, against Sussex at Hove and then looked a very good batsman indeed in scoring 176 and 78 not out against Glamorgan at The Oval, a match in which Knight recorded his first Championship hundred since returning to Surrey. David Smith hit his maiden century against Hampshire earlier in the season and Lynch, when given his first chance of the summer against the Pakistanis, similarly scored his first hundred in first-class cricket. Then John Edrich came along with his 103rd and last first-class century. But these were isolated cases. In between, the opposition bowling found the pickings all too easy, with the side being dismissed thirteen times for under 200 in the Championship; five times Surrey were not even in three figures. In successive games midway through the season, Kent dismissed Surrey for 105, 98, 95 and 75, the four innings spanning no more than 190 overs and 5 balls. Underwood took twenty wickets, including the season's only haul of 9 – for 32 runs – on a wet pitch at The Oval.

The absence of Roope did not help, though his presence in the England team for 4 Tests provided one of the small blessings, just as the absence of any Surrey men in the

David Smith.

party to tour Australia was one of the many disappointments. Also on the credit side was the efficiency of Richards, whose work behind the stumps must have pleased Arthur McIntyre as he prepared to retire after more than forty years with Surrey as wicketkeeper, coach and administrator. With Arnold gone, Jackman bore the brunt of the fast bowling. Generally he did it well, though even his willing nature was tested towards the end of the season. Whereas Intikhab and Pocock were complementary to each other in a spin department as efficient as most in the country, Jackman had only youngsters to help him. Although they did reasonably well, the new ball did not often provide deep penetration. Baker's departure from the side let in Thomas, eighteen years old and left-arm, to support Jackman. His impact was immediate, with the first four Sussex wickets for 1 run in the John Player League, but again success was fleeting. Wilson, another eighteen-year-old, but right-arm with the build of a heavyweight, took over in mid-season and held on; he usually looked the better prospect.

Within a month of the last ball of the 1978 season, Fred Titmus resigned as coach on a matter of policy. He had, he said, warned when taking over in 1977 that it would be at least two years before the performance improved to any great extent. A special committee had been set up under the chairmanship of Raman Subba Row to look into Surrey's playing strength. Titmus, who had been instrumental in obtaining the services of Sylvester Clarke could already see better results ahead. He was a member of this committee but felt his position had been undermined. Some of the senior players then approached

Derek Newton and asked him to bring Micky Stewart back to The Oval as manager. Stewart gave the proposition considerable thought and after detailed discussions came back to Surrey as manager with defined responsibilities. Pocock and Jackman believed that Stewart's appointment was necessary because attitudes at Surrey had grown lax, even irresponsible, and the outlook was bleak unless the playing side of the club could be revitalised. Anne Bickerstaff was brought in as office manager, later becoming assistant to the secretary. She had spent her life in the theatre dealing with all financial aspects and she was brought to The Oval to establish a proper foundation for the sale of tickets. What she found on the playing side, initially, disturbed her, for the players are always any club's main asset. She had come from a profession where in order to survive ambition is everything; what she found at The Oval was complacency. Her findings echoed Pocock's view that 'the attitude of many first-team players was irresponsible; the second-team players were even worse'. Roger Knight needed the backing of a dedicated and seasoned professional who could link the traditions of Surrey's past to the needs of the present and future. Before the start of the 1979 season Surrey took a three-week trip to the Far East. This helped to bring the side together, and allowed Stewart to make an assessment of the players. He set them targets and formed a good working relationship with Roger Knight.

1979

In Championship matches a limit of one bouncer per over was introduced

In the wet summer of 1979 Essex ran away with the Championship and there was never any hope of catching them, so other counties jostled for second place. Surrey held that position in the closing weeks of the season but had the misfortune to meet Essex in the match after that county had won the title. The Chelmsford ground was packed as the Essex supporters came to acclaim their heroes. Despite Geoff Howarth hitting a delightful 100 Surrey trailed by 13 runs on the first innings. Jackman and Wilson bowled Essex out for 101 in their second innings, but Lever and Phillip then bowled out Surrey for 99 and Essex won by 15 runs. This defeat condemned Surrey to third place, but after the horrors of the previous season this was almost paradise. The County made little progress in the Gillette Cup or the John Player League, but the Benson and Hedges Cup saw them fulfil a target Stewart had set them. Recovering from the loss of 3 wickets for 48, Surrey reached 205 for 4 away against Northamptonshire, thanks largely to a fine innings of 92 not out by Roger Knight. The game dragged into a third day, and Surrey eventually won by 5 runs. Combined Universities were beaten with some ease, and Essex were overcome by 7 runs with 5 balls to spare. The draw for the quarter-final took them to Worcester. Younis hit 107 and Butcher, Lynch, Howarth and Knight all scored consistently, so Surrey reached their target of 200 with 5 overs to spare and for the loss of only three wickets.

The semi-final at Derby was a much closer affair. This match revealed the positive qualities of Knight's leadership and the new-found spirit of Surrey cricket. Batting first on a slow pitch, Surrey were given a good start by Butcher and Lynch, who put on 52, but then fell away to score only 166 for 8, which hardly looked a matchwinning score. Both Derbyshire openers were soon out to Hugh Wilson but Peter Kirsten took

Monte Lynch.

complete command in an innings of 70, and with 20 overs remaining, Derbyshire were 114 for 2 and seemingly cruising to victory. All through this period Knight had maintained attacking fields with three men clustered round the bat, and the pressure began to tell on the batsmen. Kirsten's award-winning innings ended when he snicked Jackman to Richards. Sylvester Clarke, in his first season with Surrey, bowled out his 11 overs, sending back Miller, Barnett and Walters, before limping off the field, by which time Derbyshire were 141 for 8. Roger Knight took on the responsibility of bowling himself for the final stages and Hendrick went for a big hit that would have levelled the scores had he connected – he did not and he was bowled. The Surrey players leaped in the air in undisguised delight. This had been a noble victory.

There were many things stacked against Surrey in the final, not the least of which was Sylvester Clarke's inability to play because of his leg injury. David Thomas was also unfit, Wilson and Knight had been injured, and Jackman played under a severe physical handicap. Sentiment and the neutral observer were also very much on the side of Essex, who had never won a trophy and who were appearing in a Lord's final for the first time. Knight won the toss and asked Essex to bat first. Gooch and Denness gave them a bright start and, later, Gooch and McEwan played champagne cricket. Jackman was obviously struggling, Pocock had not been in the best of form, and both bowlers suffered. Hugh Wilson took four wickets but his inexperience showed, and of the Surrey bowlers Knight and Intikhab brought more restraint from the Essex batsmen. Essex's score of 290 for 6 was the highest ever made in a Benson and Hedges final. That Surrey were beaten by only 35 runs was a credit to their undying spirit and courage. Howarth and Knight batted splendidly, adding 91 at a rate which compared favourably to that of Gooch and McEwan, but Roope was left high and dry at the end of an outstanding match.

As well as his four wickets in the Essex match of the Benson & Hedges group stage, Clarke took seven wickets against Northamptonshire in the Championship before the end of a wet and miserable May. He ended the season with 6 for 90 in the first innings against Hampshire. All these performances were at The Oval, the supposed graveyard for fast bowlers, but in late June after Surrey beat Glamorgan and Warwickshire in successive matches, Clarke began a long struggle against injury. There was talk of a knee operation but this was overruled by specialists who diagnosed hip trouble. As a result, the onus returned for the best part of two months to the willing shoulders of Jackman, Wilson and Thomas. All three responded well and with Knight taking five wickets in an innings twice, the gap left by Clarke's absence was reduced to a minimum. The admirable Pocock pleased those who talked of him still as the country's best off-spinner by tearing Glamorgan apart at Cardiff with the only nine-wicket haul of the summer, for 57 runs, and he was back at his devastating best at Portsmouth in taking 13 for 122 as Hampshire were mastered. Jackman finished with 93 wickets at 17.15 each, Clarke 43 at 17.60 and Pocock 70 at 20.50. Butcher enjoyed his best season with 1,398 runs overall. The unflappable style of Clinton, in his first season with Surrey after arriving from Kent, provided a useful anchor and he combined well with Butcher. Knight, Roope, Smith and Lynch all had their moments.

During a period of four years the square at The Oval was re-laid. This produced pitches that had more pace and bounce, much to the joy of the Surrey bowlers. The ground was under the tenure of Harry Brind who had first come to The Oval in 1976 with one specific brief: that of improving the quality of The Oval pitches. In his words the square 'was as dead as a doornail'. At the end of his first year he dug up his first pitch, going down a foot, throwing all the old soil away and replacing it with eight inches of clay and four inches of topsoil. After two years it was ready to play and he had the pace and bounce he was looking for. After that Harry dug up and re-laid five pitches a year for four years. There are twenty-seven pitches on the vast Oval square, twenty of them for first-class use. Being recognised as the groundsman of the year in successive years, he was to be called upon by those who govern the game to give assistance and advice to others as the TCCB Inspector of Pitches, thereby following in the footsteps of his predecessor, Bert Lock.

1980

As the 1980 season started, the resurgence in Surrey cricket was obvious from the zest with which the players approached the game. However, finishing runners-up seldom satisfies. Winning is the thing. Yet perhaps two second-place finishes could be said to add

Graham Clinton.

up to one first for Surrey who, in chasing Middlesex home in the County Championship and going down to them in the final of the Gillette Cup, at least played second fiddle to a very good side. Indeed, Surrey could consider themselves well above the remaining fifteen counties. Nottinghamshire, third in the Championship, were the proverbial mile away, sixty-seven points adrift. Surrey were the only worthwhile challengers to Middlesex from midway through the season, and early in August, when just four points separated the sides, they had a real chance. But Middlesex had two games in hand and these cushioned them in their run-in, enabling them to win by a final margin of thirteen points.

Surrey's run to the final of the Gillette Cup was not without incident or excitement. The first round match against Northamptonshire at The Oval produced some of the finest bowling that the competition had ever known. Clarke bowled at a sizzling pace and was unerringly accurate. His first 7 overs cost only 2 runs and his final figures were 1 for 9 in 12 overs, 7 of them maidens. His fire was of considerable assistance to Robin Jackman, who dismissed Larkins and Williams with successive balls and tore the heart out of the Northants batting with the result that they lost the first 6 in their order for 28 runs, 5 of them to Jackman, who later dismissed Sharp and finished with 6 for 28. Facing 141, Surrey were never in real danger and won by seven wickets with 17 overs to spare. Jackman was again to the fore in the second-round match against Gloucestershire at The Oval, this time as an all-rounder. Butcher and Clinton gave Surrey a good start, but they fell within one run of each other, and from 71 for no wicket, the County slipped to 117 for 5. Jackman helped Knight to add 66 in 13 overs, and Surrey eventually reached 200 off the final ball of the innings. The visitors lost half their side to Knight and Jackman for

Robin Jackman.

Roger Knight.

66, but Procter and David Graveney effected a recovery, and it needed the return of Jackman to end resistance and give Surrey victory by 8 runs.

The quarter-final at Chelmsford produced one of the most incredible matches ever seen in one-day cricket. Surrey began poorly and were 58 for 3, but Clinton hit a resolute 58, and with David Smith playing with customary force for 37, the County reached 195 for 7 in their 60 overs, a far better score than had looked possible earlier in the day. They seemed to take a grip on the game when, with Jackman menacing and marauding, they reduced Essex to 35 for 4, Gooch and McEwan among those back in the pavilion. With 5 overs remaining, Essex needed only 11 runs to win and had four wickets standing, including those of Hardie and Phillip, who were in full flow. An Essex victory appeared to be a formality, but Hardie hit lazily to cover to give Jackman his fifth wicket, Phillip was insanely run out and Clarke wrecked Neil Smith's stumps. The last over began with the last Essex pair at the wicket needing 2 to win. David Thomas, who had conceded 55 runs in his previous 10 overs was the bowler, and when Ray East took a single to level the scores the game still seemed to be Essex's for the taking. With 2 balls remaining, Lever pushed Thomas to mid-off and East came charging down the wicket. He was beaten by Knight's under-arm throw and Surrey had won by virtue of having lost fewer wickets with the scores level. The semi-final was less invigorating. It spread into two days, and Yorkshire were bowled out on one of the newly laid Oval pitches in poor light for 135. Ray Illingworth, their manager, was not pleased. Surrey won by four wickets with 12.1 overs to spare.

Following the drama of the earlier rounds, the final was something of an anticlimax. The game was played in sunshine on a slow, low-bouncing pitch and therefore it was a

Sylvester Clarke.

bowler's match. Surrey were put in to bat and scored only 21 in the first 11 overs, Mike Selvey taking two wickets for 17 in a 12-over spell. A late assault by David Smith and Intikhab brought 62 runs in 8 overs, but the final score of 201 was never going to be enough. The Middlesex start was even slower than Surrey's but they had less need to hurry. Mike Brearley anchored the innings with 96 not out but the final assault by Roland Butcher with 50 not out saw Middlesex home by seven wickets with 6 overs to spare.

There was a storming finish to the Championship season by Surrey, who won 5 of their last 6 matches and also beat the Australians, who were on a short tour for the Centenary Test. Crucially, Middlesex beat Surrey by an innings at Lord's, and the return match at The Oval was ruined by rain. Just as crucial was the game at Derby in August when the home side inflicted on Surrey the only defeat that they suffered in those last 6 matches. Knight won the toss and put Derbyshire in to bat. Jackman took 5 for 43, and the last six Derbyshire wickets went down for 12 runs. The Surrey batsmen fared even worse on an uncertain pitch and, bowled out for 129, they trailed by 65 on the first innings and eventually lost by 174 runs.

Robin Jackman had a lust for life that permeated his cricket. He enjoyed every ball he bowled, batted and fielded and it showed. He could bowl for hours without a sign of weariness and without losing control or the ability to move the ball. It was not just that he was willing; he hated it when he was taken off. He was now vice-captain and very supportive of Roger Knight. Jackman bowled with a bigger heart than ever, thankful that he had a fully fit Clarke at the other end to 'soften them up' in the manner of modern West Indians. Jackman was the first to admit that the arrival of Clarke had brought an extra dimension to his own bowling, for now batsmen could no longer afford to attempt to simply survive against Jackman's fast-medium line and length and movement off the seam; there was no respite at the other end and Clarke's pace and hostility were frightening to many. Throughout the season the effort of Jackman never wavered. Fifteen times he took four or more wickets in a Championship innings, with 8 for 58 against Lancashire at Old Trafford, a new best performance for him in England. A final average of 15.40 from 121 wickets left him fourth in the national averages and only his age, thirty-five, can have prevented the selectors from sending him to the West Indies in the winter. However, Bob Willis came home injured and Jackman was called and made his Test debut in Barbados.

Sylvester Clarke's first-class average of 21.51 for 79 wickets further illustrated the power of the Surrey opening attack. He took the season's first Championship hat-trick against Nottinghamshire. As the pitches became firmer so Intikhab Alam was recalled with his leg-breaks and googlies in support of Pat Pocock's off spin. Hugh Wilson fell away after promising so much in 1979, but another of the younger school, 'Jack' Richards, kept wicket well enough to suggest an international future. The arrival of Clarke had made things difficult for Howarth, although not intentionally. He began 1980 in indifferent form and dropped down to the Second XI to regain confidence. In the meantime, Intikhab had replaced Giles Cheatle, slow left-arm, whose form had lapsed, and Howarth was unable to regain his place because Surrey had their quota of two overseas players. It was not to be the last time that Howarth encountered this problem. Alan Butcher had a fine season with the bat, as to a lesser degree did his opening partner, Grahame Clinton but too often in the early part of the season insufficient advantage was taken of good beginnings. Butcher hit his first double hundred, against Cambridge University, and accumulated a total of 1,713 runs in the season.

Surrey were influential in bringing the first 'floodlit' match to the football ground at Stamford Bridge, the home of Chelsea. However, due to other commitments, Surrey were unable to play in this exhibition match and Essex took their place.

1981

Fully covered pitches introduced, 100-over limit dropped, 16 points for a win plus bonus

Knight had been in such fine form, and Surrey had done so well, that there was disappointment in 1981 that the County did not carry off a trophy. In a wet summer there was some good cricket, but not as good as Micky Stewart felt the side was capable of playing, and there was some bad luck. There was a certain sadness at The Oval as the curtain came down on 1981. Alan Butcher marked the occasion auspiciously enough with a cover-driven boundary to complete a personal 154, as well as victory for his side over Essex, but once more Surrey had not quite made it. Runners-up in the Benson and

Hedges Cup for the second time in three years was the best they could offer. In the County Championship they dropped to sixth place and in the John Player League slipped from fifth to seventh. Micky Stewart, Surrey's manager, was too realistic to try to hide behind a bad-luck story, but there were moments of frustration with injuries that mirrored the team's performance. Not least of these was the loss of Sylvester Clarke for more than half the season. Surrey had arrived at the end of June with 63 points from 3 successive wins and were top of the Championship table when Clarke, who had been worried by acute shin soreness, entered hospital for an operation to make sure that there was no infection of the bone in the left leg. All county batsmen feared his bowling and the bowlers were not too happy to see him batting either after his 100 not out in sixty-two minutes against Glamorgan, which was to remain the fastest century of the summer. Clarke was the biggest influence in the side, giving wholehearted support and always ready and willing to bowl. He played in only 9 Championship matches, but took 44 wickets at 15.43 runs each, and his loss was devastating. Well as Butcher, Knight, Clinton and Lynch batted, and encouraging as was the bowling of Thomas, and in spite of a good spell in August with Butcher in fine form, Surrey slipped to sixth in the Championship.

The survival through the zonal round of the Benson and Hedges Cup, which was played in a very damp start to the season, involved two abandonments, a defeat and a win over Minor Counties. However, this was enough to take Surrey into the quarter-finals for the match against Nottinghamshire at Trent Bridge. Rice won the toss and asked Surrey to bat. The response was a solid, consistent batting performance founded on a 2nd-wicket stand of 104 between Knight and Clinton. Knight hit 70, followed it with the wickets of Rice and Birch for 36 and took the Gold Award. It was his tenth individual award in one-day competitions, a fact that emphasises his worth as a limited-overs all-rounder. Clarke soon bowled both Nottinghamshire openers, Todd and Robinson, and Thomas had Hassan caught at slip by the incomparable Roope. Randall and Rice flattered briefly but Jackman accounted for Randall, and finished with four wickets as Surrey won by 47 runs, Nottinghamshire being dismissed for 179 in 49.4 overs.

The semi-final was an altogether tenser affair. Roger Knight chose to bat first at The Oval when he won the toss, and Clinton and Richards, now promoted to opener for the one-day matches, gave Surrey a good start against the formidable Leicestershire pace attack. In the early stages runs came at 4 an over, but the steadiness of the bowling, supported by tight fielding, restricted progress when Surrey would have been looking to increase the rate and it took a late 55 not out from Graham Roope to take the home side to 191 for 9 in their 55 overs. It looked an indefensibly small total. The Surrey score shrank as Balderstone and Steele passed 50 for the 1st wicket. Wickets fell regularly and when the last pair, Higgs and Parsons, came together, Leicestershire needed 27 runs to win. As Jackman began his last over 12 were wanted. Parsons pulled the third ball over mid-wicket for 6 and the next ball went for 2 so that Leicestershire now had a very real chance of winning. An unwise attempt at a run off the fifth ball of the over saw Higgs run out at the bowler's end by Pocock and Surrey victorious by 3 runs.

The hero of the win over Leicestershire was Ian Payne, deputising for the injured Clarke, but he could find no place in the side for the final when Clarke was pressed into service again. Surrey's 194 for 7 hardly looked likely to be a winning score against a side

David Thomas.

of Somerset's batting power, but Jackman and Clarke raised hopes when they bowled Rose and Denning in the first 3 overs of the innings. That was really the last spark of comfort for Surrey. Viv Richards, having played himself in, began to clout the ball in all directions. Roebuck helped him to add 105, and then Richards and Ian Botham hit off the last 87 runs at a very brisk pace to bring Somerset victory with 10.3 overs to spare.

Surrey reasserted themselves late in July when beating two sides vying for the title, Hampshire and Sussex, but Clarke's return was limited to 2 games before he broke down again and the challenge fizzled out. Inconsistency in batting was a major reason for Surrey's decline in a year when they were expected to prosper. Alan Butcher ended the summer by scoring 627 runs in 4 Championship matches, which was almost half his aggregate of 1,310 from 18 such games. Grahame Clinton opened with hundreds against Cambridge University and Derbyshire and ended with another against Middlesex but he stuttered in between. His final Championship aggregate was 1,059. Roger Knight was similarly inconsistent, though he too reached four figures. Monte Lynch, who managed 2 centuries with a positive approach, provided reason for optimism. Graham Roope, happily among the leading catchers again, and David Smith impressed only in spasms. Although Geoff Howarth showed his class in scoring 90 and 110 not out against Warwickshire, he was unable to command a regular place because of the limitations on overseas players and the need to look to the future. The bowling looked thin without Clarke. Robin Jackman took only 60 wickets and it was Intikhab Alam who accounted for the most victims, 65. This was his last season before returning to Lahore to enter the textile trade. In his twelve years service with Surrey, he had scored 5,707 runs and taken 629 wickets in the first-class game and 2,439 runs and 131 wickets in limited-overs matches. He had also achieved a reputation second to none in terms of sportsmanship and loyalty. Roger Knight recalls how when he asked him to bowl in a one-day match with the new ball, which Pocock said would be very difficult for a spinner to hold, Intikhab replied, 'I'll just grip the ball harder.'

The disappointment in 1981 was compounded into sadness by the deaths at an early age of both Tom Clark and Ken Barrington. Barrington's death in the West Indies when he was assistant manager of the touring England side shocked the cricket world. Surrey set up an appeal so that his name would always be remembered at The Oval in a way in which he would have liked, giving pleasure to others.

Tom Clark had first played for Surrey in 1947 and during the Championship-winning years from 1952 to 1958 scored more runs for the county than anyone apart from Constable and May. In that period he scored 7,324 runs at 29.53 and took 64 wickets and 67 catches.

1982

Fines for slow over rates introduced

In 1982 Mackintosh, Needham and Thomas went some of the way to filling the gap left by Intikhab's retirement. Clarke, as ferocious and fast as ever, steered clear of serious injury for the first time since joining Surrey and he and Jackman became the most formidable opening attack in the country. The side was positive and confident for most of the season but, frustratingly, Pocock could play in only a third of the Championship matches because of a back injury. This meant that after the hard work of Jackman and Clarke in breaking down early opposition there was an inadequate spin attack to consolidate the position and grasp the opportunities that were offered on certain pitches. Andy Needham showed considerable promise as an off-spinner and as a batsman, but he and Duncan Pauline had to be disciplined during the season for violating what Stewart saw as the individual's responsibilities to the club. In the game against Lancashire at Old Trafford in July, Surrey were 152 for 9 when Jackman joined Needham. By the close of play on the Saturday, the pair were still together, and the score was 260. On the Monday, they took it to 324 before Jackman was bowled by David Hughes for 60. Needham finished with 134 not out, the first century of his career, and the last-wicket stand of 172 was only one short of the record set by Ducat and Sandham in 1921. Needham's day of glory did not end there, for he followed this with 5 for 91, a career best, with his well-flighted off-breaks. He suffered somewhat in the second innings when Clive Lloyd and Abrahams punished him mercilessly, and Lancashire won by four wickets. It was later revealed that, in celebrating Needham's fine all-round performance, the player himself and Duncan Pauline, who was also in the side, had stayed out beyond the prescribed hour. Both were omitted from the next match as a punishment. There were some who thought it harsh, but Stewart, Knight and the Surrey administration were firm and clear in the standards that they required of their players, and there were no complaints from the players.

Graham Roope.

Surrey were always in the top five of the Championship, and briefly in July, they were second, but the final position of fifth was realistic. In the Benson and Hedges Cup, they failed to progress beyond the zonal round. The story in the NatWest Bank Trophy was different. There were some tremors at The Oval in the first-round match against Durham when Simon Davis, an Australian pace bowler, sent back Pauline, Clinton and Knight for 16 runs in the first 6 overs. Monte Lynch, with 129, and Graham Roope, with 77, added 166 in 107 minutes for the 5th wicket and Surrey reached 279, sufficient for a comfortable victory. Lynch was now a favourite at The Oval. His cheerful attitude to the game manifested itself in his glorious aggressive batting and exciting fielding, and he won friends wherever he went. In the second round, he had to play second fiddle to David Smith, who hit 103 not out in wintry conditions to take Surrey to victory over Northamptonshire at The Oval with seven balls to spare. In the match at Southampton starting at 10.00 a.m., Roger Knight had no hesitation in asking Hampshire to bat first on a pitch that would remain damp for two to three hours under an overcast sky. Jackman used the conditions to great advantage, finishing with 6 for 22, while Graham Monkhouse in particular gave able support. David Turner batted bravely for his 51, but Hampshire were all out for 119, and Surrey went on to win by eight wickets in mid-afternoon. Only 14 overs were possible on the first day of the semi-final at The Oval when Brearley had won the toss for Middlesex and put Surrey in to bat. Surrey made only 205 for 9 which did not look to be a winning score. Within the first 11 overs of the Middlesex innings, however, the match was decided in favour of Surrey. Clarke, bowling with considerable menace, had taken 4 wickets for 8 in 6 overs and Middlesex crumbled to 80 all out.

The NatWest Bank Trophy Final of 1982 will not be remembered as one of the classic games but for Surrey it was a total triumph. They arrived at Lord's with a settled side in good form. Knight won the toss and asked Warwickshire to bat. It was a pleasant morning but the early atmosphere was heavy. No batsman managed to play himself in and by the 28th over Warwickshire were 74 for 8. The game had really been turned by Knight, who only bowled himself because Monkhouse had failed to settle, and by Thomas, a left-arm bowler who could generate a fair pace but who ultimately never achieved quite as much as he had promised. Small and Asif Din restored some pride for Warwickshire with a 9th-wicket stand of 62 in 24 overs and 158 was certainly a better score than had looked possible at 11.30 a.m. There was no nonsense about the batting of Butcher and Howarth. Helped by a generous sprinkling of no balls they reached 20 inside 4 overs and 30 inside 6. Howarth played some magnificent shots off the back foot and his driving square of the wicket was regal. His downfall was an anti-climax for he played a wretched shot at a bad ball and was caught at mid-on diving forward. Butcher batted on in majestic fashion and it was fitting that he should on-drive Kallicharran for 4 and the winning hit. Warwickshire had been outclassed.

Rounding off the season so successfully created justifiable optimism at a time of gradual change. Monte Lynch, David Smith and Jack Richards were firmly established, Dave Thomas, Andy Needham, Graham Monkhouse and Kevin Mackintosh were following along the right lines and they were all in their early or mid-twenties. Graham Roope, after the best part of twenty years of excellent service, had to make way for the younger school and was looking for another county. Roope possessed tremendous talent but lacked confidence in his own ability, always living with the fear of failure. If he never shone as an outstanding batsman in his 21 Test matches, he had a fine international record, averaging 30.71 with the bat and taking 35 catches.

There was an annoying inconsistency in the Surrey batting at the start of the season. With Intikhab's leg-spin gone for good and Pat Pocock, with his off-breaks, absent for most of the year because of a nasty back condition, the spin bowling needed to follow up an effective pace attack was inadequate. Opponents who should have been winkled out in their second innings, when pitches began to wear, were allowed to slip through the net. As a result, although Surrey occupied fourth place in the Championship table for most of the season, briefly second at the end of July, they had to settle for fifth position in the end. Pocock was by no means the only player to fall foul of injury. Grahame Clinton suffered in thumb, back and shoulder in turn, Smith had a longish lay-off with a neck complaint followed by a fractured thumb and Alan Butcher had to overcome a wrist injury before ending the season full of runs. Sylvester Clarke and Robin Jackman again proved as good an opening pair of bowlers as any in the country, taking 85 and 73 wickets respectively in three-day cricket with 25 and 22 in one-day games. Jackman was spared the Sunday frolics but did better than anybody in the knockout tournaments. His 6 for 22 against Hampshire in the NatWest was an outstanding performance. This was followed by selection for his first home Test appearance against Pakistan and subsequently a place in the side for Australia. Jackman's career statistics are as follows:

SURREY

338 matches	4,823 runs at 18.98	1,206 wickets at 22.36

61 times he took 5 wickets in an innings and 7 times 10 wickets in a match

TESTS

4 matches	42 runs at 7.00	14 wickets at 31.78

ALL FIRST-CLASS MATCHES

399 matches	5,685 runs at 17.71	1,402 wickets at 22.80

67 times he took 5 wickets in an innings and 8 times 10 wickets in a match

1983

24 Championship matches

At the end of the Australian tour Robin Jackman announced his retirement from first-class cricket and settled in South Africa. His departure severely affected Surrey's chance of enjoying the successful season that had been predicted for them, and for the first time since Stewart had become manager and Gibson had become coach, Surrey failed to make a serious challenge in any of the competitions. Kevin Mackintosh, who had been expected to assume Jackman's role, was injured and in fact disappeared from the side. Clarke, Monkhouse, Thomas and Pocock carried the bowling, and indeed even Clarke took time to get into his stride. It was a season not without trauma, but not without hope. A wet May saw Surrey make an inglorious exit from the Benson and Hedges Cup and, on the thirtieth of that month, they were bowled out for the lowest score in their history. At Chelmsford, Essex hit 287 on the Monday after a blank first day. Surrey began their innings with sixty-seven minutes to play. Butcher was caught behind off Foster off the first ball of the 3rd over. Two overs later, Foster bowled Needham. Knight lasted only 3 balls before being lbw to Phillip, and Lynch was out the same way in the 9th over by which time Surrey were 8 for 4. Three more wickets fell at the same score and only a clout for 4 by Clarke off Foster and an edged 2 by Monkhouse prevented the score of 14 all out from being the lowest in first-class history. The next day, after being 18 for 2, Surrey drew the match, Knight hitting 101 not out and sharing an unbroken 3rd-wicket partnership of 167 with Clinton.

The rest of the season was not quite as damaging as that, although some would argue that the nine-wicket defeat by Warwickshire in the second round of the NatWest Trophy was equally traumatic, but there were problems in other directions. Disturbed by his side's poor form, Roger Knight called for extra effort which brought a good response. The improvement was obvious, but there had been trouble with David Smith, who seemed unable to accept the authority of his captain. In mid-August, it was announced that Surrey had accepted his resignation. He later joined Worcestershire but was to return to The Oval, somewhat unexpectedly, in 1987 only to leave again after two seasons.

On the brighter side, there was the exciting but controlled form of Monte Lynch and a show of promise from Duncan Pauline, albeit one that was never maintained either in

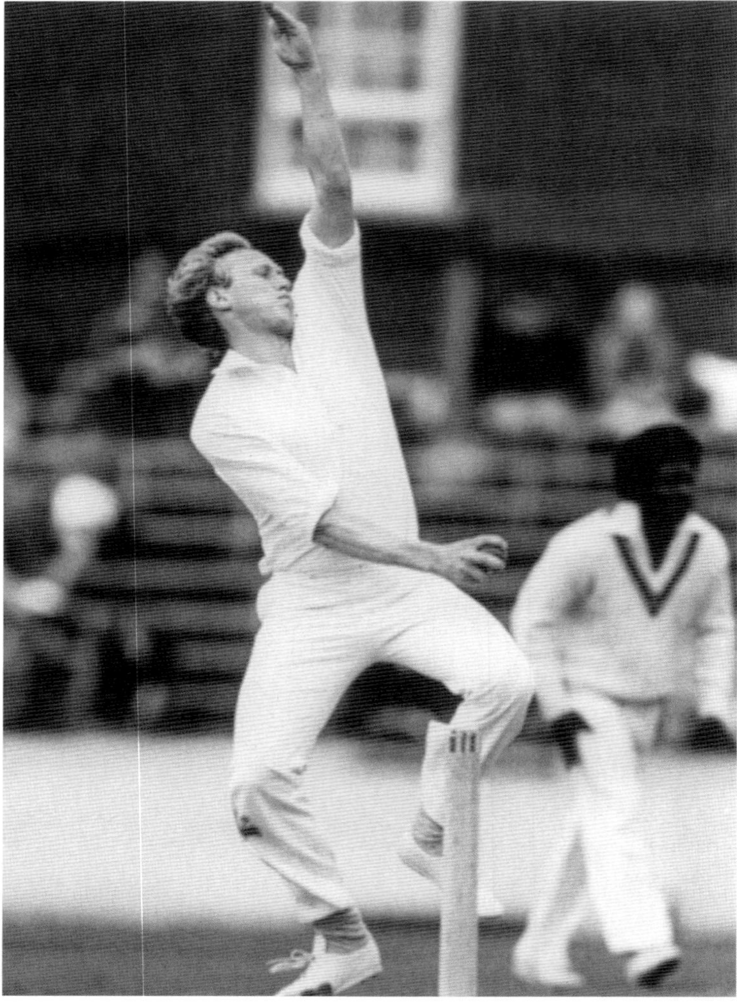
Graham Monkhouse.

his remaining days with Surrey or at Glamorgan. There was the advance of Alec Stewart, who had made his debut in 1981, and was now forcing his way more regularly into a side which had need, among other things, of his brilliant fielding, although he was also a highly competent wicketkeeper. A handsome and aggressive batsman, he hit a maiden hundred, 118 not out in three hours, against Oxford University at The Oval in June 1983. It was a happy sign for the future. As other young players like Chris Bullen and Mark Feltham began to appear in the side, there were other exciting developments at The Oval. The Ken Barrington Appeal was launched in June 1983 in an attempt to develop the Barrington Cricket Centre at the Vauxhall End of the ground. After years of struggling with bureaucrats and politicians, the club began a period of reconstruction on the ground. The perimeter wall on the gasometer side, the entrance by the Hobbs Gate and administrative offices to control the flow of the crowd had all been set in process of reconstruction and, most ambitiously, close to the pavilion a new executive suite and restaurant was developed, which was to be opened in time for the 1984 season. With plans for development of the Vauxhall End and the introduction of colourful, comfortable bucket seats, the efforts of many helped to bring the facilities at The Oval to a standard acceptable in the second half of the twentieth century.

The unveiling of the executive suite did not coincide with a marked run of success on the field. Surrey did qualify for the quarter-finals of the Benson and Hedges Cup, where they were beaten by Nottinghamshire, but only after a frighteningly close one-wicket win over Combined Universities at Oxford. Pat Pocock and Sylvester Clarke scored the 13 needed for the last wicket to win the match. In the NatWest Trophy, a good victory over Essex at Chelmsford was followed by a resounding quarter-final defeat at Edgbaston. Neither the County Championship nor the John Player League offered much comfort after a moderate start and Surrey finished eighth in the Championship. Four wins from 16 Sunday League games left them in eleventh place. The season was accepted as disappointing, and it was apparent that too much responsibility in the bowling was thrust on Pocock, who to the delight of all won back his place in the England side, and Clarke, who needed quicker, more hostile and more consistent support at the other end. The batting was generally good and entertaining, if a little inconsistent. Sylvester Clarke, despite the fact that only nine bowlers in the country bettered his 78 wickets, took a long time to get into his stride. Although Dave Thomas strove hard to fill the gap at the other end, he will be best remembered in 1983 for his batting. He hit his maiden century against Nottinghamshire in late July and then recorded another hundred at Hove, which took him into the England party at Trent Bridge, though in the event he was only made twelfth man. Graham Monkhouse returned his best figures, 7 for 51, in the Nottinghamshire match but he was soon to break a finger and, as Mackintosh was out virtually all season with back trouble, support for Clarke was seriously limited. Pat Pocock bowled his off-breaks with customary skill, but too often he was in operation after only moderate penetration by the faster men.

To some extent, the batting followed a similar pattern. Alan Butcher and Grahame Clinton never settled to make the good starts of previous years, so Monte Lynch, a strokemaker who is seldom happy sitting on the splice, had to retrain himself. To his credit, Lynch did that well, while still finding time to play some exciting innings on his way to 1,558 runs. Duncan Pauline replaced Clinton at the beginning of August and opening with Butcher against Warwickshire at The Oval started with a partnership of 136 and followed with his first first-class hundred against Sussex. Like Pauline, Alec Stewart did all that was expected of him and Roger Knight's rallying call made during the closing days of July was answered.

Roger Knight resigned the captaincy at the end of the season, but he agreed to play one more year under the new skipper Geoff Howarth before taking up a teaching appointment. He served Surrey well as player and captain. His calm and authority did much to re-establish order and discipline at a time when it was necessary. He then took up full-time teaching as housemaster at Cranleigh School and from 1990 to 1993 he was headmaster at Worksop College. In 1994 he was appointed secretary of the MCC and later became chief executive.

NINE

1984-1986

1984

Minimum 117 overs per day in Championship matches

Judged entirely on first-team results and the capturing of trophies the 1984 season was disappointing, yet to the keen observer there was excitement bubbling close to the surface. Surrey broke new ground by staging a game against Cambridge University at Banstead at the end of June. Some of the senior players stood down and with Howarth out for nothing, Surrey were struggling at 172 for 7 when Keith Medlycott joined Nick Falkner. Both players were making their first-class debuts. In 138 minutes, they shared an unbroken stand of 189, 15 runs short of the County record for the 8th wicket. Medlycott, primarily a slow left-arm bowler who had come up through all the youth structure from the Surrey schools side at the age of eleven, hit a six and 13 fours in his unbeaten 117. Falkner, who was playing on his own club ground, took 233 minutes for his 101 and hit 3 sixes and 11 fours. It was the first occasion in a first-class match in England when two batsmen have scored a century in the same innings on their first-class debuts. It had previously been achieved by O.W. Bill and L.R. Leabeater for New South Wales against Tasmania at Sydney in the 1929/30 season.

Falkner was not in the side when Surrey played Kent at Canterbury and Gloucestershire at Cheltenham in August, yet remarkably, and for the first time in history, Surrey fielded eleven players all of whom had hit a first-class century – Butcher, Clinton, Knight, Lynch, Needham, Richards, Monkhouse, Thomas, Clarke, Howarth and Medlycott. The medium-pacer 'Farmer' Monkhouse had hit 100 when batting as a night-watchman against Kent at The Oval earlier in the season while Thomas had hit a fierce century against Nottinghamshire at The Oval in 1983.

On the whole, though, the batting was a thing of bits and pieces. Monte Lynch, scorer of most runs, 1,546, hit a large proportion of them during 5 matches in mid-season, and of Alan Butcher's 4 centuries 2 came in the same match against Glamorgan at The Oval. Grahame Clinton, good one day but not the next, managed his highest score, 192, during a stand of 277 with Butcher against Yorkshire, as well as carrying his bat for 113 against Derbyshire, and Roger Knight saved his best until the last month before he gave up full-time cricket. His last 5 first-class innings were 142, 77, 114, 109 and 16. In his time he took a century off every first-class county except Yorkshire.

Sylvester Clarke again led the bowling assault, with Dave Thomas giving him better support in the latter part of the summer. Pocock earned his England recall as the best off-spinner available to the selectors, having last played for his country eight years previously. In taking 6 for 30 against Yorkshire he completed a career 1,500 first-class wickets.

Scratching deeper, there was more cause for Surrey elation for, with Geoff Arnold now back at The Oval as coach, the Second XI finished second in the Second XI Championship and the Under-25 Trophy came to Surrey after a thrilling 1-run win over a strong Middlesex side at The Oval.

1985

Minimum of 112 overs per day in Championship matches

There was abounding hope for the 1985 season, but this was dashed almost before the season began. It was found that Sylvester Clarke was suffering from disc trouble and that he would not be able to play at all during the season. The loss of Clarke was a shattering blow, for in effect he was the Surrey attack. The original plan for the faster attack was Clarke, David Thomas, Graham Monkhouse, Mark Feltham and Kevin Mackintosh, and one by one they went down. Mackintosh was always out of the running with a prolonged back injury, Feltham spent most of the summer recovering from a car accident in South Africa, Monkhouse had a wrist broken while batting against Middlesex and Thomas, incapacitated by a damaged groin, was rarely seen after the

Geoff Howarth.

beginning of July. A replacement was urgently needed, and Surrey signed Tony Gray, a 6ft 8in fast bowler who had just taken 36 wickets for Trinidad in the Shell Shield in his first full season. The registering of another overseas player meant that, under the current regulations, Gray and Howarth could not appear in the same side. Howarth, even though he was captain, had to stand down.

It must be emphasised that Howarth was fully supportive of all that was done. It was he who insisted that Surrey's need was a fast bowler, and that they needed his own batting less than they needed Gray's bowling. In fact, Geoff Howarth's last contribution to Surrey cricket was an act of chivalrous self-sacrifice. He did not appear in a Championship match, and he faded quietly from the scene. Geoff had become a good County player and then a fine Test player, at times even a great Test player. His knowledge of batting extended to the rest of cricket and he achieved his just reward in being made captain of his country. He became the most successful captain ever for New Zealand and was deservedly awarded first the MBE, and then an OBE, for his services to New Zealand cricket. Richard Hadlee commented that all the New Zealand team regarded him as having something very special to offer the team as captain. They looked upon him as a 'bit of a toff' and they would have died for him on the cricket field. Strangely, he was something of a rebel in his early days at The Oval, but Surrey cricket taught him much, and the man of quiet humour, great dignity and gentle charm repaid the club in full for all that they had done for him.

Pocock led the side for a few matches, and then Trevor Jesty, who had just joined the County from Hampshire, was appointed captain for the rest of the season when it was apparent that Howarth would not be able to take his place in the side. Jesty was signed to give middle-order experience to the team. Ian Greig was to say of Jesty: 'He was the model professional. In dress and manners, he was everything for a young player to model himself on, both on and off the field.' He was not, however, an adventurer. His captaincy was always safe. He did not make mistakes, but he took few chances.

Jesty began with a cascade of runs, but the captaincy affected him to some extent. However, he still passed 1,000 runs in Championship matches, as did Lynch, who played with excitement and maturity. At times, Monte Lynch touched brilliance, registering 7 Championship hundreds and holding 36 catches in close to the wicket fielding. Jack Richards excelled behind the stumps. Clinton, a battered and bruised model of consistency topped 1,200 runs and Needham scored 1,000 runs for the first time. Butcher, with over 1,000 runs, and Clinton, a left-handed double act, were as good an opening pair as any in the country, and the batting that followed was enterprising. For the first two months of the season, Surrey were in the top four of the Championship, and wins with maximum points over Warwickshire and Derbyshire took them to third at the beginning of August, but 4 frustrating draws followed, and in at least 2 of these matches, more penetrative bowling might have forced victories. Statistically, Surrey could still have won the Championship when they began their penultimate match against Sussex at The Oval on 4 September. Harry Brind, honoured for preparing the best wickets in the country, had given the sides a beautiful track on which to play. Sussex asked Surrey to bat first on a cold, overcast day. The wonderfully dependable Clinton hit his third Championship century of the season, and Jesty played a delightful innings of 82 and Surrey declared at

Trevor Jesty.

Tony Gray.

349 for 5. Green hit a career-best 133 for Sussex, who declared when they reached 300 in 76 overs. On the last morning, Surrey were 37 for 5, but they were rescued by a brave, positive 81 not out from Alec Stewart, and Jesty set Sussex to score 248 in 48 overs. They were 94 for 4 before Imran and leRoux hit 72 in 11 overs. Imran was superbly stumped by Richards off Monkhouse, and leRoux and Alan Wells also fell, but Ian Gould and Ian Greig scored 40 off 31 balls to bring victory to Sussex with 8 balls to spare.

This defeat ended Surrey's Championship hopes, and they finished sixth. Thomas reappeared in this match after being absent through one of a catalogue of injuries that had clouded Surrey's season, yet the event which typified the County's fortunes most in 1985 happened to the Second XI. With Bullen, Doughty, Falkner, Ward, Taylor and an impressive young fast bowler, Martin Bicknell, prominent, they played cricket of character and imagination and believed that they had won the Second XI Championship. However, TCCB deducted the 24 points they had won at Hove where, it was alleged, they had played an ineligible player, and this put them in second place, 0.1 behind Nottinghamshire.

The season ended with Stewart, Gray and Needham all receiving their county caps. Gray had taken 79 first-class wickets and proved to be an excellent acquisition. It is worth noting that Graham Gooch believed that at the end of May, when he played against Gray at The Oval, he was no more than medium place, but by the time he came to Chelmsford in late August, was very quick indeed.

Pat Pocock.

1986

Minimum of 110 overs per day in Championship matches

With Clarke fit again, Surrey were able to call upon both West Indian fast bowlers in 1986, although not in tandem because of the overseas player regulations. It did mean, however, that they always had available a potent leader of the attack, and the pair captured 99 wickets between them. Sylvester Clarke was an exceptionally fast bowler and in ten years with Surrey rapidly acquired a reputation as perhaps the most feared of them all. He bowled chest-on and he had a very big chest. His stock delivery zeroed in towards the batsman's body and his bouncer was very hard indeed to pick up, prompting persistent bar-room and dressing-room whispers about its legality. Excitingly, Martin Bicknell, 17 years old, very quick and eager to learn, forced his way into the side and belied his years and inexperience with some good performances. Tall, dark and slender, with a fine action, he took 27 wickets and would have taken more but for injury.

Pocock had taken over the captaincy in what was to be his last season, and with Micky Stewart now becoming more involved with the England side, Geoff Arnold's position as coach involved the first team while Chris Waller, another of Surrey's faithful, took over the Second XI. Three wins in 4 matches at the end of July and beginning of August took Surrey into a challenging position for the Championship, but 4 draws followed, and it was victory in the last match against Leicestershire at The Oval that enabled them to climb into third place, 39 points behind winners Essex. They had never really recovered from a poor June when they were beaten 4 times.

Lynch, despite beginning with two hundreds, was unable to reproduce his consistency of the previous season, and the regular scoring became the responsibility of Alec Stewart, who made 1,665 runs in a most stylish manner. A bonus was the batting of Jack Richards, the wicketkeeper, who passed 1,000 runs for the first time. His form won him selection for England's 2 one-day matches against New Zealand and a place on the winter tour of Australia. There was much exciting cricket being played, although not consistently, and there was disquieting news of dressing-room disharmony. Monte Lynch was suspended from a Sunday League game at the end of July and there were constant rumblings for the rest of the season which could not have made things easy for Pocock. However, he strode through all with his usual cheerful manner.

Pat Pocock played for Surrey for twenty-two years. He knew good times and bad, and he transcended the bad because he never lost his love for the game. He had a lovely high action and his off-spin was shot with variety and experiment. Like Laker, he worked his fingers until they were red and blistered. Ever cheerful, he delighted in his art and was always optimistic and refreshingly open. Perhaps it was too late for him when he became captain of Surrey. He missed his old comrades, especially Intikhab, Howarth, Knight and Jackman, and the values they represented. He said of Jackman that if anybody could find a way of bottling his energy, zest and commitment, then the future of cricket would be safe for the next century. Like Jackman, Pocock believed in the game, and one wonders if, when he wrote of his friend Jackman, 'He loved cricket as he loved life, indeed he rarely drew a distinction', he was really writing of himself. Cricket was an emptier game after he had been clapped off the field at The Oval on the evening of Tuesday 16 September. Surrey had just beaten Leicestershire by an innings, and Pat Pocock's long love affair with the game was over.

He came close to leading Surrey to a Lord's final in his last month but was denied in a game which few who saw it will ever forget. A rather close win over Cheshire had brought a match with Derbyshire who were convincingly beaten. Nottinghamshire, too, were brushed aside, and Surrey found themselves at home to Lancashire in the semi-final of the NatWest Bank Trophy.

Pocock won the toss and asked Lancashire to bat first. His reasoning was soon to become apparent when a torrid first over from Sylvester Clarke produced a single, which took Mendis to face Bicknell's first ball. The Lancashire opener slashed it into the hands of Clarke at gully. Clarke claimed the next wicket himself when he made a ball rear nastily at Fowler, who fended it off only to be caught one-handed by Richards, diving wide to his left down the leg-side. It was a breathtaking catch.

In the 15th over, Abrahams missed an in-swinger from Feltham and Lancashire were 28 for 3. Bicknell and Clarke had troubled Clive Lloyd with their pace and left him floundering, but he survived. Fairbrother did not. He fell to Thomas in the 25th over, and Lancashire were 59 for 4. Against less hostile bowling than that of Clarke and Bicknell, Lloyd and O'Shaughnessy added 99 in 21 overs. It was to prove a vital stand. Lloyd was caught behind by Pocock, Hayhurst fell to Butcher who bowled 7 tidy overs and Maynard hit a belligerent 22 before falling to Feltham, but any hopes Lancashire had of increasing their score significantly were blighted by the return of Clarke, who had O'Shaughnessy taken at slip and Allott at extra cover before bowling Simmons with the third ball of the 59th over. Lancashire were all out for 229.

Surrey were soon in trouble. Butcher hooked Allott unwisely and was caught at long leg, and Clinton edged to slip off the same bowler. Stewart was lbw to Watkinson, and Surrey were 30 for 3. Lynch and Jesty suggested recovery until Lynch insanely ran himself out. Jesty was driving handsomely, but there was much wantonness at the other end. At 173 for 7, the game was tilted in favour of Lancashire, but Clarke played a couple of thunderous shots before swatting rashly to square-leg, and when Pocock was bowled by Allott Surrey were 24 runs short of victory with only Martin Bicknell to support the limping Jesty. Having reached 76, Jesty pulled a leg muscle and then batted with a runner. The restrictions imposed upon him by the injury gave an added lustre to his stroke-play. His driving was majestic. Always a neat, elegant, unruffled batsman, he stood now like a wounded hero against the invading hordes. Young Bicknell gave him the support that any valiant squire should give to his knight.

When Hayhurst began the penultimate over Surrey needed 7 to win, and Jesty was in fine form. He hit the first ball for 2, and on the fifth he attempted a long, lofted drive towards the pavilion, but Fowler, sprinting round the boundary from long-on, held the ball as he dived and rolled over and over. Jesty had made 112 off 139 deliveries with a six and 14 fours. There was no better innings played on any ground in any competition in 1986, but Surrey had lost by 4 runs. For Jesty, twenty years in the game with never an appearance in a Lord's final, it was a sad moment. For Pocock, it was, perhaps, the most exciting memory of his last season.

Nothing could dim the brightness that was shining from the young players on the staff. The Second XI was exciting, eager and successful. Its members, as they should, were pressing for first team places, and with this in mind the County released the durable and faithful vice-captain Butcher, who went on to give good service to Glamorgan, Doughty, later to return briefly, and Monkhouse. With both captain and vice-captain gone, Surrey needed a leader.

The career statistics of Patrick Ian Pocock are as follows:

SURREY

485 matches	4,400 runs at 12.25	1,399 wickets at 25.43

53 times he took 5 wickets in an innings and 7 times 10 wickets in a match

TESTS

25 matches	206 runs at 6.24	67 wickets at 44.41

3 times he took 5 wickets in an innings

ALL FIRST-CLASS MATCHES

554 matches	4,867 runs at 11.34	1,607 wickets at 26.53

60 times he took 5 wickets in an innings and 7 times 10 wickets in a match

TEN
1987-1991

1987
Pitch ends and run-ups covered during the day when raining

In 1986, Geoff Arnold had phoned Ian Greig in Australia asking him to join Surrey as a medium-pace bowler and late middle-order batsman, for it was felt that his talents were what was needed to supplement the team and give it the boost that was required. A few weeks later, the call was repeated, but this time Greig was offered the captaincy.

Ian Greig had spent much of his career in the shadow of his brother Tony, who had captained both England and Sussex and had been prominent in the Packer revolution which, whatever else it did, certainly raised the income and status of the professional cricketer and indirectly encouraged a great deal of sponsorship into cricket. Ian Greig was thirty-one, born in South Africa and educated at Cambridge University, although his interests were sporting rather than academic. He played for Sussex from 1980 to 1985 and twice for England, and many believed he should have played more Test matches. He left Sussex in strange circumstances when, before the end of the 1985 season, the County announced they would not be retaining Ian Greig as they could not afford him. Other rumours suggested political infighting. He left Sussex and England to run an indoor sports centre in Brisbane where all the Greigs lived. His wife was Australian.

When he was offered the Surrey captaincy Ian Greig sought the advice of his elder brother Tony, for whom he had the greatest admiration. Tony Greig put three points to his brother by which he could determine whether the job was right for him:

— If you want to take the job just because it is a good financial offer, don't take it.
— If you want to be captain of Surrey just to get back at Sussex, don't take it.
— If you want to captain Surrey because you want to get back to the game you love and you think you can do a good job, say yes and start packing.

He accepted the position on the basis of the third point and the news of his appointment took all by surprise. His name had never been mentioned outside the committee room and administrative circles, but whoever first mooted the idea was responsible for one of the most inspired moves in recent Surrey cricket history.

Ian Greig's thoughts on his first season were:

> Surridge, May, Stewart, Edrich, Knight, Howarth, Pocock... what an act to follow! My first priority was to get to know the players and to quash media rumours that an unhappy atmosphere prevailed in the dressing room. This was quickly achieved; as I had suspected, it was all mainly rumour. I firmly believed from the outset that I had at my disposal a squad of richly talented players who could realistically challenge for any of the competitions at stake.

Surrey rose to fourth place in the Championship and seventh in the Sunday League. In itself this was not a position at which to rejoice, but it was certainly far better than the County had known for some years and was the product of some pulsating cricket on occasions. These achievements would, for many counties, reflect a good season. To the denizens of The Oval it was another season of unfulfilment from a side possessing an envied strike force in Sylvester Clarke and Tony Gray, and a powerful batting line-up. Lack of an experienced spinner, allied to a curious shortage of confidence, diluted their potency. This was no reflection on Greig, whose dressing-room presence was a major bonus. He proved to be a tough decision-making cricketer who won the respect of his men and eliminated the thread of disharmony that had lingered in 1986.

Surrey's failure to mount a serious bid for the Championship could be traced to an unproductive week in the second half of August. First, Kent's last-wicket pair held out for the final hour, and then Somerset denied them 11 runs off the last over. Those setbacks took on a greater significance when, after rain washed them out at Hove, the next 3 matches were won and Surrey moved into third place with one game to play. Gambling for a fourth victory, Greig set Lancashire a challenging, some felt too challenging, target, but was let down by his bowlers in the middle of a drizzle-dampening run-chase. Surrey, however, accumulated 73 bowling points and 65 for batting. Both totals were better than in 1986 when Surrey held on to third place in the final hour of the season. Clarke (66 Championship wickets) and Gray (44) both bowled impressively, but because of the registration regulations, they could never operate in tandem. Even taking into account the developing promise of Martin Bicknell, Surrey were a trifle short of firepower at one end. In the batting, there was, it seemed, a hint of complacency. Alec Stewart, Monte Lynch and Trevor Jesty all passed 1,000 runs but should really have recorded higher aggregates. With such strength in depth in the batting, enhanced by the return of David Smith to The Oval, Surrey automatically geared their strategy to fast scoring, each batsman knowing that there was run-power in reserve if he failed.

Jack Richards had a fine season, finishing second in the national wicketkeeping list. He effected a career-best ten dismissals in the home match against Sussex at the end of June and was the central figure in a piece of history, putting on 262 against Kent with Keith Medlycott at more than 5 an over to set a record for the County's 7th wicket. Medlycott, while emerging as an extremely useful lower-order batsman, took only 38 wickets in the Championship with his left-arm spin. More was expected of him as the successor to Pocock as Surrey's major spinner. Because of this shortfall, Surrey often found themselves playing on turning pitches with the opposition content that there would be no serious retaliation. Chris Bullen, with off-breaks, collected 19 wickets in addition to producing useful all-round performances in the limited-overs games. Like all the bowlers, he was supported by outstanding close catching.

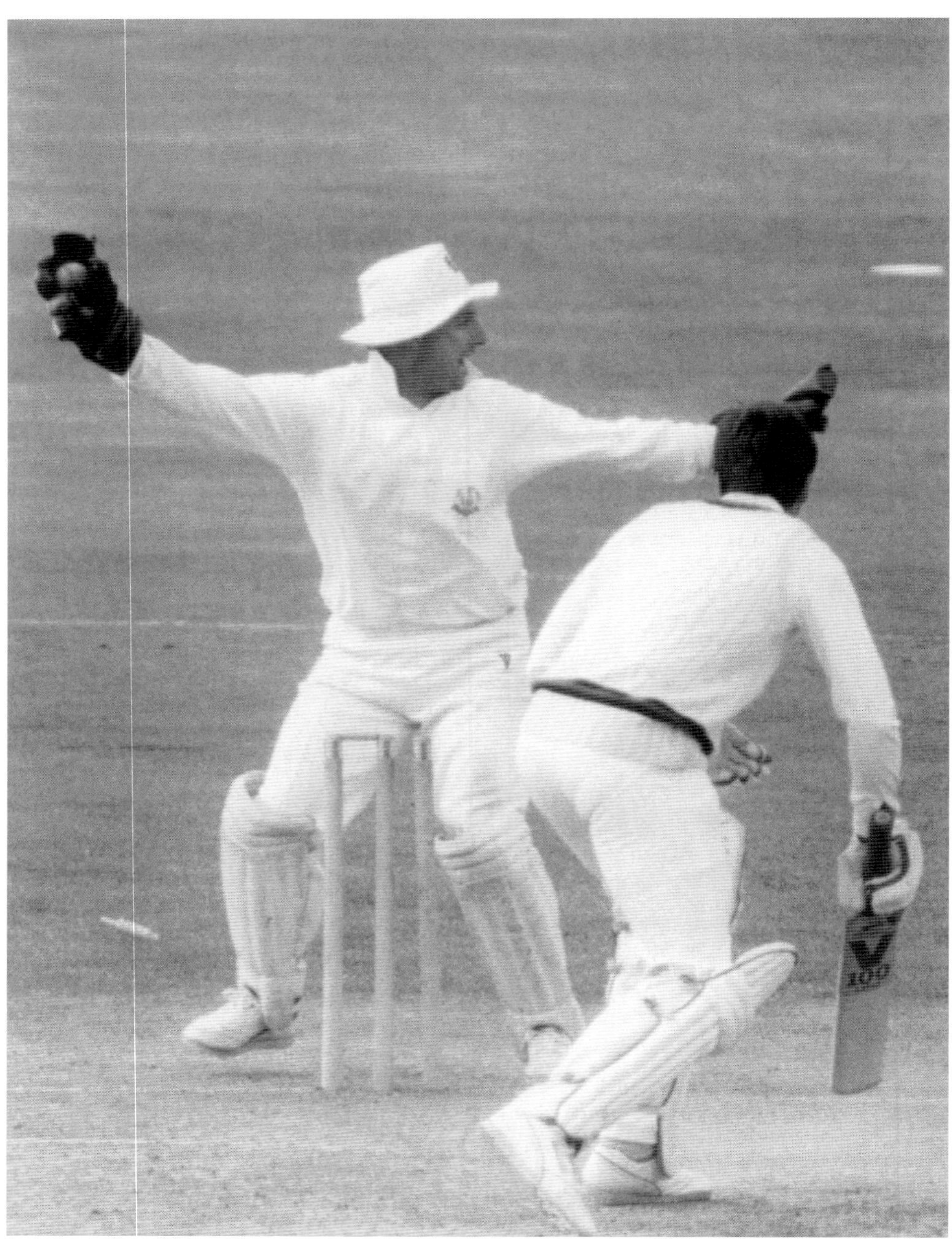

Jack Richards.

In the Sunday League playing Northamptonshire at Guildford in June, Surrey were defending a total of 220. When the last over arrived the visitors needed 4 runs to win with 6 wickets in hand. Greig handed the ball to Monte Lynch, who had not bowled an over of his off-breaks in a limited-overs game all season. It was a stroke of genius. Lynch had Harper caught behind and Williams stumped, and Geoff Cook was run out on the last ball of the match to give Surrey victory by one run. But when Surrey needed 4 runs off the last over to beat Gloucestershire, fate conspired against them. Walsh took four wickets in the September twilight.

During the year, Micky Stewart, Surrey's director of cricket, left to take up his appointment as England's team manager, but the youth policy he had nurtured was showing handsome dividends by this time.

Surrey went through to the quarter-finals of the Benson and Hedges Cup, having won all 4 of their zonal round matches. In their quarter-final they met Worcestershire at The Oval. The visitors reached an impressive 233 for 8. Darren Bicknell, a left-hander of immense promise who had made the leap from the Second XI with consummate ease, and David Smith, recently returned to the fold, put on 58 for the 1st wicket. Stewart and Lynch went quickly, but Jesty and Smith added the 159 needed for victory. Smith hit 110, Jesty 85. It was positive, confident cricket, yet the confidence did not always appear to be there, and they lost the semi-final to Yorkshire with an immature and ragged display.

HIGHLIGHTS OF THE 1987 SEASON

FIRST-CLASS MATCHES

BATTING				BOWLING				
	Runs	Ave	100s		Wkts	Ave	5wI	10wM
A.J. Stewart	1,219	38.09	3	A.H. Gray	48	15.58	2	
D.M. Smith	873	37.96	1	S.T. Clarke	67	17.31	6	2
C.J. Richards	683	37.94	1	M.P. Bicknell	42	23.74	2	
D.J. Bicknell	600	35.29	1	C.K. Bullen	21	26.86	1	
T.E. Jesty	1,074	34.65	1	M.A. Feltham	40	30.05	1	
M.A. Lynch	1,127	33.15	2	I.A. Greig	35	35.91	-	
I.A. Greig	887	30.59	1	D.J. Thomas	33	37.27	1	
G.S. Clinton	848	30.29	-	K.T. Medlycott	42	39.05	1	
K.T. Medlycott	734	29.36	1					

ONE-DAY MATCHES

BATTING				BOWLING			
	Runs	Ave	100s		Wkts	Ave	4wI
D.M. Smith	562	46.83	1	S.T. Clarke	19	23.31	2
G.S. Clinton	491	40.91	1	I.A. Greig	29	23.55	1
C.J. Richards	468	33.42	1	C.K. Bullen	20	32.90	-
T.E. Jesty	426	30.42	-				
M.A. Lynch	425	30.35	1				

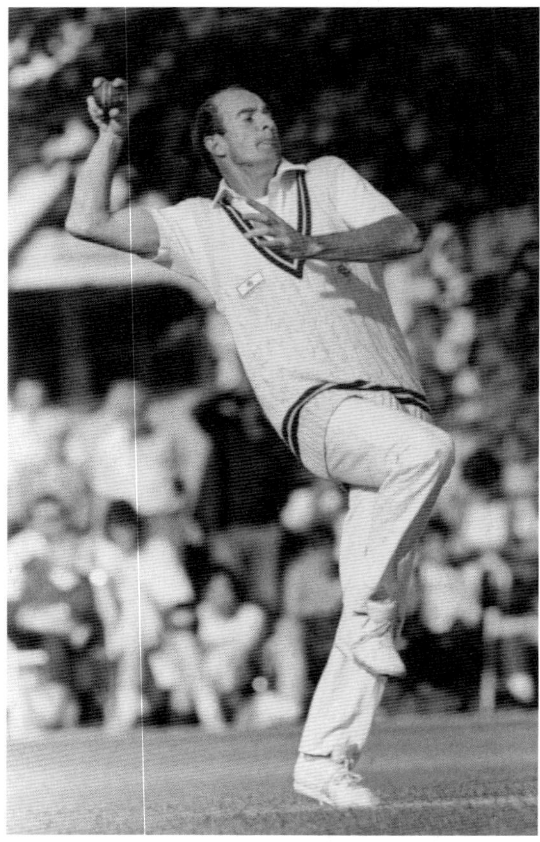

Ian Greig.

1988

Full covering of pitches re-introduced, 16 matches of three days, 6 matches of four days duration

1988 saw the emergence of four-day cricket in some County Championship matches at both ends of the season, the remainder being three-day matches. The exuberance of youth served Surrey admirably to maintain a satisfying status quo for Ian Greig's enthusiastic side. But for a frozen performance against Middlesex in their NatWest Bank Trophy semi-final, in which the shortfall in experience was strikingly evident, Surrey's fledglings would have finished the season with a feeling of greater stature. Fourth place in the Championship equalled Surrey's 1987 performance, albeit leaving members with a familiar feeling of unfulfilled promise. There had, however, been a wider availability of seasoned performers the previous season, whereas on occasions in 1988 Greig took the field with only four capped players. As the Surrey coach, Geoff Arnold, said when summing up the season: 'It was another example of getting to the last hurdle and not clearing it. But to keep the same position in the Championship and reach a semi-final, as we also did last year, with so many youngsters made it a satisfying season on which the club can build.' Surrey's problem was that they left it too late before making their run.

Keith Medlycott.

They were twelfth in mid-August before winning 3 out of 4 Championship matches by huge margins. When title contenders Kent demolished them by an innings in two and a half days at Canterbury in the last match of the campaign, there were enough points in reserve to claim a share of the prize money by finishing in fourth position.

The portents of the season looked ominous when only one win came in a strong Benson and Hedges group in May. Their lack of bowling variety, among other factors, left them without a chance in the 55-over competition. But a consistent challenge was mounted in the Sunday League. Despite losing 2 of their last 3 matches, they attained fifth place, an improvement of two places and a considerable improvement on four seasons earlier when they languished in bottom position. Arnold, his number two Chris Waller and Greig, all once with Sussex, had clearly instilled into Surrey the one-day traditions of their former county.

With Sylvester Clarke restricted to 12 Championship matches by injury and a club suspension for failing to report for the match at Swansea, and Tony Gray not bowling a single over in the Championship, it was left to Martin Bicknell, Nick Peters, Mark Feltham, Mark Frost, Keith Medlycott and Chris Bullen, all uncapped, to sustain the attack. Clarke, on his day, remained the country's most feared quick bowler and captured

63 wickets, but Gray was seemingly unable to regain his form of past years. He had suffered a broken arm in net practice during the previous autumn's World Cup, but after struggling for a time in the West Indies Red Stripe tournament he had played in the one-day series against Pakistan. However, he was passed over for the tour of England in favour of his fellow Trinidadian, Ian Bishop. Surrey, hardly surprisingly, did not offer him a new contract, nor the left-handed batsman David Smith, who when told the news gave vent to his feelings by thrashing an unbeaten 157 against Hampshire at Guildford.

Less expected was the announcement in November that the wicketkeeper, Jack Richards, was being released on the recommendation of the cricket sub-committee with a year of his contract still to run. His batting had been a bonus early in the season, when Surrey were often pinned below the halfway mark in the Championship. He had been effective opening the innings in the Sunday League and he topped the Championship averages with 861 runs at 50.65. The England selectors had recalled him for the last 2 Test matches against the West Indians. Bicknell served another rewarding term of apprenticeship, and his 9 for 45 against Cambridge University in mid-June remained the country's best bowling of the season. Medlycott's left-arm spin, blossoming batting and outstanding close catching took him close to England recognition. His self-belief and eagerness to spin the ball earned him 69 wickets, the second-highest slow-bowling return behind Marks of Somerset, but at a lower cost. Only Grahame Clinton and Stewart reached 1,000 runs for the season. Surrey collected 57 bonus points for batting, as many as Kent and two more than the champions, Worcestershire. Lynch just failed to achieve four figures, having started the summer as a member of England's Texaco Trophy squad and ending it limping towards a knee operation.

A 'Save The Oval' appeal brought in essential finance for the urgent development and general maintenance of the ground. But many members were startled by a proposed sponsorship from Courage Ltd which involved renaming the ground 'The Foster's Oval'. The cash input was believed to be around £2 million; progress held sway over tradition and agreement was carried by 1,738 votes to 322 at a special general meeting. The club was able to commence its £5.8 million West Side building programme, and the smiles were spread wide among Surrey officials when the bulldozers rumbled in halfway through September.

HIGHLIGHTS OF THE 1988 SEASON

FIRST-CLASS MATCHES

BATTING	Runs	Ave	100s
C.J. Richards	861	50.65	1
D.M. Smith	630	48.46	2
G.S. Clinton	1,054	43.92	4
M.A. Lynch	996	39.84	2
P.D. Atkins	357	35.70	1
A.J. Stewart	1,006	34.69	2
D.M. Ward	942	31.40	1

BOWLING	Wkts	Ave	5wI	10wM
S.T. Clarke	63	14.49	4	2
I.A. Greig	49	23.33	2	-
K.T. Medlycott	69	24.06	6	3
N.H. Peters	34	28.06	1	1
M.A. Feltham	56	29.98	2	
M.P. Bicknell	50	30.22	1	

ONE-DAY MATCHES

BATTING				BOWLING			
	Runs	Ave	100s		Wkts	Ave	4wI
M.A. Lynch	700	50.00	-	I.A. Greig	39	20.72	1
D.M. Smith	518	34.53	-	S.T. Clarke	24	27.63	1
A.J. Stewart	703	39.05	1	C.K. Bullen	26	31.88	-
C.J. Richards	540	31.76	1				
G.S. Clinton	301	30.10	1				

1989

25 points deducted in Championship matches for unfit pitches

Surrey finished twelfth in the Championship but there were interesting features that came to light promising a brighter future. In the NatWest Trophy, Surrey went out at the quarter-final stage, losing to Hampshire by five wickets with 2 overs left, despite having Hampshire at 23 for 3 at one stage. In the previous round Surrey had won by a single run against Yorkshire at The Oval after Darren Bicknell had scored an excellent 135 not out. In the Sunday League the County finished in sixth place with 9 victories. The lack of a strike bowler, the loss of a major batsman, Monte Lynch, after breaking a leg in a pre-season accident, and the departure of two England players, David Smith and Jack Richards, drained Surrey of vital experience. Eventually, the heavy strain this put on Ian Greig's young side told, and only 2 of the last 11 Championship matches were won. The lack of top-quality back-up bowling also contributed to Surrey's failure to qualify for the Benson and Hedges Cup quarter-finals (for the second successive season), to stem the match-wining stand by Robin Smith and Mark Nicholas in the last eight of the NatWest Trophy, or to maintain their challenge in the Sunday League. A home defeat in August by Nottinghamshire proved crucial and the victory that gave Lancashire the title on the last Sunday of the League cost Surrey fourth place. They had been occupying fourth and higher in the table for most of the 40-overs campaign.

Yet Greig, confined to just 161 Championship overs himself because of a knee complaint, was armed with a potent overseas new-ball force in a dank late April which gave no indication of the glorious summer to follow. He still had the explosive pace of the muscular Sylvester Clarke at his disposal to exploit the bouncy Oval pitches, and variation was available in the Queensland left-hander, Dick Tazelaar. For quite different reasons, however, both were lost to Surrey before the end of May. Clarke, who had captured 591 first-class wickets in his ten years at The Oval, was dismissed for alleged 'persistent breaches of the terms and conditions of his contract'. Tazelaar, who was barred by the umpires from bowling against Middlesex, at Lord's, in the second Championship match for running on the pitch, returned home with a back injury after just 4 games.

That double setback and Lynch's serious injury gave Tony Murphy, an acquisition from Lancashire, Martin Bicknell and Thorpe the chance to prove their worth. Murphy, a willing workhorse, delivered 623 Championship overs and took 65 wickets. 'He was a

revelation', enthused coach Geoff Arnold. 'He stayed fit and was always ready to do a job for us.' Thorpe's emergence, while coming earlier than expected, was no surprise to those closely acquainted with the left-hander's talent. Two hundreds and 8 fifties helped Thorpe towards an aggregate of 1,132 runs from 18 games and a place on England's 'A' tour to Zimbabwe, in company with the Bicknells. Darren, an opening batsman, hit 4 hundreds and fell just short of 1,400 first-class runs, while Martin captured 65 Championship wickets.

Senior England honours were awaiting Alec Stewart and Keith Medlycott, both of whom were selected for the winter tour to the West Indies. After an indifferent start, the free-striking Stewart came to terms with the extra responsibility of keeping wicket and scored 631 more runs than in 1988, taking a double-century off Essex at The Oval and missing another by a single run against Sussex in the final match when he ran out of partners. His keeping saw him set a County record when he caught 11 players in the match against Leicestershire.

Medlycott's left-arm spin provided nearly 700 first-class overs and 64 wickets, in addition to which he scored 928 runs. Unfortunately his close catching was not so sure as in the previous season. Greig compensated for his bowling shortfall with a four-figure batting return and was mentioned as a possible England captain for the West Indies until it was discovered he had broken the ICC qualification regulations by living in Australia

Opposite: *Darren Bicknell (far left) and Tony Murphy.*

Right: *Alec Stewart.*

between his Sussex and Surrey careers. Lynch made a popular return in mid-August, and a career best of 172 not out against Kent in the penultimate match helped to ease his frustrations.

The extra £250,000 needed to meet the £5.8 million cost of the West Side development of The Oval would, it was announced, be raised by the sale of 364 bricks to complete the sculpture of Sir Leonard Hutton to commemorate his 364 against Australia in 1938. The necessary building work was slightly behind schedule at the end of the summer, and members and cricket lovers alike were wishing away the eyesore of the giant crane at the Pavilion end which cast an unwelcome shadow across the famous turf.

A solitary trophy in the 1980s and a volume of unfulfilled ambitions throughout the decade did not leave Surrey entertaining pessimistic thoughts about the past, present or future. Instead, they were preparing to reap the harvest from a flourishing youth system sown more than ten years earlier by their former manager, Micky Stewart, and now handsomely providing eighty per cent of Surrey's current pool of players. While the club was naturally disappointed with results in 1989, which had produced a worse record than the previous season, the future, moulded around Graham Thorpe and the Bicknell brothers, was anticipated with excitement as the season ended. A feeling of optimism was backed by a growing opinion within the game that Surrey had the potential and the capacity to emerge as one of the teams of the 1990s.

HIGHLIGHTS OF THE 1989 SEASON

FIRST-CLASS MATCHES

BATTING				BOWLING				
	Runs	Ave	100s		Wkts	Ave	5wI	10wM
G.P. Thorpe	1,132	45.28	2	M.P. Bicknell	65	26.41	4	-
A.J. Stewart	1,637	44.24	4	A.J. Murphy	65	30.89	2	-
I.A. Greig	1,013	42.20	1	M.A. Feltham	36	31.22	-	-
D.J. Bicknell	1,392	35.69	4	K.T. Medlycott	64	31.64	2	-
D.M. Ward	608	25.33	1					

ONE-DAY MATCHES

BATTING				BOWLING			
	Runs	Ave	100s		Wkts	Ave	4wI
A.J. Stewart	846	38.45	2	K.T. Medlycott	22	21.63	3
G.S. Clinton	770	35.00	-	M.A. Feltham	29	22.65	1
D.J. Bicknell	366	33.27	1	M.P. Bicknell	27	24.00	1
D.M. Ward	641	30.52	-	C.K. Bullen	24	27.83	1
G.P. Thorpe	454	30.26	-	A.J. Murphy	25	27.88	1

1990

Surrey did not come to terms with the four-day format, winning only 4 matches and drawing 15 to finish in ninth place. David Ward enjoyed an excellent season, scoring 2,072 first-class runs for the County with 2 double centuries, 263 against Kent at Canterbury and 205 against Essex at The Foster's Oval. He was the first Surrey player to score 2,000 runs in a season for twenty-eight years and in the Canterbury match he shared in a stand of 413 with Darren Bicknell who scored 186. The 205 against Essex was made in the second innings after Surrey had been asked to follow-on and Surrey reached 613 for 6 with Alikhan contributing 138. It was a disappointing season for Alec Stewart and Graham Thorpe, who had returned from England tours to the West Indies and Zimbabwe respectively.

Five batsmen passed the 1,000 first-class runs mark. In addition to David Ward, Darren Bicknell scored 1,317, Ian Greig 1,259, Monte Lynch 1,227 and in his last season, Grahame Clinton 1,292. Ian Greig made the highest score of his career, 291, in the match against Lancashire at The Oval which saw Lancashire make 863 for 9 in reply to Surrey's 707 for 9 in a match which petered out in a draw.

Mark Butcher and Adam Hollioake joined the staff and in the Second XI another batsman was emerging in Alistair Brown. The most exciting newcomer burst on to the scene in July when an unknown Pakistani fast bowler, Waqar Younis, played in the quarter-final of the Benson and Hedges Cup, which Surrey lost. He then went on to take 57 wickets in first-class matches at 23.80 and 31 wickets at 12.77 in the Sunday League.

David Ward.

Mark Feltham.

Martin Bicknell with 64 wickets and Keith Medlycott with 59 were the other leading first-class wicket-takers. In the Sunday League, Surrey won 9 matches and finished seventh in the table.

HIGHLIGHTS OF THE 1990 SEASON

FIRST-CLASS MATCHES

BATTING				BOWLING				
	Runs	Ave	100s		Wkts	Ave	5wI	10wM
D.M. Ward	2,072	76.74	7	Waqar Younis	57	23.80	3	1
D.J. Bicknell	1,317	69.31	5	M.P. Bicknell	64	27.35	1	-
I.A. Greig	1,259	54.73	2	M.A. Feltham	40	28.75	2	
R.I. Alikhan	726	51.85	2	K.T. Medlycott	59	39.10	3	
A.J. Stewart	837	46.50	1	A.J. Murphy	30	45.56	2	
G.S. Clinton	1,292	46.14	1	N.M. Kendrick	25	47.76	-	
M.A. Lynch	1,227	45.44	1					

ONE-DAY MATCHES

BATTING				BOWLING			
	Runs	Ave	100s		Wkts	Ave	4wI
A.J. Stewart	640	53.33	1	Waqar Younis	38	13.50	2
C.K. Bullen	205	51.25	-	M.P. Bicknell	29	21.79	2
D.J. Bicknell	441	40.09	1	K.T. Medlycott	23	35.47	-
G.S. Clinton	439	39.90	-				
G.P. Thorpe	697	38.72	-				
D.M. Ward	550	34.37	1				

1991

It is doubtful whether anyone has bowled faster or straighter in an English season than Waqar Younis did for Surrey in 1991. Contrary to modern practice among quick bowlers, the bouncer had a minimum place in his armoury; stumps were hit and pads thumped regularly to earn the young Pakistani a rich harvest of 151 wickets in all competitions, with an astonishing two-thirds of his victims bowled or lbw. Feet and ankles were constantly in danger of bruising or worse from Waqar's wicked full-length deliveries. Many a batsman felt he had been 'Waqared', to coin a phrase.

Surrey's coach, Geoff Arnold, could think of no fast bowler in the world he rated more highly. 'He's unique: he has greater ability to swing the ball late, and at a faster pace – not to mention landing it in the blockhole – than anyone I've seen', he explained. A total of 113 batsmen fell Waqar's way, at a cost of 14.36 each, in the Championship, in which he picked up 13 returns of five wickets or more. He was most effective with the rough texture of the older ball, and he comfortably headed the national averages. On occasions he also displayed some explosive batting, as at Guildford, where his 31 from 19 balls set

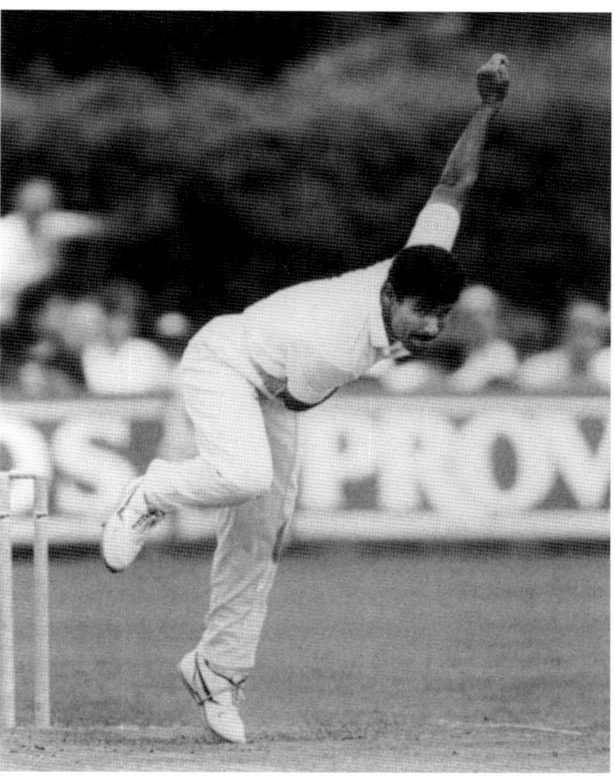
Waqar Younis.

up a last-over victory against Yorkshire, and in the NatWest quarter-final at The Oval, where his 18-ball 26 helped Surrey reach a total which Essex could not match.

The County's support bowling often spluttered, however, and they had to settle for fifth place in the Championship, which was disappointing as they shared second place in early August. Surrey fell away at the end of the season, losing their final 2 Championship matches after being beaten by Hampshire in the final of the NatWestBank Trophy, their first appearance in a Lord's showpiece since 1982. The injury-troubled Martin Bicknell, who had toured Australia with England in the winter, failed to reach 50 wickets, while Tony Murphy's 35 came at an expensive 47.62 apiece, even though earlier in the season he was Surrey's most effective one-day bowler. Keith Medlycott, after suffering a disastrous loss of control and confidence in Sri Lanka with England 'A', constantly wrestled with his action without fully mastering it. This was doubly unfortunate because pitches at The Oval were a shade slower and more conducive to spin than normal, something which made Waqar Younis's achievements all the more remarkable.

Darren Bicknell was the most consistent of the batsmen, with 5 hundreds in his 1,888 first-class runs. The friendly family man, once he became clad in the opening batsman's extensive armour, revealed a stubbornness and single-minded ability that drove opposition bowlers and fielders to distraction. It may not always have been pretty, though a

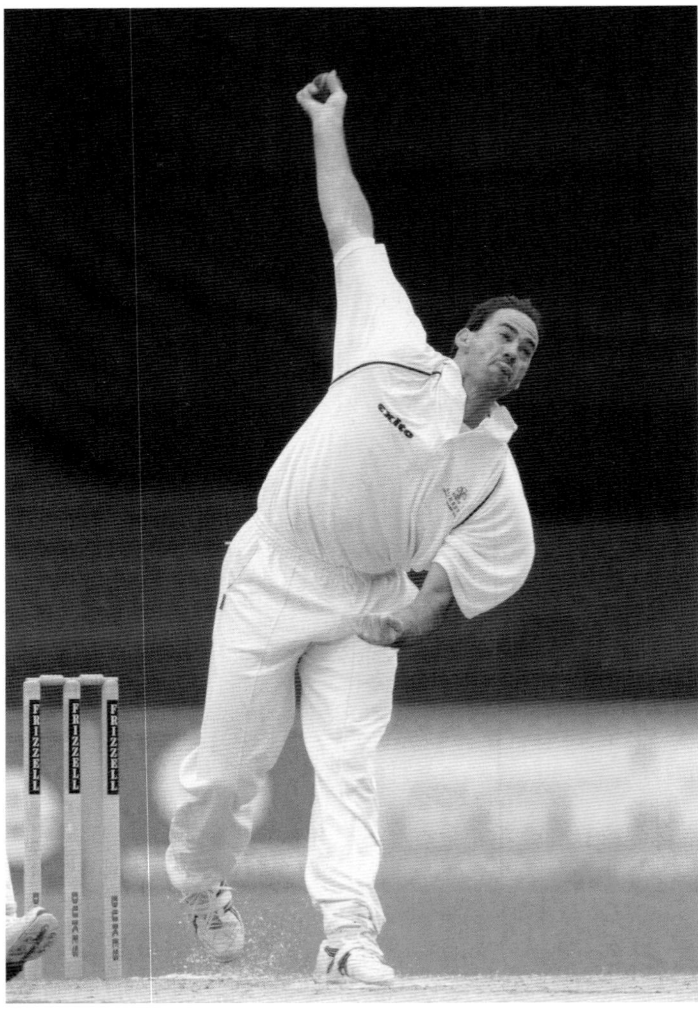

Martin Bicknell.

vintage Bicknell innings had no shortage of flowing drives and elegant glides through the legside, but offer any cricketer the chance of a long knock every day and you will find Bicknell near the front of the queue. Graham Thorpe's season finished with a flourish. He scored 3 hundreds in 5 innings, the second a career-best 177 against Sussex, and 93 in the NatWest final to convince any doubters of the temperament and ability which the selectors acknowledged with his third successive England 'A' tour. The Bicknell brothers were also selected to join him on the trip to the West Indies. David Ward was way short of his 1991 form while Alec Stewart, though regaining his England place for the last 2 Tests of the summer and making his first Test hundred, just failed to score 1,000 runs in the Championship. The lower output at the crease was reflected in the batting points column of the Championship table, where Surrey returned the meagre total of 47, marginally better than Derbyshire and Leicestershire (46) and Gloucestershire (42).

Surrey had no real voice in the Benson and Hedges Cup, in which they won only one group match, and in the Sunday League they won only 7 matches, which earned them joint eighth place. But they were a potent force in the NatWest until the final, when a four-wicket defeat was the penalty for batting too slowly in the first half of their innings. It was also a rare moment when Waqar Younis did not rise to the occasion. They had won a thrilling semi-final against Northamptonshire after Martin Bicknell's unbeaten 66 had rescued an innings in ruins at 91 for 6, and Waqar had collected five wickets in four deadly spells, the last of them going into a second day because of the deteriorating light on the first evening. Their closest shave, however, was in the first round at The Oval against the would-be giant-killers of Oxfordshire. When rain prevented a result in two attempts to play a match, the players had to move down to the indoor nets. There, Murphy, who hit the stumps twice in the bowl-out for Surrey to win 3-2, saved the first-class County from embarrassment. This was the first time in a senior cricket that a match had been decided indoors.

During the season the captain, Ian Greig, decided to step down after five years in charge, to allow Alec Stewart to emulate his father, Micky Stewart and captain the County. Greig's knee problems had restricted his bowling, which in turn upset the balance of the side, although he was retained on the staff and awarded a benefit.

At the end of July, HM The Queen, accompanied by HRH The Duke of Edinburgh, officially opened the £3 million multi-purpose Ken Barrington Centre, during the NatWest Trophy quarter-final against Essex. It was Her Majesty's first visit to The Oval since 1955, when she saw a Surrey team including Ken Barrington play the touring South Africans.

HM the Queen opening the Barrington Centre at The Oval in July 1991.

HIGHLIGHTS OF THE 1991 SEASON

FIRST-CLASS MATCHES

BATTING			
	Runs	Ave	100s
D.J. Bicknell	1,844	47.28	5
D.M. Ward	1,372	40.35	1
G.P. Thorpe	1,166	40.20	4
A.J. Stewart	936	39.00	1
R.I. Alikhan	1,055	32.96	-
K.T. Medlycott	624	24.96	1

BOWLING				
	Wkts	Ave	5wI	10wM
Waqar Younis	113	14.65	13	3
M.P. Bicknell	45	27.91	1	-
M.A. Feltham	35	30.71	-	-
K.T. Medlycott	49	34.75	2	1
A.J. Murphy	35	47.62	1	-

ONE-DAY MATCHES

BATTING			
	Runs	Ave	100s
A.J. Stewart	742	43.64	1
G.P. Thorpe	681	37.83	1
M.A. Lynch	519	28.83	-

BOWLING			
	Wkts	Ave	4wI
Waqar Younis	38	17.94	4
A.J. Murphy	25	30.12	-

ELEVEN
1992-1996

1992

Bonus points extended to 120 overs. One fast short-pitched ball per over in Championship matches

Alec Stewart had first been offered the captaincy after the 1986 season but turned it down. After the resignation of Ian Greig he took over the mantle but ran into several problems. During 1992 Surrey were punished by the Test and County Cricket Board for ball tampering. The County conducted their own enquiry and agreed that four offences had taken place over a period of three years and accepted the fine of £1,000, which was suspended for two years. It was agreed that the ball would be returned to the umpire at the end of each over and at the fall of a wicket. They recommended that all counties should adopt this procedure. In his autobiography *Playing for Keeps* Alec Stewart admits:

> We all knew that ball-tampering was going on, and some of the counties weren't innocent. Mine, for a start. Ian Greig had been our recent captain and he had seen it at first hand when he played for Sussex alongside Imran Khan. The practice was to get the fingernails into the ball and rough it up on one side so that the ball would swing late when the other side was soaked in sweat. Surrey weren't the only ones at it.

Surrey had a fluctuating season in the Championship with the County moving from bottom in June to sixth place in August but finally finishing in thirteenth place. Only 3 of the 9 matches at The Oval produced a definite result. Surrey lost in the first round of the NatWest trophy against Glamorgan despite a century by David Ward. In the Benson and Hedges competition they lost narrowly to Kent in the semi-final but achieved their best-ever position of fourth in the National League. Alistair Brown announced his arrival on the county scene by scoring 3 first-class centuries in the quick times of 79, 71 and 78 balls each. Graham Thorpe scored 13 half-centuries and in August made his maiden double-century in first-class cricket against Somerset. Monte Lynch stood in as captain when Stewart was away on Test duty and returned to his best form accumulating over 1,400 runs in the season.

Waqar Younis was not available having been called up by Pakistan for their tour of England. His replacement, South African Rudi Bryson had a very poor year with only 17 Championship wickets. His captain commented: 'I felt sorry for him. He was quick and put everything into it, but he just didn't get it right. He never threw the towel in. In the last couple of matches he was bowling as well as anyone. But it was too late by then.' Joey Benjamin, signed from Warwickshire the previous winter, took 45 wickets and bowled more overs than anyone except Martin Bicknell, who took 71 wickets. The slow left-arm bowler Neil Kendrick turned in a career-best performance of 6 for 61 against Leicestershire and was supported by off-spinner James Boiling, whose 45 wickets were enough for him to be called up for an England 'A' tour to Australia.

The Second XI had a brilliant season, winning both their competitions. Mark Butcher showed great promise for the future and Adam Hollioake was making a good impression. Surrey were desperate in their search for a wicketkeeper. David Ligertwood was tried for 4 games and then released. Neil Sargeant played for most of the season but Alec Stewart took over the gloves by the end of the year. Mark Feltham left to join Middlesex and Keith Medlycott suffered loss of form and his playing career came to an end even though he took four wickets for the Second XI in their victory in the Bain Clarkson final. The team in this final was I.A. Greig (captain), R.I. Alikhan, P.D. Atkins, J.D. Robinson, M.A. Butcher, A.W. Smith, K.T. Medlycott, A.J. Hollioake, D.G.C. Ligertwood, I.J. Ward and A.J. Murphy.

HIGHLIGHTS OF THE 1992 SEASON

FIRST-CLASS MATCHES

BATTING				BOWLING				
	Runs	Ave	100s		Wkts	Ave	5wI	10wM
G.P. Thorpe	1,863	51.75	3	M.P. Bicknell	71	25.67	4	-
A.D. Brown	740	49.33	3	N.M. Kendrick	51	30.72	3	-
M.A. Lynch	1,465	43.08	3	J. Boiling	45	35.08	1	1
A.J. Stewart	837	38.04	1	J.E. Benjamin	45	39.55	2	-
D.M. Ward	879	36.62	3					
D.J. Bicknell	1,225	34.02	1					

ONE-DAY MATCHES

BATTING				BOWLING			
	Runs	Ave	100s		Wkts	Ave	4wI
D.J. Bicknell	1,082	54.10	3	M.A. Feltham	32	22.68	1
A.J. Stewart	757	47.31	2	M.P. Bicknell	34	23.73	1
D.M. Ward	519	39.92	1	R.E. Bryson	18	27.72	2
G.P. Thorpe	686	36.10	-	J. Boiling	27	28.44	1
A.D. Brown	755	35.95	2	J.E. Benjamin	21	37.52	1
M.A. Lynch	588	28.00	1				

1993

17 four-day matches in Championship. Bonus points altered

Surrey's quest for the County Championship floundered in August 1993 with 3 defeats in a row, which ended any chance of catching Middlesex. A dismal damp finish to the

Alec Stewart (left) and Graham Thorpe.

season found them finishing in sixth place. This was a far better performance than 1992 but still very disappointing.

Much of the problem could be laid at the feet of the batsmen, highlighted by their performance in the Benson and Hedges Cup-tie against Lancashire. A record stand of 212 by Alec Stewart and Graham Thorpe had taken Surrey to within 25 runs of victory with more than 5 overs remaining, and nine wickets left. Those nine wickets fell for 18 runs. In the Championship there were similar happenings. Darren Bicknell and Alistair Brown were the only batsmen to score more than 1,000 Championship runs, although Alec Stewart and Graham Thorpe reached four figures in all first-class matches. Monte Lynch and David Ward failed to reach their former high standards. Brown performed well in his first full season, showing a good attitude at the crease, slowing down and eliminating some risk in his attacking style. As usual, Surrey did not rush into presenting him with a cap, which was to come the following year.

Martin Bicknell gained international recognition being picked for England against Australia but took only four wickets. He was the best bowler for Surrey and finished fifth in the national listings with 67 wickets. His season ended just before the Oval Test match because of a knee injury, which ultimately required surgery. The strike force of Surrey consisted of Waqar Younis, Joey Benjamin and Bicknell, who between them accounted for 187 wickets in the County Championship. Their performance only served to highlight

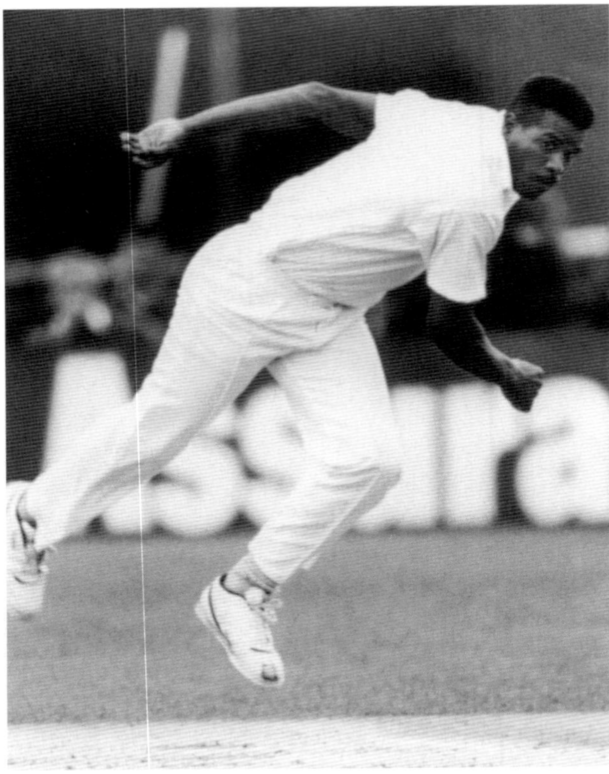

Joey Benjamin.

how the lack of runs scored meant only 6 Championship matches were won. Benjamin bowled over 600 overs, considerably more than both Waqar and Bicknell. He took a career-best 6 for 19 against Nottinghamshire and was awarded his cap. The spinners did not enjoy a good season with Neil Kendrick taking only 29 wickets in 12 matches despite a haul of seven wickets in the second innings against Nottinghamshire at Trent Bridge.

Three Surrey players, Stewart, Thorpe and Martin Bicknell, played in the Fourth and Fifth Tests of the Ashes series, the first time the County had three men in the same England side since 1972/73. Thorpe, who along with Stewart also played in the one-day internationals, made an unbeaten century in the second innings of his maiden Test at Trent Bridge as well as hitting a fifty at Edgbaston. He missed the Final Test at The Oval only because he suffered a broken thumb during nets before the start, the offending bowler being a member of Thorpe's own Farnham club.

Mark Butcher, Adam Hollioake and Andy Smith came through from the excellent Surrey youth scheme to make their debuts in the first-class game. Adam Hollioake's maiden first-class century in his first match against Derbyshire revealed some powerful stroke play coupled with a mature approach. He and Butcher batted particularly well together and the latter's unbeaten maiden half-century in the final match of the season was just reward. Graham Kersey, a wicketkeeper, was signed from Kent and soon settled in, allowing Stewart to take a permanent break from the stumper's job.

Before the season, Glyn Woodman was appointed chief executive. The coach, Geoff Arnold, left in confused circumstances, and Grahame Clinton was promoted to the vacant position. He was required to work under the wing of a new director of cricket, Mike Edwards, the former Surrey player who had been out of the first-class game for almost two decades. This appointment did not appear to end the discontent Stewart felt after Arnold's departure and he left on England's Caribbean tour without signalling his readiness to continue as captain. There were three departures among the players: Rehan Alikhan retired, while Paul Atkins and Ian Ward were released. At the end of the season the club became incorporated as an 'industrial and provident society' with the committee retaining executive powers. Woodman said members' rights would be safeguarded. This promise would be challenged in future years.

HIGHLIGHTS OF THE 1993 SEASON

FIRST-CLASS MATCHES

	BATTING				BOWLING			
	Runs	Ave	100s		Wkts	Ave	5wI	10wM
A.J. Stewart	716	47.73	2	M.P. Bicknell	63	17.11	6	2
A.D. Brown	1,382	44.58	3	Waqar Younis	62	22.69	4	-
D.J. Bicknell	1,418	42.96	4	J.E. Benjamin	64	27.85	2	-
A.J. Hollioake	352	39.11	1	A.J. Murphy	32	32.59	1	-
G.P. Thorpe	787	35.77	2	N.M. Kendrick	29	33.10	1	-
D.M. Ward	580	27.61	1					

ONE-DAY MATCHES

	BATTING				BOWLING		
	Runs	Ave	100s		Wkts	Ave	4wI
A.J. Stewart	608	55.27	1	M.P. Bicknell	31	13.74	1
G.P. Thorpe	477	36.69	1	Waqar Younis	35	19.40	2
D.J. Bicknell	469	27.58	0	A.J. Hollioake	18	20.50	1
D.M. Ward	453	34.84	1	J. Boiling	31	25.29	1
A.D. Brown	465	25.83	1				

1994

Alec Stewart resumed as captain on his return from the West Indies. Having stood at the top of the Championship at the end of July 1994 and second at the start of August, the decline which followed saw Surrey finish in seventh place. Four defeats and 2 draws in their next 6 matches followed a victory over Nottinghamshire. Three of the defeats were by an innings.

Surrey reached the semi-finals in both one-day competitions but failed to progress to the prestigious finals at Lord's. In the NatWest Trophy the semi-final provided a thrilling match with a world-record aggregate score of 707 runs after some brilliant batting in their encounter with Worcestershire. A disappointing sixth place meant the County finished outside the money in the Sunday League.

Waqar Younis had been a great asset to Surrey, but unfortunately Pakistan arranged a tour to Sri Lanka starting in July and recalled him to their national side. This coincided with a series of injuries hitting the Surrey dressing room. But for this additional tour Surrey would have had Waqar Younis for the bulk of the summer. His presence was sorely missed by an attack that was ravaged by injuries.

Martin Bicknell was the first casualty, suffering a fractured right foot after three Championship matches. Mark Butcher had a hernia that needed an operation and after two months returned to the side, not as a strike bowler but as an opening batting partner for Darren Bicknell, who had maintained his consistency. Butcher reached his maiden first-class century. He was a fine young left-hander, a clean striker of the ball and he proved he had the temperament to open the innings. Waqar's replacement was the West Indian Cameron Cuffy, but despite all his endeavours with 36 wickets he was no substitute for the Pakistani. Tony Pigott, thirty-five years old, was signed from Sussex and gained a first-team place with his swing bowling. Andy Smith found some turn on The Oval pitches and showed promise as an off-spinning all-rounder. He turned his maiden first-class century into a double hundred against Oxford University. James Boiling had moved to Durham and the opportunity was there for Andy Smith to step in as the off-spinner but, unfortunately, he was unable to rise to the challenge.

Joey Benjamin had an excellent season but even his efforts could not save the year for Surrey. His exemplary efforts were rewarded with a well-deserved England call-up, originally for the Second Test against South Africa, though he did not play until the Third, at The Oval, where he made an admirable debut. He finished sixth in the national averages, and was chosen for the Australian tour.

So the hard work put in by an exciting batting side was for nothing. Darren Bicknell was fast becoming synonymous with consistency on another front – in being overlooked by England, despite passing 1,000 runs for a sixth consecutive year. He scored his maiden double hundred, 235 not out against Nottinghamshire, but this was topped by David Ward who made a welcome return to his best form. He did not even mind being stranded half-a-dozen runs short of 300 when his captain declared against Derbyshire. Alistair Brown and Bicknell were the only batsmen to achieve four figures for Surrey. Brown was capped and Adam Hollioake's remarkable progress continued apace. Three magnificent centuries and some exciting one-day innings, as well as 26 useful Championship wickets reinforced Alec Stewart's confident prediction of an international career. Hollioake was a strokemaker of the highest calibre, comfortable on both sides of the wicket, who could destroy the most experienced attack with a few telling blows.

There was an acrimonious departure from The Oval in August when Tony Murphy, whose six-wicket performance had virtually won the NatWest quarter-final against Glamorgan, left both the club and county cricket after being overlooked for the semi-final.

Nadeem Shahid was signed from Essex and Jason Radcliffe from Warwickshire after the season, to provide cover for Thorpe and Stewart should they retain their Test places, especially as Monte Lynch had moved to Gloucestershire. Shahid could also bowl leg-spin and possibly deputise behind the stumps. The question of wicketkeeping had still to be resolved. Stewart kept in only 3 Championship matches late in the season and the specialists, Neil Sargeant and Graham Kersey, were practically inseparable statistically.

HIGHLIGHTS OF THE 1994 SEASON

FIRST-CLASS MATCHES

	BATTING		
	Runs	Ave	100s
D.J. Bicknell	1,261	50.44	3
G.P. Thorpe	897	49.83	2
A.D. Brown	1,049	47.68	2
D.M. Ward	921	43.85	1
A.J. Stewart	514	42.83	2
A.J. Hollioake	722	36.10	3
M.A. Butcher	613	36.05	1
A.W. Smith	524	32.75	1

	BOWLING			
	Wkts	Ave	5wI	10wM
J.E. Benjamin	76	20.76	5	1
A.C.S. Pigott	29	25.41	1	-
C.E. Cuffy	36	30.05	-	-
M.P. Bicknell	27	32.03	1	-
A.J. Hollioake	26	36.84	-	-
A.W. Smith	28	47.86	1	-

ONE-DAY MATCHES

	BATTING		
	Runs	Ave	100s
G.P. Thorpe	862	57.46	2
D.J. Bicknell	891	55.68	1
D.M. Ward	968	46.09	-
A.D. Brown	879	41.85	2
A.J. Hollioake	549	36.60	-
A.J. Stewart	543	36.20	1

	BOWLING		
	Wkts	Ave	4wI
A.C.S. Pigott	30	25.73	-
M.P. Bicknell	22	26.59	3
A.J. Murphy	19	28.21	1
A.J. Hollioake	24	37.83	-

1995

There was still no success on the field in 1995 and by mid-July, Surrey had gone 7 Championship games without winning and were bottom of the table. They had also been eliminated from both of the knockout competitions. At the end of the season they were twelfth in the Championship and ninth in the Sunday League, which was a fair recovery. Alec Stewart, on international duty or injured for much of the season, played in only 7 Championship matches. On rare occasions Surrey had appointed an official vice-captain and this position was now offered to Adam Hollioake, who accepted. His leadership produced 3 victories, including unlikely wins over Nottinghamshire and Yorkshire which hauled Surrey off the bottom of the Championship table and prompted speculation about the long-term future of both men.

Injuries to key players throughout the year created a problem. Martin Bicknell broke down three times in the first seven weeks and Joey Benjamin managed only 12 first-class games but still took 53 wickets to finish as the leading wicket-taker for the County.

Seventeen-year-old Alex Tudor was given a gentle introduction into the side but broke down in his fifth Championship match. By then, he had done enough to suggest that he had a good future in the game. As Waqar Younis was also injured, Carl Rackemann from Queensland was taken on and his 47 Championship wickets were a useful contribution, but overall the attack lacked penetration.

Adam Hollioake, Alistair Brown and Mark Butcher were the only batsmen to score more than 1,000 in the season but Darren Bicknell (997), who scored an unbeaten double hundred against Nottinghamshire, and Nadeem Shahid (900) were close. A glance at the Championship statistics reveals that Surrey batsmen reached half-centuries 66 times, but converted only 14 of them into hundreds. Even some of the heroes of the summer were culpable. Butcher was an opener of outstanding ability and it was thought that if he worked on his bowling, could become something of an all-rounder, but he scored only 2 hundreds. Brown passed 1,000 runs for the third consecutive season and his career-best 187 in the opening match against Gloucestershire revealed a marked improvement in temperament. Nadeem Shahid had a productive season and Graham Kersey established himself as the wicketkeeper/batsman the side needed. Jason Ratcliffe had his first season and Chris Lewis was signed at the end of the year on a two-year contract.

In early October, a large group of members called for a special general meeting. One of the motions was a demand for a more democratically-run organisation. The vote on this issue was won in the hall but lost on the postal ballot. Mike Soper had taken over as chairman following the resignation of Brian Downing and was taken aback by the depth of feeling at the meeting. He promised to listen sympathetically to the views of the

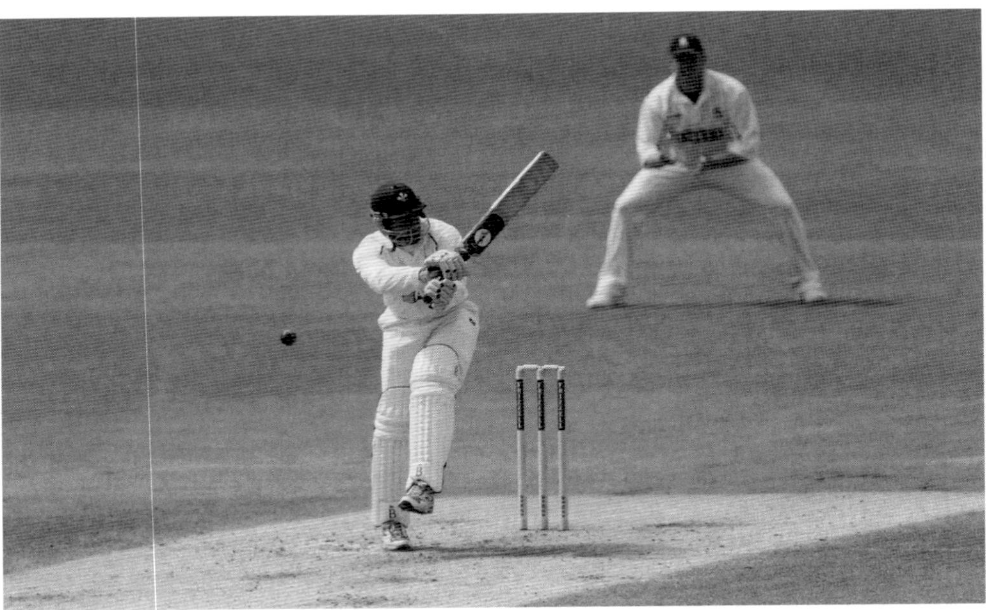

Adam Hollioake.

members, and the club had also asked Sir Peter Imbert, the former Metropolitan Police commissioner to lead a review into the management of the club. His report included 44 recommendations, some of which suggested a change in the role of the chief executive, Glyn Woodman, particularly regarding cricket matters. Glyn Woodman resigned as he felt his position had become untenable and was immediately succeeded by Paul Sheldon, who had been taken on the staff to organise the club's 150th anniversary. The anniversary was celebrated with a dinner at Grosvenor House and special additional matches at The Oval including a three-day match game against New South Wales captained by Mark Taylor. A large fundraising scheme was organised and with help from the National Lottery the goal was achieved to build the Cricket Development Centre in Guildford.

HIGHLIGHTS OF THE 1995 SEASON

FIRST-CLASS MATCHES

BATTING				BOWLING				
	Runs	Ave	100s		Wkts	Ave	5wI	10wM
A.J. Stewart	534	44.50	2	A.J. Tudor	14	22.85	1	-
A.D. Brown	1,054	42.16	3	M.P. Bicknell	41	23.85	3	-
D.J. Bicknell	997	39.88	2	J.E. Benjamin	53	25.01	3	-
G.P. Thorpe	717	39.83	2	C.G. Rackemann	48	29.79	1	-
Nadeem Shahid	900	39.13	2	A.C.S. Pigott	22	30.31	2	1
A.J. Hollioake	1,094	39.07	1	A.J. Hollioake	21	34.33	-	-
M.A. Butcher	1,185	38.22	2	R.W. Nowell	32	39.50	-	-

ONE-DAY MATCHES

BATTING				BOWLING			
	Runs	Ave	100s		Wkts	Ave	4wI
D.J. Bicknell	779	48.68	1	J.E. Benjamin	19	25.89	2
Nadeem Shahid	398	44.22	1	A.J. Hollioake	24	27.75	2
A.J. Stewart	266	38.00	-	S.G. Kenlock	20	31.30	2
A.J. Hollioake	443	34.07	-				
G.P. Thorpe	404	31.07	1				
A.D. Brown	604	30.20	1				

1996

Minimum of 104 overs per day. 3 points for a draw in Championship matches

Surrey won the Sunday League for the first time in 1996. Even so, it was very close. Surrey and Nottinghamshire finished on the same number of points and Surrey won the title due to a higher run rate. They both won 12 of the 17 matches and there was one No Result. Ironically it was the game between Surrey and Nottinghamshire at Trent Bridge that was abandoned. In the 12 matches won the opposition was dismissed on 10 occasions. Their match at Stockton-on-Tees against Durham can illustrate one reason

Graham Kersey.

why Surrey finished with a higher run rate. David Ward and Adam Hollioake advanced the Surrey score by 80 runs in 24 balls during the 36th, 37th, 38th and 39th overs of the innings. The trophy was received in the final game of the season at Cardiff when Surrey won by seven wickets with over 7 overs to spare.

By mid-August, the mood at The Oval was more buoyant than for many years as the County was on course to complete a treble by collecting the Championship and the NatWest Trophy as well. But the disappointment of their NatWest semi-final capitulation to Essex, despite Alec Stewart's unbeaten hundred, was a foretaste of further failure. The Championship slipped from their grasp, first with a draw in the rain at Trent Bridge, then with a share of the spoils at Cardiff, where Surrey's need for a top-class spinner was starkly revealed. The rain-soaked final match against Worcestershire was reduced to a money-chase; second place was the best they could hope for and, despite a brave effort, they finished third. At least Surrey had rid themselves of the monkey that had clung to their backs for the last 14 years, in which they won nothing but criticism for unfulfilled potential. They ended the season with the belief that the Sunday League should be the first of many trophies for this talented team.

The contribution of Australian bite to Surrey's summer cannot be underestimated. The shrewdest signing was that of former Test fast bowler David Gilbert in the role of cricket manager. He began by ordering the demolition of the wall between the capped and non-capped players' dressing rooms. Having taken that first dramatic step towards uniting his squad Gilbert saw the players respond swiftly to his canny man-management skills. Another key figure was Australian all-rounder Brendon Julian, who overcame an alarming propensity to bowl no-balls and wides and completed an impressive double by passing 500 runs and 50 wickets. Meanwhile, Australian-born Adam Hollioake began the season at Taunton with a century in each innings, the twelfth Surrey batsman to achieve the feat, and led Surrey to 4 of their 8 Championship victories and 5 Sunday League wins. He was rewarded by being named captain of England 'A' for their winter tour to Australia.

Surrey had an unpleasant five weeks before getting things right. They drew their first 4 Championship matches and lost the 5th to the team who were already their *bête noire* for the season, Yorkshire. They lost their Sunday League game with Yorkshire and less than a fortnight earlier had been outbatted, outbowled and outplayed by them in the Benson and Hedges quarter-finals. In mid-June, they stood thirteenth in the Championship. After that, they finally woke up to their capabilities.

Adam Hollioake and the prolific Mark Butcher, who both scored over 1,500 Championship runs, led the batting. Due to England commitments Graham Thorpe played in only 9 Championship games but still scored over 1,000 runs. However, their strength was in the bowling. They took sixty-four bowling points, more than any other county, and the maximum of four in 14 of their 17 matches. This was despite the unenviable landmark of conceding more than 1,000 extras, believed to be a first for any county, and the lack of a top-class spinner; Richard Pearson toiled, but lacked the penetration required at this level.

Martin Bicknell stayed injury-free and was back to his best, with 66 wickets at 24.74. Joey Benjamin, seemingly as ageless as ever, provided some superb support and Darren Bicknell compensated for missing out on 1,000 runs by revealing himself as an orthodox slow left-hand bowler who should not be taken lightly. His 16 wickets will have been all the sweeter because, coming at an average of 23.00, they beat his brother into second place in the averages. Chris Lewis produced enough magic moments to convince everyone he had plenty more to offer. His rehabilitation was helped by an England recall. The TCCB tried to persuade Surrey to omit him from their team after England had dropped him for arriving late during the Oval Test. The club's response was to make him captain and he led the County to victory over Warwickshire in three days.

Adam Hollioake's eighteen-year-old brother, Ben, made a big impact in his first season with 13 Sunday League wickets and but for England Under-19 calls it could have been a lot more. Irish seamer Mark Patterson was another addition to the young squad. Inevitably, there were departures, most notably that of beneficiary David Ward, a long-time favourite of Oval crowds. He still managed to leave his mark, with hundreds in Sunday League victories over Kent and Durham, and was to be sorely missed, as much for his sense of fun as for his big hitting. His buddy Alistair Brown had a spring to remember but a summer to forget. A century for England in the one-day series with India was followed by precious little for his county. He hit an unprecedented run of poor form, with just 3 fifties in the Championship. He admitted that being dropped late in the season came as a relief.

After all that, an unseasonably warm autumn buzzed with rumours. The most persistent said that leg-spinner Ian Salisbury was going to tread a well-worn path from

Sussex to The Oval. In November, that turned out to be true, and it was felt that the appointment would solve Surrey's most serious shortcoming. Another rumour claimed that the captaincy was once more an issue, with the cricket committee apparently in favour of Adam Hollioake succeeding Stewart. There was certainly a case for Hollioake taking over: apart from his impressive record when left in charge, there was the matter of continuity – Stewart's reign had always been interrupted by England calls. In 1997, though, there was the possibility that Hollioake could also become a regular in the Test squad, in which case he would be away just as often.

HIGHLIGHTS OF THE 1996 SEASON

FIRST-CLASS MATCHES

BATTING				BOWLING				
	Runs	Ave	100s		Wkts	Ave	5wI	10wM
G.P. Thorpe	1,044	69.60	5	D.J. Bicknell	16	23.00	-	-
A.J. Hollioake	1,521	69.13	5	M.P. Bicknell	66	24.74	3	-
M.A. Butcher	1,540	53.10	3	B.C. Hollioake	10	25.20	-	
B.P. Julian	759	36.14	2	B.P. Julian	61	28.88	3	-
D.J. Bicknell	969	34.60	2	J.E. Benjamin	39	31.20	-	
Nadeem Shahid	535	33.43	1	C.C. Lewis	29	33.68	1	-
				R.M. Pearson	31	48.67	1	-

ONE-DAY MATCHES

BATTING				BOWLING			
	Runs	Ave	100s		Wkts	Ave	4wI
A.J. Stewart	778	64.83	4	A.J. Hollioake	48	15.97	5
C.C. Lewis	289	48.16	-	C.C. Lewis	25	18.48	-
A.D. Brown	943	42.86	1	J.E. Benjamin	24	22.25	-
M.A. Butcher	404	40.40	-	B.P. Julian	33	25.42	1
G.P. Thorpe	369	33.54	-	M.P. Bicknell	31	27.35	-
D.M. Ward	433	27.06	2				

The cricketing progress of Alec Stewart had been through the ranks. Tiffin School, junior Surrey sides, Surrey second team during his final school year and finally, when he left school at eighteen, joining the Surrey staff. Alec came from a family environment likely to produce a sportsman – his mother, Sheila, was a top netball and hockey player and his father had been a stalwart at Surrey for many years.

Simultaneously, he began an association with Australian grade cricket at the Midland-Guildford club in Perth. Alec called Perth his second home and credits it with being the finishing school for his cricket education. He played grade cricket from 1980 to 1989 and was such a fixture that they named a stand after him at their Lilac Hill ground.

If he learned his batting skills at The Oval, it was the Aussie school of hard knocks that instilled in him a mental toughness, a desire to give as good as he got and to mix it verbally. So when on his first England tour, and playing only his second Test, he crossed

Mark Butcher.

swords with Desmond Haynes at Trinidad, Haynes by no means got the better of him. No one can say that success has come easily to Stewart. He has always appeared to be a well-organised, busy, bat-twirling player, capable of making entertaining runs but lacking, apparently, the commitment to register the big scores that get noticed. The first ten years of his career had brought him just 16 first-class centuries. Had he not developed his wicketkeeping he might not have received his chance in international cricket. Yet even having made the squad it was not easy to establish himself. Dropped after the disastrous tour of Australia in 1990/91, he was recalled, much to his surprise, to keep wicket in the Final Test against West Indies that summer. It was an opportunity he could not afford to miss, and he took it. England won memorably. Two weeks later he scored his first Test century, against Sri Lanka, and in the 17 Test innings after his return he scored 952 runs at an average of 68.00.

Over the years, Stewart filled a plethora of roles for England. He was vice-captain to Atherton and Gooch and captained the side himself for the first time against India in 1993. He was officially appointed captain in 1998 and led England for 14 Test matches altogether, including a series victory at home against South Africa. He also skippered them in the 1999 World Cup, standing down afterwards. He batted in all positions from No.1 to No.7 without complaint, for the good of the England side. At Bridgetown, in 1994, he became the first Englishman to score a century in each innings against the West Indies, scores of 118 and 143 steering England to victory. His highest score of 190 came against Pakistan at Edgbaston in 1992. Originally drafted into the squad as a batsman-cum-wicketkeeper in an all-rounder role, he became accepted as a wicketkeeper of international standing. He was a consistent performer for Surrey, maintaining a batting average of around 40, with 26 centuries, his most successful years being in the late 1980s and early 1990s. In one-day cricket his average was 37.17, second only to Mark Ramprakash and Graham Thorpe of the current squad. When not keeping wicket, he was an excellent fielder, both close to the wicket and in the outfield.

TWELVE

1997-1998

1997

In 1997 Dave Gilbert was in the second year of his contract as coach with the club. Much had already been achieved and apart from success in one-day competitions in successive years he had made an impression in other areas. He made two important additions to the playing staff that would bear fruit over the forthcoming years: Ian Salisbury was signed from Sussex and Saqlain Mushtaq was recruited as the overseas player from Pakistan. Ian was a rarity, an English leg-spinner and a successful one too at county level. He bowled well-flighted leg-breaks, had a well-disguised googly and generally maintained good length and line. Not a big spinner of the ball, he relied on variation of length and pace. A useful bat, he often contributed runs in the lower order without really being considered an all-rounder. He had played his early cricket for the village of Brixworth, near Northampton, and appeared for Northamptonshire at junior levels up to the Under-19s. His first-class debut with Sussex was in 1989 and he gained his cap in 1991. His best bowling performance for them was 8 for 75 against Essex at Chelmsford and his highest score was 83 against Glamorgan at Hove. Ian's success was rewarded with a Test against Pakistan and his first scalp was a notable one, Javed Miandad. He played in 15 Tests spread over the next few years, touring India and the West Indies but failing to make a significant impact. His move to Surrey in 1997 revitalised his career and joining Saqlain Mushtaq saw the formation of a very effective spin partnership.

Saqlain joining Surrey was a step he considered to have been wholly beneficial. He made an immediate impression, taking ten wickets in a match in both his fifth and sixth first-class games for the County. Pakistan benefited from his fine performances over the year, having first call on his services but Saqlain, being a loyal and enthusiastic member of the team, was always back to play for Surrey at every available opportunity. He was born in Lahore, the son of a government clerk, and his two elder brothers taught him the rudiments of the game. An off-spinner of the new school who loved variation, Saqlain Mushtaq mastered a mystery ball that was delivered with an off-spinner's action but that spun away from the batsman.

Saqlain made his first-class debut in 1994/95 aged seventeen, when he took 52 wickets in his first season and was picked to represent Pakistan 'A' in a one-day tournament in Dhaka. Full international recognition came quickly in September 1995 with his Test

Ian Salisbury.

Saqlain Mushtaq.

Ben Hollioake.

debut in Peshawar, where he took four wickets, followed by five in the next match. He holds the record for being the bowler to reach 100 one-day international wickets in fewer matches than anyone else.

In 1997, Surrey took the season's first trophy when they crushed Kent by eight wickets in the final of the Benson and Hedges Cup. As Wisden reported:

> An innings of innocent near genius from Ben Hollioake – a reprise of his international debut on the same ground in May – created a one-sided victory for Surrey. On a clammy morning, the ball swung for Surrey's spirited bowlers and Kent's fragile top order was quickly exposed.

Thanks to innings from Llong and Ealham Kent reached 212 in their 50 overs.

> Surrey's batting suggested no total was beyond them. Though they lost Brown in the first over, Ben Hollioake and Stewart then carried the match away from Kent. Hollioake's only previous appearance at Lord's had produced a half-century for England, this time, he almost completed a whole one. Upright and poised and driving the ball from the top of its bounce, he made 98 from 112 balls, with 15 fours. When he was second out at 161, Surrey were 51 short of Kent's total, and Stewart, who made 75 not out, emerged from Hollioake's long shadow to see his side home. The team dedicated what was only their second Benson and Hedges Cup to the memory of their colleague, Graham Kersey.

The tragic death of the popular Graham Kersey the previous winter had left an aching void in the dressing room. He had died in Australia on 1 January from injuries sustained in a road accident. Not only had he been a fine cricketer but he was known as one of the most popular and reliable players in the game. Born in Plumstead in south-east London he joined Kent for the 1990 season. With Steve Marsh as their regular keeper opportunities for first-class cricket were limited and he played only four such matches for Kent. He joined Surrey in 1993 to act as backup for Alec Stewart when he was called up for international duties. In his four seasons for Surrey he claimed 155 catches and 11 stumpings in first-class matches with 30 catches and 4 stumpings in limited-overs games. He was a true and much missed servant of the club.

Apart from gaining this victory the season was rather disappointing for a team that now had ten international players. They finished joint eighth place in the Championship and fifth in the Sunday League and were eliminated from the NatWest Trophy in the second round, bowled out for 154 by a modest Nottinghamshire attack. Again it was difficult to maintain consistency in light of the inevitable calls of the national side. Adam and Ben Hollioake joined Alec Stewart and Graham Thorpe for the one-day internationals in May and all four, plus Mark Butcher, were required at various times for Test matches. That may have accounted for an appalling start, which saw Surrey lose 2 games and draw 5 before claiming their first victory against Nottinghamshire in the last week of June. Surrey were fifteenth in the table after 7 games. Almost inevitably, there was a late surge. Three consecutive victories in August took Surrey to the fringes of the title race, but a bad-tempered draw against Glamorgan put them out of contention.

It took some time for Adam Hollioake to come to terms with full-time captaincy and his personal form fell away. After the all-conquering performances of 1996 he finished the season with only 15 first-class wickets and just one century, against Middlesex.

Surrey's biggest problem was that none of the batsmen came anywhere near scoring 1,000 runs for the club, although Thorpe's impressive England performances lifted him to 1,160 at 61.05 overall. Alistair Brown, who made a delayed entry into the side, was the most productive with 848 runs and 3 centuries. He also produced some thunderous one-day innings, a Surrey-record 157 not out in a Sunday game against Leicestershire, which he soon surpassed with 203 against Hampshire, the first double-century in the competition's twenty-nine seasons. But Brown's first-class opportunities came partly at the expense of the slower-scoring Darren Bicknell, who spent half his season piling up runs for the Second XI. When Bicknell did get a chance in the Championship, he was his usual reliable self, maintaining his high career average with 594 runs at 39.60. Stewart hit a superb 271 not out against Yorkshire, his first Championship hundred since June 1995, as well as keeping wicket. But then he joined the Ashes campaign and left Surrey with a dilemma they could not resolve. James, the son of Alan Knott did not fulfil his early promise and Jonathan Batty still had much to learn at the highest level.

Among the bowlers, only Saqlain Mushtaq excelled. He finished fifth in the national first-class averages being easily the best spinner with 32 wickets at 19.28, and would have taken more if his season had not been interrupted by one-day appearances for Pakistan. He was signed late and missed Surrey's final 2 matches, both of which they lost, as well as a fortnight in mid-season. With Ian Salisbury sewing up a couple of victories in his first season at The Oval, and Rupesh Amin emerging as an orthodox left-armer, there was suddenly no shortage of slow-bowling talent. Chris Lewis finished his two-year contract and opted to return to Leicestershire, his first county. He had picked up only 33 wickets during the season at just under 30, although Leicestershire must have noticed his successful leadership of the side in the absence of Hollioake and Stewart. Martin Bicknell took only 44 first-class wickets and there was little support from Joey Benjamin, Alex Tudor and Ben Hollioake.

Dave Gilbert left at the end of the season in a move to Sussex and Surrey needed to find a new coach. They opted for Keith Medlycott, who had built up a strong reputation as manager of the Second XI, without being as well known as many of the cricketers that he had to manage.

HIGHLIGHTS OF THE 1997 SEASON

FIRST-CLASS MATCHES

BATTING				BOWLING				
	Runs	Ave	100s		Wkts	Ave	5wI	10wM
G.P. Thorpe	707	70.70	2	Saqlain Mushtaq	32	19.28	4	2
A.J. Stewart	726	55.84	2	M.P. Bicknell	44	26.68	1	-
A.D. Brown	848	42.40	3	C.C. Lewis	33	29.39	1	-
D.J. Bicknell	594	39.60	2	A.J. Hollioake	13	29.84	-	
A.J. Hollioake	731	38.47	1	I.D.K. Salisbury	30	31.20	2	-
J.D. Ratcliffe	759	31.62	1	A.J. Tudor	16	32.87	1	
M.A. Butcher	659	31.38	-					

ONE-DAY MATCHES

BATTING				BOWLING			
	Runs	Ave	100s		Wkts	Ave	4wI
G.P. Thorpe	552	39.42	1	C.C. Lewis	31	19.70	1
A.J. Stewart	641	45.78	-	M.P. Bicknell	36	21.05	2
A.D. Brown	877	38.13	2	Saqlain Mushtaq	18	23.50	-
B.C. Hollioake	472	26.22	-	A.J. Hollioake	27	24.07	1
A.J. Hollioake	546	27.30	-	I.D.K. Salisbury	23	29.13	1
J.D. Ratcliffe	345	26.53	-	J.E. Benjamin	17	32.29	1
M.A. Butcher	386	25.73	-	B.C. Hollioake	20	39.25	-

1998

Top 8 teams in Championship qualify for 1999 Super Cup (used for only one season)

The whole of the 1998 season boiled down to one game at home to Leicestershire in September. Leicestershire had steadily gained ground on Surrey during the season and it was now time to discover which was the best side. By the third day of the match Surrey were left in no doubt as to where they stood, out of the money and a long way short of

Left: *Nadeem Shahid.*

Above: *Jason Radcliffe.*

Opposite: *Alex Tudor.*

being Champion County. Though they won 10 matches, and led the table from May to the start of September, fifth place was an accurate reflection of their year. Of their 5 Championship defeats, 4 were at the hands of the sides that finished above them. They had under-performed earlier in the season, against Somerset, Lancashire and, especially, Yorkshire, but nothing had prepared anyone for the wretched show they put up against a team that everyone had been calling a bits-and-pieces side. In the end, it was Surrey who were shredded by Leicestershire by an innings and 211 runs.

The Championship would have been a remarkable achievement. Surrey were without their dependable opener Darren Bicknell, who took most of the summer to recover from a back operation. International calls deprived them of more key personnel, notably Alec Stewart, Mark Butcher, Graham Thorpe (who then dropped out with another back injury), and, during the one-day series, Alistair Brown and Adam Hollioake.

For long spells, they rose above their handicaps. The squad system held firm, and the reserve players, Jason Radcliffe, Nadeem Shahid, James Knott, Ian Ward and, latterly, Joey Benjamin did more than anyone could have hoped. They kept Surrey on top of the Championship until, ironically, after the final Test match. But the return of most of their

England men coincided with a poor showing against Yorkshire, and they would have done far better to have remained loyal to one of the lesser players rather than bring back a half-fit Thorpe for the final game.

The weather hit everyone, restricting the harvest of bonus points. Surrey, though, missed out without any help from the climate. They achieved maximum points with the bat in just half a dozen matches; on five occasions, they were bowled out for less than 200 runs in the first innings and got none. Only Brown passed 1,000 runs for the County and

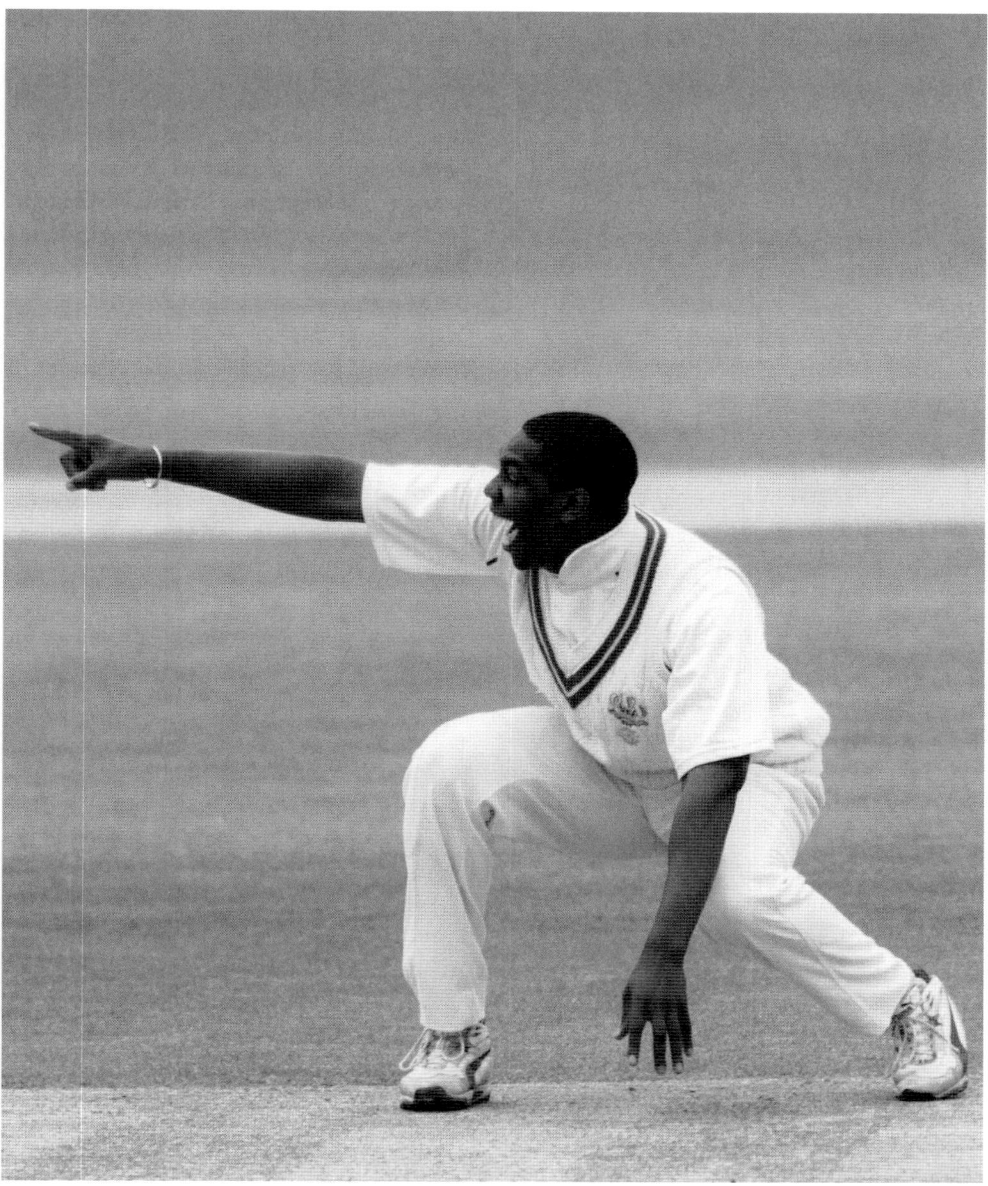

a hugely respectable average of 49.33; no one else was remotely near. Butcher reached the mark due to his England form and Stewart finished just 37 short. The Surrey batsmen scored only 11 hundreds in the Championship, 4 of them by Alistair Brown.

The bowling was the key to Surrey's apparent superiority for so much of the summer, and Saqlain Mushtaq must take pride of place, despite the noble efforts of Martin Bicknell. Saqlain played in 5 fewer matches than Bicknell, Surrey's only ever-present, but his bowling, at times unreadable, brought him 63 wickets, compared with Bicknell's 65. In 3 games (all at The Oval), he finished with eleven-wicket returns, all match-winning performances. His departure before the showdown with Leicestershire, for yet another meaningless money-spinning one-day tournament, was particularly galling. When Saqlain had been signed, it was implied that Pakistan would not call on him if Surrey were in contention for the Championship.

Another blow to Surrey's cause was the stress fracture of the foot suffered by improving fast bowler Alex Tudor, who took 29 wickets in the 10 games he did play. He showed enough promise to earn a place on the Ashes tour, and a Test debut in Perth. Ian Salisbury's decline in form, as well as an injury, also hit hard. On the soft pitches of early summer, when it was least expected, he was bowling as well as he ever has, especially in tandem with Saqlain. But his unsuccessful return to Test cricket and subsequent loss of confidence left Surrey in still more of a mess. It was again up to Martin Bicknell, who had not done so badly with the bat either, to lead the way.

The Benson and Hedges Cup semi-final was the earliest manifestation of Leicestershire as Surrey's nemesis, ending a run of 13 consecutive wins in the tournament. The NatWest Trophy quarter-final tie at home to Derbyshire was a woeful display. Wickets, and thus the game, were cast away wilfully. But nothing could match the depths to which Surrey sank in the Sunday League. Regardless of the fact that the final half of the season was used to try out new players, there could be no justification for their incompetent showing. They finished bottom, for only the second time, and it was all they deserved. They won just one game before September. Thanks to the unseasonable weather, they sometimes fell foul of the Duckworth/Lewis method. But there was so much talent in the squad that excuses are absurd. The Duckworth/Lewis System had been introduced to set a fair target score for the side batting second in a weather-interrupted limited-overs match.

HIGHLIGHTS OF THE 1998 SEASON

FIRST-CLASS MATCHES

	BATTING				BOWLING			
	Runs	Ave	100s		Wkts	Ave	5wI	10wM
A.D. Brown	1,036	49.33	4	Saqlain Mushtaq	63	17.76	3	3
A.J. Stewart	464	42.18	-	M.P. Bicknell	65	20.61	2	-
G.P. Thorpe	251	41.83	1	I.D.K. Salisbury	36	21.27	2	-
M.A. Butcher	661	38.88	2	B.C. Hollioake	34	23.29	-	-
Nadeem Shahid	683	35.94	2	A.J. Tudor	29	25.41	1	
A.J. Hollioake	684	34.20	1	J.E. Benjamin	22	28.45	1	-
J.D. Ratcliffe	449	32.07	1					

ONE-DAY MATCHES

BATTING				BOWLING			
	Runs	Ave	100s		Wkts	Ave	4wI
A.J. Stewart	584	36.50	1	A.J. Tudor	10	15.10	1
G.P. Thorpe	345	34.50	-	B.C. Hollioake	32	23.68	-
I.J. Ward	395	28.21	-	I.D.K. Salisbury	23	25.47	-
A.J. Hollioake	623	27.08	-	Saqlain Mushtaq	15	26.46	1
M.A. Butcher	301	23.15	-	A.J. Hollioake	30	26.53	2
A.D. Brown	494	20.58	-	M.P. Bicknell	23	28.08	1

THIRTEEN

1999-2000

1999

County Championship: 12 points for a win, 4 points for a draw plus bonus points

To summarise the season one can do no better than refer to the book by Trevor Jones entitled *The Dream Fulfilled* where he states:

> This book could just as easily have been entitled '*How to Win a County Championship*' since an exceedingly well-conceived plan was so well carried out by a fine squad of players. Seldom has the Championship been so utterly dominated by one county as it was by Keith Medlycott's men in 1999. Generally speaking, it is true to say that statistics never tell the whole story, but the expressive list of facts and figures below is worthy of closer inspection nevertheless.
>
> — Surrey bowled the opposition out twice in every match that they won.
>
> — Surrey claimed 304 wickets out of a maximum 340 in the season. Twenty-five of the thirty-six they did not take were denied them by rain - at Worcester, Surrey were only able to bowl five overs, taking one wicket in that time, while Leicestershire were down to their last six wickets when the final day of the game was washed out.
>
> — These impressive bowling statistics were achieved despite the fact that the full first-choice attack of Martin Bicknell, Alex Tudor, Saqlain Mushtaq and Ian Salisbury played together in only ONE match - against Hampshire at Guildford.
>
> — Tudor and Saqlain played in a combined total of just sixteen matches - less than a full season.
>
> — Surrey, in fact, were more affected by injuries and international calls than any other county.
>
> — Only Derbyshire (25) and Worcestershire (22) used more players than Surrey's twenty-one.
>
> — Surrey (6) won fewer tosses than every other county, bar Glamorgan (5).
>
> — While Surrey remained unbeaten throughout the whole season, every other county lost at least one game at home and at least two away from home.
>
> — If the 1998 points scoring system, which was more generous in the way it rewarded a team for winning the match, had still been in use then Surrey would have won the title by a massive seventy-two points, with 307 to second-placed Lancashire's 225.
>
> — Hampshire were the only county to bowl Surrey out twice in the season.

— Only Somerset (371) averaged more runs per innings than Surrey (353).
— Surrey scored their runs at a faster rate (3.44 runs per over) than any other team in the Championship.
— Surrey (219) conceded fewer runs per innings than any other county.
— No side could match Surrey's strike rate of a wicket every 48 balls bowled.
— Surrey were also number one in terms of economy rate, conceding just 2.75 runs per over.

Is there anyone who still believes that this title was not fully deserved? Perhaps there are occasions when statistics give a true picture after all.

There were one or two people who felt that Surrey could not have won the title without the brilliant Saqlain Mushtaq, but the argument just doesn't hold water. It is worth remembering that when he rejoined the Club after the World Cup, Surrey were already top of the table, having won five matches out of eight with the other three having been potential victories but for the intervention of rain. Although the next seven matches were all won with the assistance of Saqlain's mastery, it would take a very brave (or foolish!) man to suggest that Surrey would have won fewer that four, even without the presence of the talented off-spinner.

Nevertheless, it is worth recording his figures in these seven matches.

The 1999 Surrey team. From left to right, back row: K.O.A. Barratt, R.M. Amin, I.E. Bishop, M.W. Patterson, G.J. Batty, C.G. Greenidge. Middle row: K.R. Booth (scorer), J. Gloster (physio), J.A. Knott, J.N. Batty, M.A.V. Bell, A.J. Tudor, B.C. Hollioake, G.P. Butcher, I.J. Ward, K.T. Medlycott (manager), A.R. Butcher (second-team coach). Front row: J.D. Radcliffe, A.D. Brown, J.E. Benjamin, D.J. Bicknell, A.J. Stewart, A.J. Hollioake, M.A. Butcher, M.P. Bicknell, G.P. Thorpe, N. Shahid, I.D.K. Salisbury.

SAQLAIN MUSHTAQ: 7 MATCHES, 58 WICKETS

		1st Innings	2nd Innings
v. Durham	The Foster's Oval	5 for 72	7 for 38
v. Hampshire	Guildford	1 for 77	6 for 44
v. Warwickshire	Edgbaston	2 for 58	5 for 32
v. Glamorgan	The Foster's Oval	2 for 14	5 for 18
v. Sussex	Hove	7 for 19	3 for 78
v. Derbyshire	Derby	3 for 36	5 for 59
v. Nottinghamshire	The Foster's Oval	3 for 15	4 for 100

Total: 290.5 overs, 90 maidens, 660 runs, 58 wickets

So Surrey had left the twentieth century as they entered it – as champions. One hundred years after winning the 1899 County Championship Surrey did it again. But the more significant date in everyone's mind was 1971, Surrey's last Championship. It took twenty-eight years for the sequence of failure to be broken.

Surrey went to the top of the table on 5 June and stayed there for the remainder of the season. Finishing unbeaten (even the legendary Surrey sides of the 1950s never managed this) with 264 points, well ahead of Lancashire, who finished second on 208 points. They reached their moment of fulfilment with 2 matches to spare and in celebration at The Oval for the final match against Yorkshire, the prices in the Members bar were set at 1971 levels so a pint of beer cost twenty pence and a bottle of wine £1.50. Despite this match being interrupted by rain one and all had a good time. With the problems encountered by injuries and international calls, including the World Cup, Surrey operated a squad system and captain Adam Hollioake and cricket manager Keith Medlycott contrived to mould the players available into a winning co-operative.

Three Surrey bowlers figured in the national top 10, five in the top 30. Some commentators suggested that the Oval pitches, once hard and true, were now playing false, lacking pace and primed to help off-spinner Saqlain Mushtaq and wrist-spinner Ian Salisbury. But although Saqlain did take plenty of wickets in his 7 matches for the County only 3 of these were at The Oval. Salisbury, one of the three ever-presents, did his bit, as 60 wickets bore witness. So did Martin Bicknell, who finished with 71, the eighth time in a fourteen-year career he had reached 50 first-class wickets. Alex Tudor's season may be best remembered for his unbeaten 99 in the Edgbaston Test, but he took 39 wickets in 9 games for Surrey before he was struck down with a knee injury. The bowling 'discovery' of the season was Jason Ratcliffe, an innocuous-looking medium-pacer, who made up for poor batting form with a career-best 6 for 48 against Sri Lanka 'A'; he actually finished above Bicknell in the national averages!

The batting was solid, if not spectacular. Ali Brown scored 1,000 first-class runs for the fifth time, with 4 more hundreds, including a career-best of 265 against Middlesex at Lord's. In the same drawn match Mark Ramprakash scored 209 not out for the home side. Mark Butcher captained the side until Adam Hollioake's interest in the World Cup ended, leading Surrey to 5 of their 12 victories. He scored a maiden double hundred at Leicester and his county success was some consolation for a traumatic summer with England.

Carl Greenidge.

Like Butcher, Ian Ward completed 1,000 first-class runs, including, after a rash of fifties, his maiden hundred. He proved a fine, at times brilliant, fielder. A few years ago, an unforgiving and shortsighted Surrey management had thoughtlessly dumped Ward. He had returned in 1996 and now, aged 26, made the most of his chance to succeed and was rewarded with an England 'A' tour. Graham Thorpe averaged 51 when England could spare him, though Alec Stewart had a disappointing season. Jon Batty proved an able wicketkeeper, with 50 Championship dismissals.

Among the seamers, twenty-one-year-old Carl Greenidge, the son of the West Indian Test batsman Gordon Greenidge, had pace and showed promise for the future. On the downside Ben Hollioake made little progress, although he did manage a five-wicket haul and 4 fifties before injury cut short his season. Joey Benjamin did not have his contract renewed and Darren Bicknell, a Surrey man through and through, left for greener pastures at Trent Bridge, after losing his place to Ward. Martin Bicknell took 71 Championship wickets despite not taking five wickets in an innings all season.

Again, Surrey had little success in the one-day game. The National League changed by moving many games away from Sundays and introducing floodlight matches. Winning only 5 games they remained in the second division. Their Super Cup campaign was a virtual non-starter, while their NatWest run ended in a crunching and unexpected semi-final defeat by Somerset. The Super Cup, sponsored by Benson and Hedges, was played for in only this one season. But despite their poor form in the one-day game Surrey were overjoyed to be able to hoist the County Championship pennant in the year 2000.

HIGHLIGHTS OF THE 1999 SEASON

FIRST-CLASS MATCHES

BATTING				BOWLING				
	Runs	Ave	100s		Wkts	Ave	5wI	10wM
A.D. Brown	1,127	51.22	4	Saqlain Mushtaq	58	11.37	7	2
G.P. Thorpe	561	51.00	2	J.D. Ratcliffe	15	17.93	1	-
M.A. Butcher	991	47.19	2	M.P. Bicknell	71	18.95	-	-
I.J. Ward	1,018	37.70	1	A.J. Tudor	39	21.43	3	-
A.J. Hollioake	534	33.37	1	I.D.K. Salisbury	60	21.91	2	-
D.J. Bicknell	504	31.50	2					

ONE-DAY MATCHES

BATTING				BOWLING			
	Runs	Ave	100s		Wkts	Ave	4wI
G.P. Thorpe	682	68.20	-	Saqlain Mushtaq	20	10.30	3
A.J. Stewart	371	28.53	-	I.E. Bishop	11	22.09	1
M.A. Butcher	423	26.43	-	A.J. Tudor	11	27.00	-
A.D. Brown	488	25.68	1	M.P. Bicknell	18	27.22	1

2000

Introduction of two divisions in the County Championship. Introduction of Central Contracts for England players

One of the defining matches of the year was played at Oakham School. Surrey won the toss and batted first only to lose their first seven wickets for 190. Ali Brown was still at the wicket and in partnerships with Alex Tudor, who scored 22 runs, Ian Salisbury 12 and Saqlain Mushtaq 66 added 315 runs for the last three wickets to reach a total of 505. This was on the way to the highest score of his career, 295 not out, which is also the largest score by a Surrey batsman in the second century of the club. He batted for eight and a half hours, receiving 392 balls and scoring 32 fours and 1 six. It was a classic innings with no false strokes and should have convinced all his detractors that he was not merely a one-day player. Saqlain was particularly disappointed to be dismissed before Brown reached 300, a milestone that has only been achieved by five Surrey players throughout their long history. This list is Bobby Abel 357 not out, Walter Read 338, Jack Hobbs 316 not out, Tom Hayward 315 not out and Andy Ducat 306 not out. Bearing in mind that Leicestershire were dismissed for 143 and 184 it can be seen how vital this period of play was in determining the result of the match. At this point in the season Surrey went to the head of the table and stayed there to the end.

The 2000 season had seen the introduction of two-division County Championship cricket. Being defending champions Surrey were naturally in Division One and had to play their eight opponents twice, once at home and once away. They had a very poor start to the year, losing to both Durham and Derbyshire in away matches. In between they won at home against Hampshire. After the Derbyshire game they had a purple patch with 7 wins in a row but the destiny of the Championship was not resolved until the final game when Surrey emerged as champions for the second season in succession.

In contrast, Surrey had the National League Division Two title parcelled up by the end of August and could use their remaining matches to blood some younger players. After their unbeaten run of 13 League games from the start of the season, the losses they subsequently suffered raised a few eyebrows, but did not spoil the supporter's enjoyment. Promotion was their compensation for the disappointment that followed earlier Benson and Hedges Cup semi-final and NatWest Trophy quarter-final defeats.

Alistair Brown.

Jonathan Batty.

The first year of two-division Championship cricket was certainly a proving ground. For only the third time in more than a century, no Surrey batsman reached 1,000 runs, but determination and experience gave them depth down the order. No other team in the first division collected as many batting bonus points; only second-division Warwickshire picked up more. Alistair Brown emerged as the top run-maker for the fourth successive season with 935. Ian Ward's 894 first-class runs merited as much praise, and earned him his second England 'A' tour in a row. He scored 3 hundreds and forged a formidable left-handed opening partnership with Mark Butcher. Butcher struggled to find his touch until mid-season, when his unbeaten hundred at Southampton launched a more consistent run. Alec Stewart's Championship season was restricted to just 3 games early on and Graham Thorpe followed him into the England team at the end of June after signalling he was returning to his old self with 115 against Somerset. Wicketkeeper Jonathan Batty hit his maiden hundred in the same match.

Thanks to runs from Adam Hollioake, Nadeem Shahid and Martin Bicknell, Stewart and Thorpe's absence was hardly an issue. Martin Bicknell scored 500 runs for the first time, and his 60 wickets at 17.53 raised his status to that of a genuine all-rounder. He had a memorable game against Leicestershire on his home ground at Guildford, claiming the best match return by an England bowler, 16 for 119, since Jim Laker's 19 for 90 against

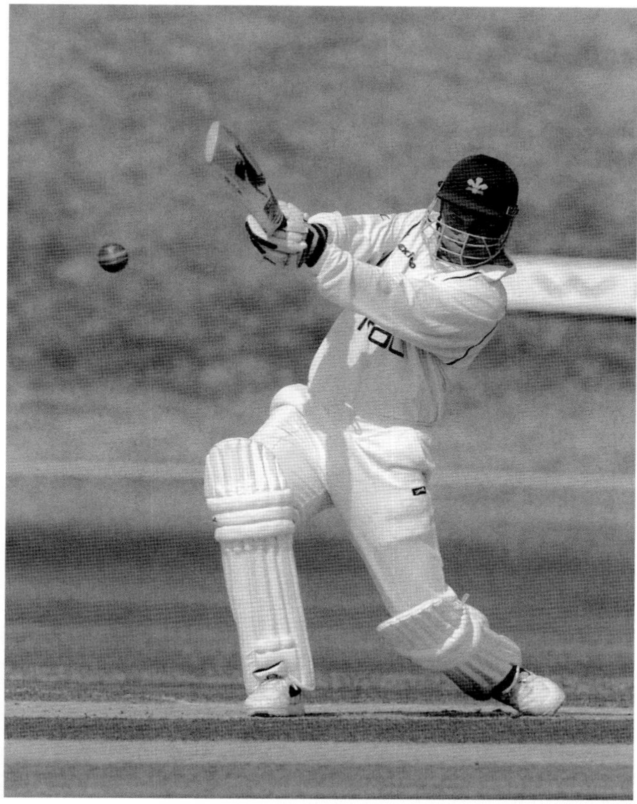

Ian Ward.

Australia in 1956. To many a Surrey supporter the way he was ignored by England selectors was a complete mystery but a great bonus for Surrey for whom he contributed so much. Instead, the selectors returned their attention to Ian Salisbury's leg-spin for England's winter tours to Pakistan and Sri Lanka, attracted by his 52 Championship wickets at 18.92. As a foil to Saqlain Mushtaq's masterful off-spin and bewitching variations, which brought 66 wickets at 15.39, Salisbury enjoyed an impressive domestic season, but he was found wanting in Pakistan, doing neither himself nor his County figures justice in the 3 Tests. He was not taken to Sri Lanka. Alex Tudor went close to 50 Championship wickets, enough to win a place in the England 'A' team and then an upgrade to the senior side when Andrew Flintoff was unfit to bowl. The Butcher brothers did their bit with the ball as well. Not called on to bowl until the final Championship match of the season, against Lancashire at Old Trafford, Mark Butcher claimed five in an innings for the first time in his career. But it was younger brother Gary who made the headlines, taking four wickets in four balls against Derbyshire at The Oval. He later hit a half-century at Old Trafford to remind everyone of his all-round ability, and unintentionally underlined the sorry situation of the man he replaced, Ben Hollioake who in 2000 was but a shadow of the exciting, naturally gifted cricketer who had captured the country's imagination three years earlier. His 285 runs and 24 wickets in 24 first-team games in 2000 were inadequate returns for someone of his talent, and yet it was difficult to pinpoint what had gone wrong. It might just have been one of those seasons; most players have one at some time. Trevor Jones produced another book entitled *Doubling Up with Delight*, which graphically detailed all the matches played by the County in the season.

Central contracts for England players were introduced whereby selected players were paid by the ECB and could only play for their county when released by the England coach, who at the time was Duncan Fletcher. During the years from 2000 to 2003 this affected three Surrey players, Alec Stewart, Graham Thorpe and Mark Butcher, for varying lengths of times. It is worth noting their contribution to Surrey in Championship matches during the period of their international careers.

ALEC STEWART

YEAR	TESTS	LOI	COUNTY CHAMPIONSHIP		%
			PLAYED	TOTAL	
1990	0	2	12	22	54.5
1991	1	0	17	22	77.2
1992	2	5	13	22	59.0
1993	6	3	10	17	58.8
1994	6	3	10	17	58.8
1995	3	3	7	17	41.1
1996	1	6	9	17	52.9
1997	6	3	9	17	52.9
1998	6	6	8	17	47.0
1999	1	5	7	17	41.1
2000	**7**	**7**	**3**	**16**	**18.7**
2001	**7**	**6**	**5**	**16**	**31.2**
2002*	7	7	4	16	25.0
2003	**7**	**0**	**6**	**16**	**37.5**

GRAHAM THORPE

YEAR	TESTS	LOI	COUNTY CHAMPIONSHIP		%
			PLAYED	TOTAL	
1993	3	0	11	17	64.7
1994	2	2	14	17	82.3
1995	6	3	10	17	58.8
1996	6	5	9	17	52.9
1997	6	3	8	17	47.0
1998	3	0	6	17	35.2
1999	4	5	9	17	52.9
2000	3	7	8	16	50.0
2001	**3**	**0**	**2**	**16**	**12.5**
2002	**4**	**3**	**4**	**16**	**25.0**
2003	1	0	11	16	68.7

MARK BUTCHER

YEAR	TESTS	LOI	COUNTY CHAMPIONSHIP PLAYED	TOTAL	%
1997	5	0	13	17	76.4
1998	4	0	12	17	70.5
1999	3	0	13	17	76.4
2000	0	0	16	16	100.0
2001	5	0	10	16	62.5
2002	7	0	6	16	37.5
2003	**7**	**0**	**6**	**16**	**37.5**

The years in which these players were awarded central contracts are in bold. The asterisk by Alec Stewart's 2002 season indicates that he was contracted later during that summer following the injury to James Foster, who had been given a contract at the start of the year. The interesting aspect of having central contracts is that when the England coach asks the county to give one of the players a championship game the county could refuse as it is upsetting the balance and morale of the team. This happened on at least two occasions. The England players took part in nearly all the one-day games in the Benson and Hedges Cup and the NatWest Trophy but less in the Sunday League. Again it is interesting to read the comments of Alec Stewart on central contracts in his book *Playing for Keeps* (pp. 175-6).

HIGHLIGHTS OF THE 2000 SEASON

FIRST-CLASS MATCHES

	BATTING				BOWLING			
	Runs	Ave	100s		Wkts	Ave	5wI	10wM
A.D. Brown	935	51.94	2	Saqlain Mushtaq	66	15.39	6	2
M.A. Butcher	891	42.42	2	M.P.Bicknell	60	17.53	3	1
I.J.Ward	894	40.63	3	I.D.K.Salisbury	52	18.92	3	2
Nadeem Shahid	434	36.16	-	A.J.Tudor	47	22.78	3	-
M.P. Bicknell	500	31.25	-					
A.J. Hollioake	689	29.95	-					

ONE-DAY MATCHES

	BATTING				BOWLING		
	Runs	Ave	100s		Wkts	Ave	4wI
A.J. Stewart	513	64.12	-	A.J.Hollioake	32	12.84	3
G.P.Thorpe	482	53.55	1	M.P.Bicknell	23	16.21	-
Nadeem Shahid	239	47.80	1	Saqlain Mushtaq	21	16.95	-
I.J. Ward	497	31.06	-	A.J.Tudor	25	19.60	1
A.J. Hollioake	403	31.00	1				

FOURTEEN
2001-2003

2001

John Major was in his second year as a very proud president of the club and after their success in the previous two seasons was expecting Surrey to perform well in 2001, but by the middle of the season they were in danger of being relegated from Division One of the County Championship. However, they eventually finished fourth thanks to an excellent team spirit and spirited play by several individuals. They had been unbeaten until August but a string of poor draws did not help their cause. In the National League a disastrous year saw them drop straight back into Division Two.

Poor weather in the first few weeks did not help and they recorded only 2 wins in the first 10 Championship games. Saqlain Mushtaq was on duty with Pakistan and missed 7 matches. His season's contribution of 43 Championship wickets at 22.13 was useful but there were no specific match-winning performances.

With Surrey having a squad containing many international players, the demands of the England team had a serious effect on the strength of the County. To provide backup for the batting Mark Ramprakash had been signed from Middlesex, but he played so well in the first half of the year with a couple of marvellous hundreds and several fifties that he too was given another chance in the England set-up. Mark Butcher forced himself into the England team, made a magnificent comeback and scored 1,300 first-class runs at 56.52 in the season.

Alec Stewart and Graham Thorpe played in a total of only 7 Championship matches between them due to their central contracts. England also called on the services of four other Surrey players for various matches, Ian Ward, Alex Tudor, Alistair Brown and Ben Hollioake. The one player who continued to be overlooked by the national selectors was Martin Bicknell, but this was a great advantage to the County. He had developed into a full-blown all-rounder and again topped Surrey's bowling averages. He was the country's second-highest wicket-taker, and showed his batting colleagues a clean pair of heels until some established practitioners hauled him back at the finish. Bicknell's 748 runs at 46.75, coupled with 72 wickets at 21.36, reinforced the impression that he was not only getting older, but also better. According to reports, he was within twenty minutes of an England call for the Fourth Ashes Test, but it was not to be. To cap a triumphant year he hit his maiden first-class hundred, against Kent at Canterbury, after having picked up four first-innings wickets. Ed Giddins had been recruited to bolster the attack but did not have quite the desired impact, his 30 Championship wickets costing 36 runs apiece, and those expected to challenge for regular first-team places were disappointing. Slow left-armer Rupesh Amin and fast bowlers Carl Greenidge and Ian Bishop were released, along with Gary Butcher, despite some handy performances in his three seasons at The Oval. There was little doubt that more personnel changes would be necessary, and Leicestershire's England seamer Jimmy Ormond was signed to reinforce the squad.

Jason Ratcliffe, one of the unsung heroes of the consecutive Championship triumphs, missed the season through a long-term knee injury. Tudor struggled for much of the time with a side strain, although it did not prevent him making his maiden first-class hundred. Ian Salisbury did not miss a match but he was troubled by painful toe and finger problems that affected his technique and form, while, midway through the season, Brown broke his thumb while fielding against Northamptonshire at Guildford. It did not stop him scoring a fine hundred, and because of all the injuries in the squad he continued to play in subsequent matches, but his next half-dozen innings produced barely 50 runs. An unbeaten century from him had seen Surrey win their Benson and Hedges quarter-final at Hove. In the semi-final a total of 361, a competition record by one first-class county against another, saw off Nottinghamshire, led by former Surrey stalwart Darren Bicknell, to set up the Lord's showdown against holders Gloucestershire. In the final Surrey batted first and made 244 with Ian Ward scoring 54, Mark Ramprakash and Adam Hollioake each contributing 39. Ben Hollioake scored an excellent 73 to take the Man of the Match

The 2001 Benson and Hedges Cup-winning team. From left to right: Ed Giddins, Mark Butcher, Jonathan Batty, Alec Stewart, Alex Tudor, Saqlain Mushtaq, Martin Bicknell, Adam Hollioake, Alistair Brown, Ian Ward, Ben Hollioake, Mark Ramprakash.

award. Despite a gritty innings of 62 by Russell, Gloucestershire were always short of the chase. Tudor, Giddins and Saqlain took three wickets each.

Surrey now had a trophy in the cabinet by mid-season, but they lost disappointingly to Yorkshire in the Cheltenham & Gloucester Trophy. The feeling of sadness around The Oval at losing their Championship title was heightened by the death in October of a Surrey legend, Alf Gover, at the age of ninety-three. As a fast bowler and subsequent club president, Gover had been associated with the County for more than seventy years, witnessing many of their triumphs including the most recent, the Benson and Hedges Cup victory in July. After his retirement from playing first-class cricket Alf Gover served on various committees over a period of forty years at Surrey, eventually becoming president in 1980. He had moved into journalism and coaching and ran the very successful Gover Cricket School at Wandsworth from 1938 to 1959. Cricketers of all abilities, from humble club players to international stars, were welcomed and benefited from his coaching expertise.

HIGHLIGHTS OF THE 2001 SEASON

FIRST-CLASS MATCHES

	BATTING				BOWLING			
	Runs	Ave	100s		Wkts.	Ave	5wI	10wM
M.A. Butcher	844	60.28	2	M.P. Bicknell	72	21.36	3	1
M.R. Ramprakash	776	55.42	3	Saqlain Mushtaq	43	22.13	4	-
M.P. Bicknell	748	46.75	1	E.S.H. Giddins	30	36.73	1	-
A.J. Hollioake	758	39.89	-	A.J. Tudor	19	38.52	1	-
A.D. Brown	630	31.50	3	I.D.K. Salisbury	27	42.63	1	

ONE-DAY MATCHES

	BATTING				BOWLING		
	Runs	Ave	100s		Wkts	Ave	4wI
M.R. Ramprakash	529	48.09	-	A.J. Hollioake	26	19.15	2
B.C. Hollioake	563	46.92	-	B.C. Hollioake	28	19.67	-
A.D. Brown	787	43.72	4	A.J. Tudor	20	21.35	1
G.J. Batty	317	35.22	-	M.P. Bicknell	24	23.66	-
I.J. Ward	548	34.25	-	E.S.H. Giddins	25	32.20	-

2002

In March 2002 Ben Hollioake died in a car crash in Australia and the news had a devastating effect on the club. Ben had been a very popular member of the squad and everyone was determined to play that extra dimension for him and his grieving brother and family.

To watch the team play in 2002 was an exceptional experience and it came as no surprise that they lifted the Championship title for the third time in four years. They also

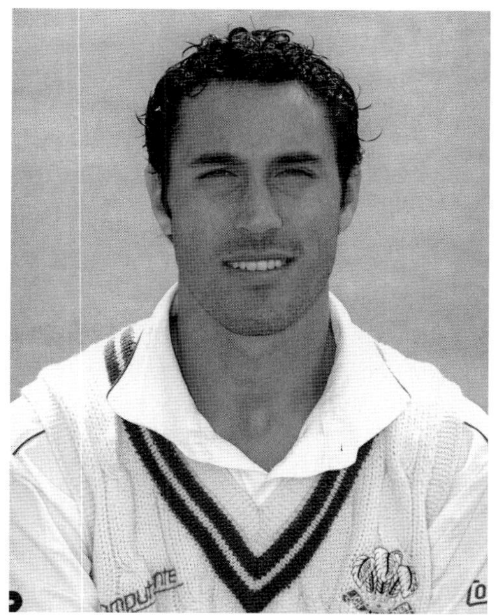

Ben Hollioake (left) and Azhar Mahmood.

gained promotion from the Second Division of the National League. New players were emerging, namely Rikki Clarke and Scott Newman, who both scored maiden hundreds.

The early part of the season took place without the captain, Adam Hollioake, who remained with his family in Australia until June, by which time his wife Sherryn had given birth to their daughter, Bennaya. When he did return, he played with unfettered ease and confirmed his reputation as one of the most astute, innovative and flexible captains in the modern game. His philosophy was to entertain, and several sensational innings rekindled memories of the way he had burst on the scene in the early 1990s. His unbeaten 117 in the C&G at Hove were not unlike his brother Ben at his best: brutal but beautiful. 'Adam played', wrote one observer, 'like a man possessed.' Nor were his fireworks confined to the short game. He thrashed 738 Championship runs off just 812 balls, scoring 66 per cent of his runs – 86 fours and 24 sixes – in boundaries. He crowned his season with a magnificent double hundred against Leicestershire in the final Championship innings, and his deceptive, varied medium-pacers were back to their best with two one-day five-fors. Throughout one of the most traumatic periods of his life, Hollioake displayed dignity, composure and professionalism, and these qualities filtered through to the whole squad.

The frequent absences of Saqlain Mushtaq on international duty were a blessing in disguise because his replacements, both fellow Pakistanis, proved astute signings. Azhar Mahmood claimed 20 wickets in 3 Championship matches, including a stunning eight-wicket haul to beat Lancashire. And near the end of the season, Mushtaq Ahmed's leg-spin was crucial in the victory at Leicester. Not even a cruel injury to Martin Bicknell – out for eight weeks from late June after stumbling in his delivery stride against Sussex and

Alistair Brown.

breaking his right wrist – could stop an exhilarating team from lifting the title. They headed the table after every round save one.

The C&G campaign was crammed with excitement, records and entertainment. It ended in the semi-final at Headingley, but only after an unprecedented decision to designate a fourth day for the tie. For reasons best known to themselves, Yorkshire switched pitches from the original choice, and cantered to victory. Before that, Surrey had produced some scintillating cricket, particularly against Glamorgan at The Oval, where both sides topped 400 – a world record – and Alistair again blazed his way into the history books with a phenomenal 268 from just 160 balls. After Surrey had scored 438 for 5 in their 50 overs Glamorgan made a spirited reply which saw the match going to the penultimate ball of the last over, being all out for 429. The performance in the Benson and Hedges Cup was understandably muted, coming so soon after the loss of Ben Hollioake, who more than anyone had won it for Surrey in 1997 and 2001.

Alistair 'Ali' Brown had attended Caterham School and played for the various Surrey age groups from Under-11 up to Young Cricketers. His father played for Surrey Young Amateurs in the 1950s. Standing 5ft 10in, an attacking right-hand bat, commanding the crease and using his strong arms to build a bat speed which sent the ball to the boundary or, not infrequently, some way over it. A more mature approach had taught him though

Scott Newman.

that major innings require foundations. An excellent fielder, he specialised at being close on the leg side and was also an occasional wicketkeeper. He played for England in 16 one-day internationals with a highest score of 118 against India in his debut season of 1996, thereby gaining his reputation as a one-day specialist. In the second century of the club he now holds the record for the highest individual scores in the following competitions:

County Championship:	295 not out *v.* Leicestershire at Oakham School, 2000
C&G Trophy:	268 *v.* Glamorgan at The AMP Oval, 2002
National League:	203 *v.* Hampshire at Guildford, 1997

The manner in which he scored his runs made him a favourite with the crowds, a dashing and daring player who could quickly resuscitate a moribund match.

In the Championship, Scott Newman's 5 innings revealed a powerful strokemaker of the highest calibre. He became only the third Surrey player to hit 99 in his first Championship innings, and needed just three more attempts to score a century, and a big one at that: 183 against Leicestershire at The Oval.

Rikki Clarke followed a maiden first-class hundred on his debut, against Cambridge, with a fine unbeaten 153 at Taunton. He produced some promising spells of fast-medium

Rikki Clarke.

bowling and was rewarded with a winter at the ECB Academy. The Cricket Writers' Club named him Young Cricketer of the Year, and Surrey were delighted when he signed a new five-year contract.

The emergence of Tim Murtagh and Philip Sampson as promising seamers meant that, when Bicknell eventually retires, there are others capable of assuming his onerous mantle. Once again, Surrey's success was very much a team effort. It began with the stand-in captain, Mark Butcher, who enjoyed an unbeaten run of 4 Championship matches before handing over to Ian Ward. The defining match in the Championship was against Kent at Canterbury starting on 19 July.

The fixture began in controversy as Surrey disregarded England's request that Graham Thorpe be given match practice. It ended in triumph as Ian Ward's eight-hour vigil, scoring 168 not out in the second innings with solid support from Rikki Clarke, Saqlain Mushtaq and James Ormond, saw Surrey move to an extraordinary victory. This was after they had only narrowly avoided the possibility of being asked to follow on thanks to a century from Adam Hollioake. Kent thought they were in a winning position and enforced the extra half-hour on the third day to finish the match to no avail.

Andrew Symonds had helped put Kent in a sound position but Saqlain's bowling performances were commendable. It was Surrey's highest fourth-innings score to win a match, 410 for 8 wickets. Ward's innings surpassed his ultimately less meaningful career best, made on the same ground two years previously, and the Ward-Ormond partnership

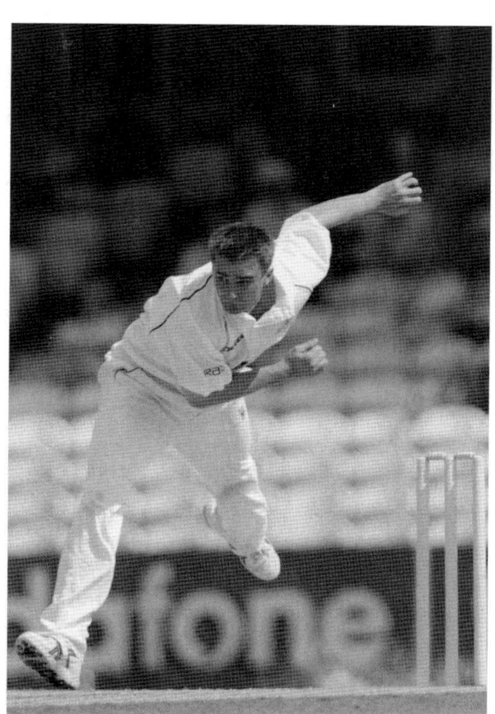

Tim Murtagh.

James Ormond.

replaced a ninety-six-year old record against Kent. In all, 202 runs were scored after the 7th wicket fell in the second innings.

Ian Ward made 6 other centuries in the Championship – including 4 in as many innings at the end of the season – and was the country's highest first-class run-scorer with 1,759. Brown was often in explosive form, hammering 5 Championship centuries to go with his world-record 268, and passing 1,000 runs for the sixth time. Jonathan Batty, for so long an unsung hero, caught the eye with two thoroughly good centuries, the second coming when he was not just standing in for Alec Stewart but also deputising as opener for Butcher. Behind the stumps he was as tidy as his teammates could have wished. Mark Ramprakash also passed 1,000 runs, with double hundreds in successive matches, and Nadeem Shahid was a stand-in who would have been a linchpin at many counties.

Surrey picked up maximum bowling points in every Championship match. Generally, the wickets were shared around, although Saqlain and Ian Salisbury took 90 wickets between them. In his first season with Surrey, Jimmy Ormond passed 50 wickets, and against Warwickshire took ten in a match for the first time. Bicknell and a resurgent Alex Tudor picked up more than 30 each, but Ed Giddins disappointed in the final year of his contract and left in November to join Hampshire. The slow left-hander Rupesh Amin, released in 2001, was re-signed, only to be re-released at the end of the season; he joined Leicestershire.

HIGHLIGHTS OF THE 2002 SEASON

FIRST-CLASS MATCHES

	BATTING				BOWLING			
	Runs	Ave	100s		Wkts	Ave	5wI	10wM
A.J. Hollioake	738	67.09	2	Azhar Mahmood	20	17.25	1	-
I.J. Ward	1759	62.82	7	T.J. Murtagh	17	24.94	1	-
M.R. Ramprakash	1194	56.85	4	Saqlain Mushtaq	53	25.64	3	1
R. Clarke	711	50.78	2	A.J. Tudor	42	26.76	1	-
A.D. Brown	1211	50.45	5	M.P. Bicknell	34	31.38	2	
Nadeem Shahid	712	37.47	2	I.D.K. Salisbury	37	32.21	-	-
J.N. Batty	742	35.33	2	J. Ormond	51	34.90	2	1

ONE-DAY MATCHES

	BATTING				BOWLING		
	Runs	Ave	100s		Wkts	Ave	4wI
G.P. Thorpe	175	87.50	1	A.J. Hollioake	30	14.86	4
M.R. Ramprakash	952	56.00	2	M.P. Bicknell	22	20.18	1
A.D. Brown	899	37.45	1	E.S.H. Giddins	34	22.62	2
A.J. Hollioake	351	35.10	1				

2003

The year of 2003 is seen as a watershed year for professional cricket in England, Wales and Scotland. It stands out in history alongside 1963, when the Gillette Cup changed the landscape forever. Then came 1969, when the John Player League proved that one-day cricket would become a staple food for county cricket, the game for the family, the sprat to catch the mackerel. 2003 saw the introduction of Twenty20 cricket, which repeated the success of those two pioneering competitions. Blessed with extremely fine weather none of the matches were affected by rain or bad light and the crowds came out in droves to all venues. Many asked what tactics the competing teams would adopt but it came down to straightforward batting, bowling and superb fielding. As befitted the current status of Surrey, recognised as the best county side in the country, they went through the whole event unbeaten and won the trophy in the final at a canter.

In a competition that was hailed as being made for batsmen it was the bowlers that called the tune. Adam Hollioake publicly apologised for his round-arm bowling of mixed speeds but by bowling straight he ended the series as the highest wicket-taker with 16. The inspired spells by James Ormond in both the semi-final (1 for 21) and final (4 for 11) at Trent Bridge set up the victories. During the various matches there were fifties scored by Azhar Mahmood, Scott Newman, Mark Ramprakash and Graham Thorpe. In

The 2003 Twenty20 Cup-winning team.

the final Alistair Brown and Ian Ward both scored fifties in a century opening stand enabling Surrey to win in 10.4 overs.

Surrey won the National League, winning 12 of their 16 matches and losing 3, with 1 match being abandoned. As cricket manager Keith Medlycott stated in the Yearbook:

> As a newly promoted side we had to establish ourselves against sides who had played good cricket the year before and knew each other's strengths and weaknesses. We did this from the outset and found that it was indeed tough – of our 12 wins, almost all were incredibly close games. To win each one of these matches was a great achievement and the culmination of everything we set out to do in one-day cricket. From the start we had the mechanics of a great team in place – in the bowling department we possess two quality finishers – Adam Hollioake and Azhar Mahmood – who showed their skill and bravery time and time again – and bowlers able to make early breakthroughs. In the batting we had two explosive starters, followed by Mark Ramprakash and Graham Thorpe who are always likely to build you a solid foundation. Our numbers 5,6 and 7, all genuine all-rounders, were real powerhouses – we'd been looking for that sort of devastating middle order for some time. Azhar and Adam performed in the skilful and belligerent manner we have become accustomed to over the years and Rikki Clarke confirmed his burgeoning reputation, putting his hand up with the ball as well towards the end of the season, and bowling beautifully at some awkward times. And then of course there was Jon Batty and the bowlers contributing valuable runs when necessary. All in all, a very powerful line-up that performed admirably all summer long.

Having played for Northern Transvaal in 1988/89, Keith Medlycott returned to South Africa to become their manager from 1995 to 1997. He then came back to England as manager and coach at Surrey. His record as manager must have been the envy of all the other counties. In 1997 the Second XI won the Aon Risk Trophy, and then the First XI lifted the County Championship in 1999, 2000 and 2002, won the Benson and Hedges Cup in 2001 and the National League and Twenty20 Cup in 2003. To assist his coaching, Keith had the use of a computer programme called Cricstat to help iron out the Surrey players' technical flaws. Cricstat is a cricket programme that analyses every delivery of each day's play. It is a logging system detailing the type of delivery, where the ball pitches, what type of shot is played, how many runs are scored and whereabouts on the field the ball goes. All the information is then analysed and players are able to look at the footage to sort out problems in their technique. Several of the players were taking advantage of this modern development.

However, despite winning two trophies there was a sense of disappointment in the camp as the most important trophy, the County Championship, eluded the team when Surrey finished in third place after being in a commanding position for most of the season. It started to go wrong at Leicester in August. After scoring 501 in their first innings Surrey dismissed Leicestershire for 166 and enforced the follow-on. John Maunders and Brad Hodge then put on 281 for the 2nd wicket and the occasional bowlers were brought on to try and force a declaration but to no avail as the game petered out in a draw. Travelling to Old Trafford Surrey were then comprehensively beaten by Lancashire when key players

Alec Stewart celebrating his final Test appearance at The Oval.

were missing through Test match calls and injuries. Martin Bicknell had been recalled to the England team, long overdue, and was in the team that beat South Africa at The Oval to win the series. His swing bowling was one of many key factors along with the return of Graham Thorpe to the international fold marked by an excellent faultless century. Martin had become a special record holder when he played in the Test match at Headingley, as England had played 114 Tests since his last appearance for his country against Australia in 1993. Another pleasing first for him was that his portrait was hung in the Long Room at The Oval, this being the first occasion when a current player had received this honour. By the end of the season he had taken 982 first-class wickets in his career and looked forward to joining the elite 1,000-wicket club in 2004.

The Oval Test match also saw the last international appearance of Alec Stewart. His record for his country had been outstanding. The benchmark for batsmen at Test match level is regarded as being an average of 40 or above. Alec almost achieved this at 39.93 and had been an excellent servant for his country, batting in any position asked, keeping wicket and captaining the side on 15 occasions. His first Test match was in February 1990 at Sabina Park, Kingston, when England beat West Indies, their first victory against them for sixteen years and 30 Tests. Alec Stewart was disappointed that he never played in an Ashes-winning series, or a World Cup-winning side, but he was proud to have captained his country in a series victory against South Africa in 1998 and to have been part of the team that won back-to-back series against Pakistan and Sri Lanka in 2000/01. He decided that this was the time to retire from first-class cricket. Alec Stewart's career statistics are as follows:

SURREY CAREER			
266 matches	15,016 runs at 39.93	26 centuries	Ct. 395 St. 12
TESTS			
133 matches	8,463 runs at 39.54	15 centuries	Ct. 263 St. 14
ALL FIRST-CLASS MATCHES			
447 matches	26,165 runs at 40.06	48 centuries	Ct. 721 St. 32
ONE-DAY INTERNATIONALS			
170 matches	4,677 at 31.60	4 centuries	Ct. 159 St. 15
ALL ONE-DAY MATCHES			
507 matches	14,787 runs at 35.04	19 centuries	Ct. 443 St. 48

Travelling down to Canterbury at the start of September, Surrey were short of five players due to Test calls (four to England and one to Pakistan) and three key bowlers became injured, two before the match and one during it. The challenge was too much for the reserve players and Kent won comfortably by an innings and 155 runs. The final match at The AMP Oval against Essex continued the trend as Ian Salisbury captained what was virtually the Surrey Second XI.

Mark Ramprakash was also missing from this game through injury, but had maintained his excellent form in the first-class game during the year. He was the only Surrey batsman to score more than 1,000 runs in the season, with 1,239 at an average of 68.83. This included a record 279 not out against Nottinghamshire at Whitgift School. This was the debut first-class match at Whitgift and Mark established another record in that his score is the highest ever made the first time a ground had been used for a first-class match. Surrey won the match with ease and Mark's score was higher than each of the innings scores of the opponents which were 240 and 242. To emphasise how much Ramprakash had contributed to Surrey in his three seasons with them, this was his fourth double-century and he had scored 3,414 first-class runs at 63.22 and 2,231 runs in limited-overs matches at 55.77.

At the end of the season, Adam Hollioake announced that 2004 would be his last year playing cricket as he planned to return to Australia after his benefit year to pursue a business career. The Committee decided that a new captain should be appointed for 2004 and Jonathan Batty was given the position. Ian Ward left for pastures new in Sussex. Keith Medlycott, the coach and cricket manager, then announced that he was leaving The Oval with a year remaining on his contract. He stated:

> I now feel that following Adam's decision to stand down as captain the time is right for me to leave. I formed a fantastic winning partnership and it's now time for me to pursue other opportunities and fresh challenges. I believe I have taken Surrey as far as I can and that under a new manager and captain in Jonathan Batty the club can continue to be successful.

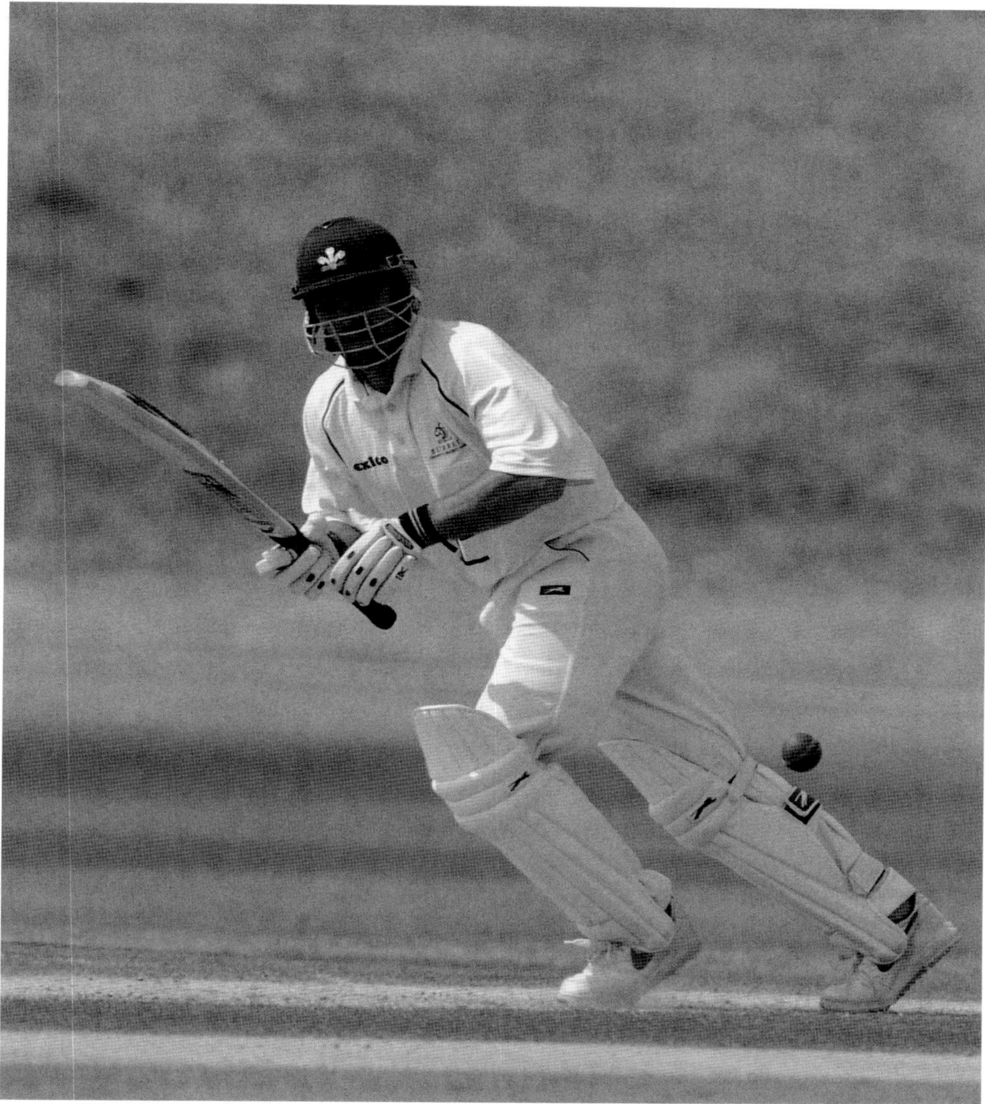

Mark Ramprakash.

How then were the players in this successful side remunerated? In the accounts for 2002, the Cricketers Employment Costs were listed as £1,542,000, of which approximately £1,200,000 relates to direct wages. This gives an average salary of £54,500 for each of the twenty-two cricketers on the staff. Surrey were not responsible for the salary of any player who had a 'central contract' with ECB. This compared with the Average National Earnings for 2002 of £24,400 culled from National Statistics. All capped players were provided with a sponsored car.

HIGHLIGHTS OF THE 2003 SEASON

FIRST-CLASS MATCHES

	BATTING			BOWLING				
	Runs	Ave.	100s		Wkts.	Ave.	5wI	10wM
M.R. Ramprakash	1444	76.00	6	M.P. Bicknell	40	27.77	3	
M.A. Butcher	572	63.55	2	J. Ormond	51	28.00	3	-
A.J. Stewart	451	64.42	-	Azhar Mahmood	35	31.34	1	-
J.N. Batty	968	56.94	3	Saqlain Mushtaq	41	33.26	3	-
G.P. Thorpe	895	52.64	1	I.D.K. Salisbury	33	37.09	-	-
M.P. Bicknell	421	52.62	2					
R. Clarke	551	39.35	2					
A.J. Hollioake	688	38.22	2					

ONE-DAY MATCHES

	BATTING			BOWLING			
	Runs	Ave.	100s		Wkts.	Ave.	4wI
M.R. Ramprakash	750	62.50	2	A.J. Hollioake	28	19.50	2
G.P. Thorpe	522	52.20	1	Azhar Mahmood	24	24.08	2
M.A. Butcher	130	32.50	1	J. Ormond	18	30.50	-
I.J. Ward	371	30.91	1				
A.D. Brown	496	27.55	-				

So what had been the contribution of Adam Hollioake to Surrey? In 2003 he was named as one of the *Wisden* Five Cricketers of the Year. Many of the comments by Simon Wilde in his appreciation in *Wisden* are appropriate and are repeated here.

> In July 1995, Surrey hit rock bottom, tumbling to 18th place in the table. It was a custom at The Oval not to appoint an official vice-captain, even though the then captain, Alec Stewart, was an automatic choice for England. That July, the task of standing in for Stewart was handed to a 23-year-old all-rounder, Adam Hollioake. Stewart was the ultimate Surrey insider, son of Micky, who had led the team to the 1971 Championship and later became manager. Hollioake, raised in Australia until he was 12, was much more of an outsider, as was the new coach, Dave Gilbert. Hollioake's approach was refreshingly positive and results improved almost immediately. Surrey won three first-class games and hauled themselves to 12th in the Championship and ninth in the Sunday League.
>
> Stewart remained in place but Hollioake, now officially vice-captain, played a larger role. In 1996, he led the team to four Championship victories as Surrey climbed to third, and they confounded *Wisden* and other observers by winning the Sunday League. In 1997, Hollioake was appointed captain and Surrey won the Benson and Hedges Cup. In 1999, finally, they won the Championship. Unlike 1971, this was not an isolated triumph: they

Opposite: *Adam Hollioake.*

retained the title in 2000, won the B & H again in 2001 and the Championship for the third time in four years in 2002. They had become the most successful team in the country.

If Hollioake changed one thing, it was to defenestrate the tired thinking prevailing in most county dressing rooms. 'It was the blame culture', he reflects, 'Captains and managers pointing the finger for not winning. People covering their tracks. We would not be like that. We'd do everything to win but there's been no aimless stuff. No five-hour fielding practice for the sake of it. If we were fielding well, we wouldn't bother. We asked ourselves what we needed to do to win and suggestions could come from anyone. No one questioned another's desire to win. Democracy's hard to get in county cricket. It comes through trust. If we have to sit around in pink underwear for half an hour beforehand, we will.'

The collective realisation of what was required brought with it a need for collective maturity. Martin Bicknell, Alistair Brown, Mark Butcher and Graham Thorpe were all aged 24 to 28 when Hollioake's reign began; they have grown wiser together. Hollioake was helped by his outsider's perspective, by two key confidants – his father, John, and Alec Stewart, who could have been old-laggish but went along with the new broom. Both had experience of Australian grade cricket and espoused its virtues. 'I grew up with the Australian view', Adam says. 'The main thing was to win, not how. I have carried that with me.'

Subsequently Matthew Fleming commented on Hollioake 'Adam didn't necessarily increase Surrey's popularity on the pitch but he certainly increased the levels of respect that people had for Surrey and for him. He turned Surrey from a talented and pretty arrogant club into one of the most successful clubs of all time.'

Within his very talented group of players were some pretty substantial egos, and it took a strong person to harness them and keep them under control. He quickly earned the respect of his players and encouraged them to respect themselves. He also had no fear of failure, and because he wasn't afraid of it, it didn't become an option very often.

ADAM HOLLIOAKE AS CAPTAIN

1997	Appointed captain of Surrey
	Wins Benson and Hedges Cup
1999	Wins County Championship
2000	Retains County Championship
2001	Wins Benson and Hedges Cup
2002	Wins third County Championship
	Wins National League Division 2
2003	Wins inaugural Twenty20 Cup
	Wins National League Division 1

SURREY'S CHAMPIONSHIP RESULTS UNDER HIS CAPTAINCY

MATCHES	WON	LOST	DRAWN
102	48	17	37

FIFTEEN

THE OTHER SURREY TEAMS AND THE FUTURE OF THE OVAL

The history of Surrey County Cricket Club is not just confined to the performance of the First XI. From 1946 until 1958 the Surrey Second XI played in the Minor Counties Championship. This Championship was formed in 1895 for all counties not then recognised as first-class. In December 1898 it was decided that the Second XIs of first-class counties should be included and Surrey were the first to take advantage of this change in 1899. They only won this competition four times: in 1939, 1950, 1954 and 1955.

The principal performances of the Second XI since 1946 have been:

— In 1947 they reached the Challenge match held between the teams finishing first and second in the Championship. They lost to Yorkshire Second XI but Stuart Surridge took seven wickets for 107 runs in the match.
— In 1950 they were Champions, finishing top of the table. The Challenge match against Bedfordshire ended in a draw. Geoff Whittaker scored 253 not out against Gloucestershire at The Oval.
— In 1952 Surrey finished third, McMahon taking 56 wickets in the season.
— When winning in 1954, Ken Barrington had a batting average of 58.28 and Micky Stewart 51.70.
— During the following season, 1955, when they were again champions, Henry Kelleher took 59 wickets and David Halfyard 54.

In 1959 Surrey withdrew from the Minor Counties Championship and started playing in the newly formed Second XI Championship restricted to the Second XIs of the first-class counties. Surrey had the enviable record of winning the title outright more times than any other county. The years of success were 1966, 1968, 1975, 1988 and 1992.

In the Second XI Cup (55-over) competitions they won three times under different sponsors. In 1992 they won the Bain Dawes Trophy, in 1997 and 2001 the AON Risk Services Trophy.

Highlights from these competitions have been:

— David Sydenham took 60 wickets in 1959, 46 in 1960 and 38 in 1962.
— Roger Harman took 41 wickets in 1963.
— In the Championship year of 1966, David Marriott took 54 wickets.
— 1967 was a good year for Ian Finlay, with 936 runs at 62.40, and Robin Jackman with 40 wickets.

— Champions again in 1968 and Randolph Ramnarace took 65 wickets.
— David Gibson took 49 wickets in 1969 and Robin Jackman 50 as Surrey finished as runners-up.
— Surrey slipped to fourth in 1970 but John Hooper scored 779 runs at 64.91 and Mohammad Iqbal 700 runs at 43.75, while Chris Waller took 53 wickets.
— Chris Waller went on to take 47 wickets in 1971, 41 in 1972 (Surrey finished second) and 59 in 1973.
— In 1975, a Championship year, Alan Butcher scored 2 centuries and Roy Baker took 36 wickets.
— Christopher Aworth scored 765 runs at 47.81 in 1976.
— Grahame Clinton scored 3 centuries in his 588 runs at 65.33 in 1983 when Surrey finished third.
— In 1984 and 1985 Surrey finished second and in 1985 Chris Bullen scored 2 centuries out of 650 runs at 50.00. Nicholas Taylor took 45 wickets in both 1984 and 1985.
— David Ward scored 1,042 runs for the Second XI in 1987 at 49.62.
— In 1987, David Ward then scored 1,161 runs at 64.50 and Darren Bicknell 850 runs at 65.38.
— 1988 was a championship year when Darren Bicknell scored 883 runs at 49.06 with 3 centuries. Mark Frost took 53 wickets and Neil Kendrick 45.
— 1989, although Surrey finished sixteenth in the table, saw Frost taking 53 wickets and Kendrick 48, with Rehan Alikhan scoring 1,283 runs at 55.78.
— Rehan Alikhan had another good season in 1990 with 497 runs at 71.00.
— Paul Atkins scored 744 runs at 82.70 and Keith Medlycott took 39 wickets in the 1992 Championship-winning season. The same year, Surrey's Second XI won the 55-over competition where Alistair Brown accumulated 680 runs at 113.30 including 210 not out against Kent at The Oval.
— In 1993 Rehan Alikhan made 770 runs at 77.00.
— Graham Kersey headed the averages in 1994 with 759 runs (64.08) and Monte Lynch scored 1,072 runs (51.04) and 553 runs (55.30) in the 55-over competition.
— Nadeem Shahid in 1995 scored 660 runs (110.00) and Gregor Kennis 783 (39.15) boosted by 258 against Leicestershire at Kibworth. Ben Hollioake took 33 wickets and Alex Tudor 30.
— Gregor Kennis was to the fore again in 1996 with 1,107 runs (39.53) and Ian Ward scored 956 runs at 53.11. Richard Nowell took 53 wickets.
— Although Surrey finished in only sixth place in 1997, 4 double centuries were scored: Darren Bicknell 244 against Gloucestershire out of 960 runs (106.66) for the season; Nadeem Shahid 200 not out *v.* Nottinghamshire at Trent Bridge out of 973 (60.81); Ian Ward 217 against Sussex at Hove out of 969 (46.14); and Gregor Kennis 210 in the same match, when they added 392 for the 2nd wicket.
— Gary Butcher had a good all-round season in 1999 scoring 623 runs at 36.64 and taking 35 wickets. Martin Bell took 39 wickets.
— In 2000 Gary Butcher scored 627 runs (44.78) and Gareth Batty 761 (34.59). Carl Greenidge took 37 wickets in the championship and 10 wickets in the limited-overs competition.

— Scott Newman made 719 runs (55.30) in 2001 and Gareth Batty took 32 wickets. In the AON Risk Trophy, won by Surrey, Batty scored 492 runs (70.28).
— Scott Newman continued in good form in 2002 scoring 1,209 runs (60.45) in the championship and 425 (85.00) in the limited-overs series. Rupesh Amin took 32 wickets and 13 wickets in the two competitions.
— Scott Newman with 1,228 runs (58.47) was in company with Nadeem Shahid with 1,269 (66.78) and James Benning on 933 runs (54.88) in 2003 when Neil Saker took 36 wickets.

The following extract, written by Jenny Booth, is taken from the Surrey Yearbook for 2003:

> In 2003 Scott Newman and Nadeem Shahid opened the Surrey first innings against Derbyshire at The Oval in reply to the visitors' impressive first innings total of 580-7 who declared at 12.45 on the second day of this three day match. Before lunch they posted 50 runs from 5.4 overs. For the rest of the day they scored at approximately 50 runs from every six overs. The day closed with the score at 547-0 after they had blocked the last few overs to ensure that they would both still be at the wicket the following morning. However, the stand was broken after only 12 minutes on the third day when Nadeem Shahid fell to a slip catch by Kerr off the bowling of Tucker. His 266 came from 271 balls and included 41 fours and 3 sixes. Newman batted on before he was bowled by Havell for 284, the fifth highest individual score recorded in the second eleven championship. With 49 fours and three sixes his innings lasted for 360 minutes and 292 balls.
>
> The first wicket stand of 552 in 91 overs easily outdistanced the previous highest partnership for the first wicket in this competition (438* by S Hutton and M A Roseberry for Durham at Abergavenny in 1998) and is also the highest partnership for any wicket in the second eleven Championship. Surrey now holds the record for both the first and second wicket partnerships as the second wicket record of 392 was set by Gregor Kennis and Ian Ward against Sussex at Eastbourne in 1997. On each occasion, both batsmen completed double centuries.

From 1946 and into the 1960s Surrey ran three other sides, these being the Colts, the Young Amateurs of Surrey and the Club and Ground. The Colts invariably played some 16-20 matches in the season and were a proving ground for the junior players under review by the County. Those who represented the Colts who eventually graduated to the First XI included John Edrich, Graham Roope, Bill Smith, Roy Swetman, David Sydenham and Derek Taylor. The Young Amateurs of Surrey played only 5 or 6 matches each season in August and September, drawing their players from public or independent schools. A thirteen-year-old Colin Cowdrey and a sixteen-year-old Peter May each played one game in 1946. In later years Raman Subba Row, Micky Stewart, Brian Parsons, Mike Edwards and Richard Jefferson made their first appearances for the County in this team. The Club and Ground side saw amateur members of the club being assisted by professionals to play club sides and schools within the county.

Over the years various changes have taken place in the organisation of county sides and now the emphasis has turned to the development of structured age groups. Surrey fields

The coaching team of 2003: Gareth Townsend, Alan Butcher, Adam Hollioake and Keith Medlycott.

teams at the following age levels: Under-19, Under-17, Under-15, Under-13, Under-11 and Under-9. The club organises a range of courses for boys and girls at schools throughout the county, many in Lambeth, coached by the club's cricket development officers. These include Outreach Schools Coaching, for 250 primary and secondary schools, involving 10,000 children. There are selected talent identification courses, which cater for around 450 children; in-service training for around 450 teachers; and five different Kwik Cricket competitions played by over 300 schools, involving in excess of 3,000 schoolchildren.

The club runs coaching courses for county-standard players aged from under eight to under seventeen, including girls' cricket, with a total of eighty courses organised annually for nearly 2,000 players. The extent of the cricket being played throughout the county at all age levels is detailed in the 2003 Surrey Yearbook under the watchful eyes of Gareth Townsend and development manager Chris Bullen.

In 2002 the ECB awarded a three-year licence to Surrey to set up a Cricket Club Academy. Under their director, Gareth Townsend, The County Academy focuses on the development of the most talented thirteen- to eighteen-year-old cricketers. It is a player-focused, coach-led, performance-based programme, accredited by the ECB and delivered by Surrey CCC. Up to twelve players will be selected by the academy director at the end of July in each year, ready for a start in September. The academy director consults with the County first-team coach and director of cricket before agreeing final selection.

The County Club is also involved in many local projects near The Oval. In the summer of 2002, as part of a major initiative to give local people the chance to play the game, the Kennington Community Cricket Ground was developed in a unique public-private collaboration between Lambeth Council, Channel 4, Surrey CCC, The Lord's Taverners and the United Cricket Association. A ground was set up in little over a year, with Surrey CCC lending their expertise to make sure it was in a fit state for cricket to be played.

The AMP Oval Health and Fitness Centre provides fitness facilities and tuition for the local community, and membership is at over 400, with all members either living or working in Lambeth.

Over a quarter of a million people have used the Ken Barrington Centre inside the Oval during the last ten years. The activities include cricket coaching, nets practice, cricket courses, five-a-side football for clubs and local teams; badminton for schools, firms, and charities; and basketball for schools. The centre also provides facilities for Lambeth Community Cricket, the London Schools Cricket Association and a number of disadvantaged groups including the Federation of Disabled Cricketers and England blind cricketers.

Surrey CCC formed a groundbreaking partnership with The Prince's Trust, the Prince of Wales' charity which helps disadvantaged young people make a success of their lives. On an annual basis, a group of local youngsters, aged between sixteen and twenty-five, descend on the ground for a twelve-week personal development course.

The club have also worked closely with the Southwark Police in the 'Karrot Project'. Developed by the Southwark Police partnership team, working closely with the London Borough of Southwark, the youth offending team and schools across the borough, the Karrot Project rewards eleven- to fifteen-year-olds for good behaviour. Some of the rewards on offer are tickets to Surrey cricket matches, as well as other sporting events in the capital.

The future of Surrey County Cricket Club is inevitably linked to the development of cricket nationally in England. With the proliferation of international cricket in the last few years the status of county cricket is coming under close scrutiny.

Lord MacLaurin, the chairman of the England and Wales Cricket Board (ECB) produced a report in 1998 entitled 'Raising the Standard'. The purpose of the report was to highlight how the structure of cricket in England could be altered to encourage more people to play the game and build a system to feed the best talent through to the national team. Some of his recommendations have already been actioned but others have subsequently been taken up by the self-styled Cricket Reform Group. This Group is in discussion with the ECB and their proposals are being analysed by the Domestic Structure Review Group. The reform group suggests that counties play 10 four-day games, with more money going to the 'elite' six than to the other twelve, who would play 10 games in north and south divisions, the winners of each playing-off to decide who is promoted to the 'premiership'. Over the years, many have suggested that there should be fewer professionals in the English game, with more amateur or semi-professional players on the fringes of the game.

As Christopher Martin-Jenkins recently argued in his regular article in The Times, the devil lies in the detail, especially where professional and recreational cricketers meet. Proposals to abolish the First Class Forum, the body that represents the eighteen first-class counties, plus all county Second XI and Minor County cricket, will meet stern opposition.

However, Surrey County Cricket Club has faith in the future of the game as they are committed to a major building development at The Oval. A large new stand is being built at the Vauxhall End that will increase the capacity of the ground to 23,000. The playing area has been reduced and as a result the ground can no longer claim to have the largest playing area in the Northern Hemisphere.

A dramatic, lightweight roof that will become an important new cricketing landmark will cover the new stand. This stand will follow the natural shape of the site, tapering at either side to retain visual interest and rising to a maximum of four storeys to incorporate significant open elements. Within the stand there will be an improved media facility, a new classroom and additional, significantly shared, community space. Two banqueting suites, each capable of accommodating 500 people will also have views of the ground.

An innovative 'living screen' will wrap around the rear of the stand. A range of climbing and trailing plants will be grown over this screen to provide a changing seasonal display and significantly improving the approach to The Oval along Harleyford Road.

The lower seating deck should be completed by 10 August 2004 in time for the Test match against the West Indies and the whole scheme will be finished by 31 May 2005 for the one-day internationals in June 2005 when England meet Australia.

The new era at The Oval for 2004 started when a new sponsor was announced for the club. Brit Insurance have invested a considerable sum of money to help in raising the profile of Surrey cricket, and the ground at Kennington was consequently renamed 'The Brit Oval'.

Jonathan Batty has been appointed captain for the 2004 season under a new manager, Steve Rixon, recruited from Australia. Steve Rixon, forty-nine, has been coach for New

Above: *An artist's impression of how The Oval will look by 2005.*

Right: *Jonathan Batty.*

South Wales in recent years and was the coach for the New Zealand national team from 1996 to 1999. His playing career included 13 Test matches for Australia from 1977 to 1985.

The season of 2004 will be a challenging one for Surrey, particularly if they lose players to the England squad for the planned 7 Test matches and 28 one-day internationals. Hopefully, the next written history of Surrey CCC will record the continuing success of the club.

STATISTICS

SURREY CAREER RECORDS OF PLAYERS WHO HAVE REPRESENTED THE COUNTY IN FIRST-CLASS CRICKET SINCE 1946

	Career	M	I	NO	Runs	HS	Ave	100	50	Runs	Wkts	Ave	Best	5wI	10wM	Ct	St
Alikhan, R.I.	1989-1993	45	78	6	2,346	138	32.58	2	16	165	5	35.00	2-43	-	-	23	
Allom, A.T.C.	1960	1	1	1	0	0*	-	-	-	53	0	-	-	-	-	-	
Amin, R.M.	1997-2002	15	18	8	35	12	3.50	-	-	1,108	27	41.03	4-87	-	-	6	
Arnold, G.G.	1963-1977	218	217	52	2,302	63	13.95	-	4	14,857	745	19.94	8-41	32	2	76	
Atkins, P.D.	1988-1993	24	44	3	1081	114*	26.36	1	4							9	
Aworth, C.J.	1974-1976	26	47	4	965	115	22.44	1	5	353	5	70.60	2-23	-	-	9	
Azhar Mahmood	2002-2003	14	18	3	541	98	36.06	-	5	1,442	55	26.21	8-61	2	-	20	
Baker, R.P.	1973-1978	54	56	30	563	91	21.65	-	2	2,942	104	28.28	6-29	1	-	24	
Barling, H.T.	1927-1948	389	605	54	18,995	269	34.47	34	96	530	7	75.71	3-46	-	-	171	
Barrington, K.F.	1953-1968	362	564	99	19,197	207	41.28	43	100	4,729	133	35.55	5-46	4	-	382	
Barton, M.R.	1948-1954	110	183	13	3,975	132	23.38	5	12							79	
Batty, G.J.	1999-2001	2	4	1	80	25*	26.66	-	-	58	2	29.00	2-45	-	-	2	
Batty, J.N.	1997-2003	82	119	18	3,009	168*	29.79	6	11	61	1	61.00	1-21	-	-	223	30
Bedser, A.V.	1939-1960	370	429	148	4,108	126	14.61	1	9	27,918	1,459	19.13	8-18	72	11	226	
Bedser, E.A.	1939-1961	443	669	78	14,148	163	23.93	9	60	19,831	797	24.88	7-33	24	4	227	
Benjamin, J.E.	1992-1999	96	118	35	925	49	11.14	-	-	9,147	313	29.22	6-19	13	1	17	
Bennett, N.H.	1946	31	45	2	688	79	16.00	-	4	25	1	25.00	1-1	-	-	6	
Benning, J.G.E.	2003	2	3	0	87	47	29.00	-	-	81	1	81.00	1-39	-	-	-	
Bicknell, D.J.	1987-1999	195	343	33	12,464	235*	40.20	31	57	789	23	34.30	3-7	-	-	73	
Bicknell, M.P.	1986-2003	254	304	77	5,639	141	24.84	3	22	22,837	947	24.11	9-45	40	4	88	
Bishop, I.E.	1999-2000	6	8	4	21	12	5.25	-	-	347	7	49.57	2-45	-	-	3	
Boiling, J.	1988-1994	43	53	22	425	34*	13.70	-	-	3,192	79	40.40	6-84	2	1	38	
Brazier, A.F.	1948-1954	36	56	11	979	92	21.75	-	4	7	0	-	-	-	-	10	
Brown, A.D.	1992-2003	183	286	27	10,958	295*	42.30	32	44	461	2	235.50	1-11	-	-	189	1
Brown, F.R.	1931-1948	106	159	16	3,982	212	27.84	9	15	10,548	429	24.58	8-34	30	5	68	
Brown, G.E.	1986-1988	10	11	8	59	13*	19.66	-	-							19	2
Bryson, R.E.	1992	11	13	2	257	76	23.36	-	1	1,256	23	54.60	5-48	2	-	-	
Bullen, C.K.	1982-1991	30	35	7	663	65	23.68	-	4	1,078	38	28.37	6-119	1	-	30	
Butcher, A.R.	1972-1998	284	481	43	14,605	216*	33.34	29	69	4,689	125	37.51	6-48	1	-	130	
Butcher, G.P.	1999-2001	13	20	2	484	70	26.88	-	4	280	9	31.10	5-18	1	-	3	
Butcher, M.A.	1992-2003	131	218	19	8,611	259	43.27	17	52	3,496	107	32.67	5-86	1	-	138	
Butcher, M.S.	1992	1	0							2	0	-	-	-	-	1	
Carberry, M.A.	2001-2002	8	14	1	534	153*	41.07	1	1							8	
Cheatle, R.G.L.	1980-1983	20	13	9	62	27*	15.50	-	-	894	27	33.11	5-28	2	-	11	
Clark, T.H.	1947-1959	260	421	35	11,458	191	29.68	12	58	2,233	73	30.58	5-23	1	-	104	
Clarke, R.	2002-2003	21	32	4	1,262	153*	45.07	4	5	1,160	28	41.42	4-21	-	-	19	
Clarke, S.T.	1979-1988	152	155	18	2,130	100*	15.55	1	3	11,226	591	18.99	8-62	37	6	97	
Clinton, G.S.	1979-1990	234	392	50	11,838	192	34.61	20	66	192	2	96.00	2-77	-	-	84	
Constable, B.	1939-1964	434	681	81	18,224	205*	30.37	26	91	2,585	49	52.75	3-68	-	-	174	
Cosh, N.J.	1969	6	9	1	165	55	20.62	-	1							6	

	Career	M	I	NO	Runs	HS	Ave	100	50	Runs	Wkts	Ave	Best	5wI	10wM	Ct	St
Cox, D.F.	1949-1957	42	52	17	660	57	18.85	-	4	2,316	68	34.05	7-22	2	1	39	
Crouch, H.R.	1946	1	1	0	4	4	4.00	-	-							-	
Cuffy, C.E.	1994	12	15	8	42	10	6.00	-	-	1,082	36	30.05	4-70	-	-	1	
Cumbes, J.	1968-1969	29	22	13	76	25*	8.44	-	-	1,989	93	21.38	6-35	5	-	11	
Curtis, I.J.	1983-1984	14	11	5	23	7	3.83	-	-	726	18	40.33	6-28	1	-	3	
Cuthbertson, J.L.	1963	7	9	3	118	34	19.66	-	-	204	3	68.00	1-13	-	-	1	
Davies, A.G.	1985	1	1	1	26	26*	-	-	-							3	
de la Peña, J.M.	1995	2	3	3	2	2*	-	-	-	208	6	34.66	3-53	-	-	-	
Dernbach, J.	2003	1	1	0	3	3	3.00	-	-	74	1	74.00	1-74	-	-	-	
Doughty, R.J.	1985-1987	27	33	4	631	65	21.76	-	3	2,047	66	31.02	6-33	1	-	22	
Edrich, J.H.	1958-1978	410	716	80	29,305	226*	46.07	81	138	16	0	-	-	-	-	242	
Edwards, M.J.	1961-1974	236	415	24	10,581	137	27.06	12	51	34	0	-	-	-	-	262	
Falkner, N.J.	1984-1987	16	24	3	734	102	34.95	2	2	9	1	9.00	1-3	-	-	10	
Feltham, M.A.	1983-1992	114	142	38	2526	101	24.28	1	7	9,266	292	31.73	6-53	6	-	48	
Finlay, I.W.	1965-1967	23	35	3	654	103	20.43	1	1	56	1	56.00	1-19	-	-	10	
Fishlock, L.B.	1931-1952	347	588	41	22,138	253	40.47	50	120	433	9	48.11	4-62	-	-	187	
Fletcher, D.G.W.	1946-1961	300	494	40	13,646	194	30.05	21	72							174	
Frost, M.	1988-1989	13	13	1	22	7	1.83	-	-	1,005	25	40.20	5-40	1	-	2	
Gibson, D.	1957-1969	183	211	45	3,143	98	18.93	-	11	12,213	550	22.20	7-26	26	1	76	
Giddins, E.S.H.	2001-2002	19	21	12	59	9*	6.55	-	-	1838	52	35.34	5-48	1	-	3	
Gover, A.R.	1928-1947	336	386	154	2,170	41*	9.35	-	-	34,101	1,437	23.73	8-34	87	15	164	
Gray, A.H.	1985-1990	48	34	6	245	35	8.75	-	-	4,234	199	21.27	8-40	11	2	18	
Greenidge, C.G.	1999-2000	5	5	0	29	14	5.80	-	-	337	12	28.08	5-60	1	-	3	
Gregory, R.J.	1925-1947	413	622	76	18,978	243	34.75	38	96	13,877	434	31.97	6-21	11	1	282	
Greig, I.A.	1987-1991	115	157	27	4,298	291	33.06	4	22	4,280	118	36.27	6-34	2	-	64	
Griffin, N.F.	1963	1	2	1	90	83*	90.00	-	1	45	0	-	-	-	-	-	
Hall, J.K.	1958-1962	13	11	3	19	5	2.37	-	-	787	36	21.86	5-30	1	-	7	
Hansell, T.M.G.	1975-1977	14	26	5	319	54	15.19	-	1							2	
Harman, R.	1961-1968	141	144	50	924	34	9.82	-	-	8,708	369	23.59	8-12	18	3	84	
Hollioake, A.J.	1993-2003	148	224	19	8,511	208	41.51	17	51	4,365	107	40.79	5-62	1	-	142	
Hollioake, B.C.	1996-2001	66	100	4	2,267	118	23.61	1	13	3,376	104	32.46	5-51	1	-	58	
Holmes, E.R.T.	1924-1955	198	298	40	8,837	206	34.25	15	47	6,135	173	35.46	6-16	3	-	145	
Hooper, J.M.M.	1967-1971	21	36	10	406	41*	15.61	-	-	10	1	10.00	1-10	-	-	14	
Howarth, G.P.	1971-1985	188	323	25	9,284	183	31.15	18	47	848	16	53.00	3-20	-	-	109	
Humphrey, R.G.	1964-1970	2	2	1	63	58	63.00	-	1							4	1
Intikhab Alam	1969-1981	232	338	45	5,707	139	19.47	4	19	18,871	629	30.00	8-74	25	2	73	
Jackman, R.D.	1966-1982	338	386	132	4,823	92*	18.98	-	15	26,969	1,206	22.36	8-58	61	7	152	
Jefferson, R.I.	1961-1966	76	106	23	1,663	136	20.03	2	3	5,582	206	27.09	6-25	7	1	27	
Jesty, T.E.	1985-1987	68	102	14	3,281	221	37.36	7	14	884	29	30.48	6-81	1	-	37	
Judd, P.	1960	1	0							14	0	-	-	-	-	1	
Julian, B.P.	1996	16	23	2	759	119	36.14	2	3	1,762	61	28.88	6-37	3	-	9	
Kelleher, H.R.A.	1955	3	0							179	12	14.91	5-23	2	1	-	
Kember, O.D.	1962-1963	4	7	2	56	19*	11.20	-	-							6	2
Kendrick, N.M.	1988-1994	55	72	19	862	55	16.26	-	3	4,825	133	36.27	7-115	6	1	47	
Kenlock, S.G.	1994-1996	7	10	2	55	12	6.87	-	-	666	11	60.54	3-104	-	-	4	
Kennis, G.J.	1994-1997	6	11	1	140	29	14.00	-	-	4	0	-	-	-	-	6	
Kersey, G.J.	1993-1996	49	79	12	1,509	83	22.52	-	9							155	11
Kirby, G.N.G.	1948-1953	19	17	8	141	32	15.66	-	-							38	8
Knight, R.D.V.	1968-1984	174	290	32	8,712	142	33.76	15	52	5,549	163	34.04	5-44	2	-	137	
Knott, J.A.	1995-1998	12	20	7	273	49*	21.00	-	-	2	0	-	-	-	-	12	2
Laker, J.C.	1946-1959	309	387	70	5,531	113	17.44	2	15	24,236	1,395	17.37	10-88	93	24	223	
Lewis, C.C.	1996-1997	22	34	3	932	94	30.06	-	5	1,947	62	31.40	5-25	2	-	23	
Lewis, R.M.	1968-1973	38	68	9	1,746	87	29.59	-	13	7	0	-	-	-	-	26	
Ligertwood, D.G.C.	1992	4	7	0	63	28	9.00	-	-							7	1

	Career	M	I	NO	Runs	HS	Ave	100	50	Runs	Wkts	Ave	Best	5wI	10wM	Ct	St
Loader, P.J.	1951-1963	298	291	87	1,827	81	8.95	-	2	20,685	1,108	18.66	9-17	65	13	99	
Lock, G.A.R.	1946-1963	385	451	100	5,391	70	15.35	-	16	29,835	1,713	17.41	10-54	123	31	533	
Long, A.	1960-1975	352	409	90	4,999	92	15.67	-	10							702	103
Lynch, M.A.	1977-1994	304	491	59	15,674	172*	36.28	33	76	1,251	24	52.12	3-6	-	-	314	
McEntyre, K.B.	1965-1966	3	3	0	33	15	11.00	-	-							-	
McIntyre, A.J.W.	1938-1963	376	544	75	10,893	143*	23.22	7	50	180	4	45.00	1-10	-	-	615	147
McKelvey, P.G.	1959-1960	2	0							19	1	19.00	1-7	-	-	1	
Mack, A.J.	1976-1977	10	9	0	42	16	4.66	-	-	760	7	108.57	2-50	-	-	-	
Mackintosh, K.S.	1981-1983	14	12	9	117	31	39.00	-	-	1,135	36	31.52	6-61	1	-	5	
McMahon, J.W.J.	1947-1953	84	106	52	344	23*	6.37	-	-	6,903	234	29.50	8-46	9	1	55	
Majendie, N.L.	1963	8	6	1	11	6	2.20	-	-							26	3
Marriott, D.A.	1965-1967	19	13	6	88	24*	12.57	-	-	1,244	43	28.93	4-45	-	-	3	
May, P.B.H.	1950-1963	208	327	46	14,168	211*	50.41	39	75							182	
Mays, C.S.	1987-1988	4	3	2	20	13*	20.00	-	-	303	3	101.00	1-36	-	-	3	
Medlycott, K.T.	1984-1991	134	173	37	3,586	153	26.36	3	21	10,726	331	32.40	8-52	17	5	88	
Mobey, G.S.	1930-1948	77	105	19	1,526	75	17.74	-	6						125	10	
Monkhouse, G.	1981-1986	74	85	33	1,158	100*	22.26	1	2	4,589	170	26.99	7-51	2	-	35	
Murphy, A.J.	1989-1994	67	67	32	298	38	8.51	-	-	6,666	175	38.09	6-97	6	-	11	
Murtagh, T.J.	2001-2003	11	16	7	122	22	13.55	-	-	906	29	31.24	5-39	1	-	3	
Mushtaq Ahmed	2002	2	3	0	66	47	22.00	-	-	305	8	38.12	5-71	1	-	1	
Nadeem Shahid	1995-2003	79	130	10	3,782	150	31.51	7	20	1,065	18	59.16	3-93	-	-	87	
Needham, A.	1977-1986	91	132	17	2,620	138	22.78	4	10	5,079	104	48.83	6-30	5	-	42	
Newman, S.A.	2002-2003	5	9	1	364	183	45.50	1	1	5	0	-	-	-	-	5	
Nowell, R.W.	1995-1996	12	22	3	162	28*	8.52	-	-	1397	34	41.08	4-43	-	-	5	
Ormond, J.	2002-2003	28	32	9	434	47	18.86	-	-	3,208	102	31.45	6-34	5	-	8	
Owen-Thomas, D.R.	1970-1975	73	118	14	2,604	112	25.03	3	10	6	0	-	-	-	-	31	
Parker, J.F.	1932-1952	334	512	70	14,068	255	31.82	20	78	15,387	538	28.60	6-34	8	-	317	
Parsons, A.B.D.	1958-1963	119	203	18	5,307	125	28.68	3	31	4	0	-	-	-	-	48	
Patterson, M.W.	1996-1999	2	3	0	6	4	2.00	-	-	163	10	16.30	6-80	1	-	-	
Pauline, D.B.	1979-1985	49	76	6	1,803	115	25.75	1	13	595	16	37.18	5-52	1	-	18	
Payne, I.R.	1977-1984	29	37	5	338	43	10.56	-	-	1,127	26	43.34	5-13	1	-	30	
Pearson, R.M.	1996-1997	15	15	9	143	37	23.83	-	-	1,599	33	48.45	5-142	1	-	4	
Peters, N.H.	1988-1989	16	18	8	101	25*	10.10	-	-	1,246	40	31.15	6-31	1	1	7	
Pierpoint, F.G.	1936-1946	8	11	7	15	4	3.75	-	-	592	13	45.53	3-60	-	-	3	
Pigott, A.C.S.	1994-1995	14	22	1	236	40	11.23	-	-	1404	51	27.52	6-46	3	1	2	
Pocock, P.I.	1964-1986	485	503	144	4,400	75*	12.25	-	3	3,5577	1,399	25.43	9-57	53	7	154	
Pratt, D.E.	1954-1957	9	12	4	171	33	21.37	-	-	392	13	30.15	6-119	1	-	4	
Pratt, R.E.C.	1952-1959	69	102	14	1,900	120	21.59	1	6	138	3	46.00	1-8	-	-	53	
Rackemann, C.G.	1995	13	20	12	120	20*	15.00	-	-	1,430	48	29.79	6-60	1	-	3	
Ramprakash, M.R.	2001-2003	39	62	8	3,414	279*	63.22	13	12	147	0	-	-	-	-	17	
Ransom, V.J.	1951-1955	2	2	0	3	2	1.50	-	-	82	1	82.00	1-21	-	-	-	
Ratcliffe, J.D.	1995-2002	58	100	6	2,698	135	28.70	2	17	676	23	29.39	6-48	1	-	21	
Richards, C.J.	1976-1988	256	328	79	7,142	172*	28.68	7	33	219	5	43.80	2-42	-	-	534	66
Robinson, J.D.	1988-1992	31	49	10	898	79	23.02	-	5	1,152	28	41.14	3-22	-	-	12	
Robson, A.G.	1991	2	3	0	3	3	1.00	-	-	103	1	103.00	1-72	-	-	-	
Roope, G.R.J.	1964-1982	342	554	118	16,226	171	37.21	22	87	7,725	211	36.61	5-14	3	-	513	2
Rose, F.A.	2003	1	2	0	37	36	18.50	-	-	101	3	33.66	3-101	-	-	-	
Rushworth, W.R.	1946	1	1	0	0	0	0.00	-	-	86	2	43.00	1-15	-	-	3	
Russell, S.G.	1967	1	0							77	2	38.50	2-63	-	-	2	
Sadiq, Z.A.	1988-1989	7	11	0	213	64	19.36	-	1							5	
Saker, N.C.	2003	2	3	0	6	5	2.00	-	-	179	1	179.00	1-71	-	-	-	
Salisbury, I.D.K.	1997-2003	101	127	22	2,345	101*	22.33	2	9	7,568	275	27.52	8-60	10	2	50	
Sampson, P.J.	2002-2003	3	5	2	78	42	26.00	-	-	261	11	23.72	3-52	-	-	-	
Saqlain Mushtaq	1997-2003	72	89	25	1,418	69	22.15	-	8	7,087	356	19.90	8-65	30	10	26	

	Career	M	I	NO	Runs	HS	Ave	100	50	Runs	Wkts	Ave	Best	5wI	10wM	Ct	St
Sargeant, N.F.	1989-1995	52	67	11	786	49	14.03	-	-	88	1	88.00	1-88	-	-	120	16
Scott, B.J.M.	2003	2	3	1	79	58*	39.50	-	1							6	
Selvey, M.W.W.	1968-1971	6	8	4	19	14*	4.75	-	-	445	21	21.19	6-58	1	-	-	
Skinner, L.E.	1971-1977	71	115	14	2,255	93	22.32	-	11							108	13
Smith, A.W.	1993-1996	38	59	7	1,379	202*	26.51	1	6	2,435	43	56.62	5-103	1	-	12	
Smith, D.M.	1973-1988	169	260	57	6,723	160	33.12	11	30	1,463	27	54.19	3-40	-	-	109	
Smith, W.A.	1961-1970	144	242	18	5,024	103	22.42	2	23	1	0	-	-	-	-	51	
Squires, H.S.	1928-1949	402	643	44	18,636	236	31.11	36	101	10,496	297	35.34	8-52	7	-	137	
Stewart, A.J.	1981-2003	266	425	49	15,016	271*	39.93	26	91	424	3	141.33	1-7	-	-	395	12
Stewart, M.J.	1954-1972	498	844	91	25,007	227*	33.20	48	125	48	1	48.00	1-4	-	-	605	
Stockley, A.J.	1968	3	2	0	5	5	2.50	-	-	194	10	19.40	4-74	-	-	3	
Storey, S.J.	1960-1974	315	468	58	10,402	164	25.37	12	53	12,903	490	26.33	8-22	11	2	319	
Subba Row, R.	1953-1954	41	58	11	1,663	128	35.38	3	5	131	1	131.00	1-10	-	-	35	
Surridge, S.S.	1978	1	1	1	2	2*	-	-	-							1	
Surridge, W.S.	1947-1959	254	316	32	3,697	87	13.01	-	10	13,753	464	29.64	7-49	19	1	361	
Swetman, R.	1954-1961	129	178	29	3,073	93	20.62	-	13							230	38
Sydenham, D.A.D.	1957-1972	142	131	64	483	24*	7.20	-	-	9,548	481	19.85	9-70	26	3	52	
Taylor, D.J.S.	1966-1969	10	8	1	137	56	19.57	-	1							16	5
Taylor, N.S.	1984-1985	10	9	3	63	21*	10.50	-	-	833	28	29.75	7-44	1	-	3	
Tazelaar, D.	1989	4	4	1	65	29	21.66	-	-	417	10	41.70	3-88	-	-	1	
Thomas, D.J.	1977-1987	135	172	35	2,850	119	20.80	2	7	10,155	303	33.51	6-36	6	1	47	
Thompson, D.J.	1994	1	2	0	39	22	19.50	-	-	123	3	41.00	2-37	-	-	-	
Thorpe, G.P.	1988-2003	178	291	38	11,497	222	45.44	30	58	1,185	23	51.52	4-40	-	-	141	
Tindall, R.A.E.	1956-1966	172	256	38	5,383	109*	24.69	2	27	4,846	150	32.30	5-41	2	-	130	
Titmus, F.J.	1978	1	2	2	4	4*	-	-	-	35	1	35.00	1-35	-	-	1	
Todd, M.J.	2003	1	1	1	6	6*	-	-	-	92	1	92.00	1-92	-	-	-	
Topley, T.D.	1985	1	1	1	6	6*	-	-	-	64	2	32.00	2-42	-	-	1	
Tudor, A.J.	1995-2003	65	87	19	1,525	116	22.42	1	5	5,493	205	26.79	7-48	11	-	15	
Verrinder, A.O.C.	1974-1976	3	2	0	0	0	0.00	-	-	105	4	26.25	2-42	-	-	2	
Wait, O.J.	1950-1951	7	9	3	11	4	1.83	-	-	400	14	28.57	3-27	-	-	3	
Waller, C.E.	1967-1973	40	31	13	173	47	9.61	-	-	2,195	96	22.86	7-64	4	-	13	
Waqar Younis	1990-1993	45	47	16	447	31	14.41	-	-	4,420	232	19.05	7-33	20	4	11	
Ward, D.M.	1985-1996	155	244	34	8,078	294*	38.46	16	32	113	2	56.50	2-66	-	-	120	3
Ward, I.J.	1992-2003	92	154	12	5,738	168*	40.40	14	31	197	3	65.66	1-1	-	-	50	
Waterman, P.A.	1983-1985	11	6	3	7	6*	2.33	-	-	727	18	40.38	3-22	-	-	4	
Watts, E.A.	1933-1949	240	350	68	6,005	123	21.29	2	27	18,757	722	25.97	10-67	24	2	152	
Westerman, P.	1949-1951	9	12	5	25	10*	3.57	-	-	596	21	28.38	5-49	2	-	1	
Wheatley, G.A.	1947	5	7	1	119	37*	19.83	-	-							5	2
Whittaker, G.J.	1937-1953	124	183	18	4,584	185*	27.78	6	22	47	1	47.00	1-31	-	-	46	
Willett, M.D.	1955-1967	172	273	45	6,535	126	28.66	8	35	1,105	23	48.04	3-36	-	-	94	
Willis, R.G.D.	1969-1971	34	34	20	228	33	16.28	-	-	2,428	96	25.29	5-78	1	-	13	
Wilson, P.H.L.	1978-1982	37	23	15	80	15	10.00	-	-	1,814	55	32.98	4-39	-	-	6	
Winterborne, G.	1986	1	0							47	0	-	-	-	-	-	
Yeatman, R.H.	1946-1947	5	8	1	53	21	7.57	-	-	18	0	-	-	-	-	1	
Younis Ahmed	1965-1978	262	448	63	14,112	183*	36.65	19	83	602	17	35.41	4-10	-	-	144	

BATTING RECORDS

HIGHEST INDIVIDUAL INNINGS

295*	A.D. Brown	*v.*	Leicestershire	Oakham	2000
294*	D.M. Ward	*v.*	Derbyshire	The Foster's Oval	1994
291	I.A. Greig	*v.*	Lancashire	The Foster's Oval	1990

279*	M.R. Ramprakash	*v.*	Nottinghamshire	Whitgift School, Croydon	2003
271*	A.J. Stewart	*v.*	Yorkshire	The Foster's Oval	1997
265	A.D. Brown	*v.*	Middlesex	Lord's	1999
263	D.M. Ward	*v.*	Kent	Canterbury	1990
259	M.A. Butcher	*v.*	Leicestershire	Leicester (GR)	1999
255	J.F. Parker	*v.*	New Zealanders	The Oval	1949 (2)
253	L.B. Fishlock	*v.*	Leicestershire	Leicester (GR)	1948
235*	D.J. Bicknell	*v.*	Nottinghamshire	Trent Bridge	1994
233*	H.T. Barling	*v.*	Nottinghamshire	The Oval	1946
230	M.A. Butcher	*v.*	Glamorgan	Cardiff (SG)	2001
228*	D.J. Bicknell	*v.*	Nottinghamshire	Guildford	1995
227*	M.J. Stewart	*v.*	Middlesex	The Oval	1964
226*	J.H. Edrich	*v.*	Middlesex	The Oval	1967
222	G.P. Thorpe	*v.*	Glamorgan	The Foster's Oval	1997
221	T.E. Jesty	*v.*	Essex	The Oval	1986
218	M.R. Ramprakash	*v.*	Somerset	Taunton	2002
216*	A.R. Butcher	*v.*	Cambridge University	Fenner's	1980
216	J.H. Edrich	*v.*	Nottinghamshire	Trent Bridge	1962
216	G.P. Thorpe	*v.*	Somerset	The Foster's Oval	1992
211*	P.B.H. May	*v.*	Nottinghamshire	Trent Bridge	1954
210*	M.R. Ramprakash	*v.*	Warwickshire	The AMP Oval	2002
210	H.S. Squires	*v.*	Derbyshire	The Oval	1949
210	L.B. Fishlock	*v.*	Somerset	The Oval	1949
208	D.M. Ward	*v.*	Essex	The Foster's Oval	1990
208	A.J. Hollioake	*v.*	Leicestershire	The AMP Oval	2002
207	P.B.H. May	*v.*	Cambridge University	The Oval	1954
207	K.F. Barrington	*v.*	Nottinghamshire	The Oval	1964
206*	A.J. Stewart	*v.*	Essex	The Foster's Oval	1989
205*	B. Constable	*v.*	Somerset	The Oval	1952
205*	J.H. Edrich	*v.*	Gloucestershire	Bristol (Phoenix)	1965
205	M.R. Ramprakash	*v.*	Loughborough UCCE	The AMP Oval	2003
204*	J.F. Parker	*v.*	Derbyshire	The Oval	1947
202*	A.W. Smith	*v.*	Oxford University	The Foster's Oval	1994
200*	M.J. Stewart	*v.*	Essex	The Oval	1962

CENTURIONS FOR SURREY

81	J.H. Edrich
48	M.J. Stewart
43	K.F. Barrington
39	P.B.H. May
33	M.A. Lynch
32	A.D. Brown
31	D.J. Bicknell
30	G.P. Thorpe
29	A.R. Butcher
28	L.B. Fishlock (50)
26	B. Constable, A.J. Stewart
22	G.R.J. Roope
21	D.G.W. Fletcher
20	G.S. Clinton
19	Younis Ahmed
18	G.P. Howarth
17	M.A. Butcher, A.J. Hollioake, J.F. Parker (20)

16	D.M. Ward
15	R.D.V. Knight
14	I.J. Ward
13	M.R. Ramprakash
12	T.H. Clark, M.J. Edwards, S.J. Storey
11	D.M. Smith, H.S. Squires (36)
9	E.A. Bedser,
8	H.T. Barling (34), M.D. Willett
7	T.E. Jesty, A.J.W. McIntyre, Nadeem Shahid, C.J. Richards
6	J.N. Batty, G.J. Whittaker
5	M.R. Barton
4	R. Clarke, I.A. Greig, Intikhab Alam, A. Needham
3	M.P. Bicknell, R.J. Gregory (38), E.R.T. Holmes (15), K.T. Medlycott, D.R. Owen-Thomas, A.B.D. Parsons, R. Subba Row
2	R.I. Alikhan, N.J. Falkner, R.I. Jefferson, B.P. Julian, J.C. Laker, J.D. Ratcliffe, I.D.K. Salisbury, W.A. Smith, D.J. Thomas, R.A.E. Tindall
1	P.D. Atkins, C.J. Aworth, A.V. Bedser, M.A. Carberry, S.T. Clarke, M.A. Feltham, I.W. Finlay, B.C. Hollioake, G. Monkhouse, S.A. Newman, D.B. Pauline, R.E.C. Pratt, A.W. Smith, A.J. Tudor

NB: Figures shown in brackets indicate total number of centuries scored for Surrey in career (balance before 1939).

CENTURY IN EACH INNINGS

186	118*	K.F. Barrington	*v.* Warwickshire	Edgbaston	1959
117*	114	A.R. Butcher	*v.* Glamorgan	The Oval	1984
112	124	J.H. Edrich	*v.* Nottinghamshire	Trent Bridge	1959
143	113*	J.H. Edrich	*v.* Worcestershire	Worcester	1970
111	124	J.H. Edrich	*v.* Warwickshire	The Oval	1971
140	115	J.H. Edrich	*v.* Kent	The Oval	1977
129	112	L.B. Fishlock	*v.* Leicestershire	Leicester (GR)	1946
111	118	L.B. Fishlock	*v.* Nottinghamshire	Trent Bridge	1949
128	117*	A.J. Hollioake	*v.* Somerset	Taunton	1996
167	103*	P.B.H. May	*v.* Essex	Southend-on-Sea	1951
109	103*	G.J.R. Roope	*v.* Leicestershire	Leicester (GR)	1971
112	156	I.J. Ward	*v.* Hampshire	The Rose Bowl	2002

CARRYING BAT THROUGH A COMPLETED INNINGS

			Total			
J.N. Batty		154*	337	*v.* Lancashire	Old Trafford	2003
D.J. Bicknell	(2)	145*	268	*v.* Essex	Chelmsford	1991
		129*	299	*v.* Worcestershire	The Foster's Oval	1996
M.A. Butcher	(2)	109*	245	*v.* Somerset	Taunton	1998
		145*	281	*v.* Glamorgan	The Oval	2001
T.H. Clark		81*	135	*v.* Yorkshire	The Oval	1956
G.S. Clinton	(2)	113*	260	*v.* Derbyshire	The Oval	1984
		84*	171	*v.* Yorkshire	Headingley	1986
J.H. Edrich	(2)	79*	122	*v.* Northamptonshire	The Oval	1963
		61*	108	*v.* Essex	Southend-on-Sea	1978
L.B. Fishlock		81*	141	*v.* Australians	The Oval	1948
D.G.W. Fletcher		127*	271	*v.* Yorkshire	Bradford	1947
A.B.D. Parsons		30*	71	*v.* Leicestershire	The Oval	1961

MOST CENTURIES IN CONSECUTIVE INNINGS

Four

I.J. Ward	114		*v.* Warwickshire	Edgbaston	2002
	112	156	*v.* Hampshire	The Rose Bowl	
	118		*v.* Leicestershire	The AMP Oval	

Three

J.H. Edrich	139	*v.* New Zealanders	The Oval	1965
	121*	*v.* Oxford University	The Parks	
	205*	*v.* Gloucestershire	Bristol (Phoenix)	

1,000 RUNS IN A SEASON

18	J.H. Edrich
14	M.J. Stewart
12	B. Constable
10	K.F. Barrington
8	M.A. Lynch
7	A.R. Butcher, G.S. Clinton, L.B. Fishlock (12), P.B.H. May, J.F. Parker (9), G.R.J. Roope, Younis Ahmed
6	E.A. Bedser, D.J. Bicknell, A.D. Brown, T.H. Clark, R.D.V. Knight
5	M.J. Edwards, A.J. Stewart, S.J. Storey
4	D.G.W. Fletcher, H.S. Squires (11), G.P. Thorpe
3	G.P. Howarth, A.B.D. Parsons, M.D. Willett
2	H.T. Barling (9), M.R. Barton, M.A. Butcher, I.A. Greig, A.J. Hollioake, T.E. Jesty, A.J.W. McIntyre, M.R. Ramprakash, D.M. Ward, I.J. Ward
1	R.I. Alikhan, R.J. Gregory (9), E.R.T. Holmes (5), A. Needham, C.J. Richards, D.M. Smith, W.A. Smith, R.A.E. Tindall, G.J. Whittaker

NB: Figures shown in brackets indicate number of times the player has scored 1,000 runs in a season throughout his career.

HIGHEST WICKET PARTNERSHIPS FOR SURREY

1st Wicket

359	M.A. Butcher (191) & I.J. Ward (144)	*v.* Durham	The Foster's Oval	2000
321	D.J. Bicknell (169) & G.S. Clinton (146)	*v.* Northamptonshire	The Foster's Oval	1990
277	A.R. Butcher (118) & G.S. Clinton (192)	*v.* Yorkshire	The Oval	1984
266	A.R. Butcher (216*) & G.S. Clinton (89)	*v.* Cambridge University	Fenner's	1980
260	L.B. Fishlock (210) & E.A. Bedser (154)	*v.* Somerset	The Oval	1949
256	D.J. Bicknell (63) & D.M. Ward (181)	*v.* Oxford University	The Parks	1990
255	R.E.C. Pratt (120) & M.J. Stewart (155*)	*v.* Cambridge University	Guildford	1956

2nd Wicket

316*	M.J. Stewart (200*) & K.F. Barrington (130*)	*v.* Essex	The Oval	1962
316*	A.R. Butcher (187*) & D.M. Smith (105*)	*v.* Warwickshire	Edgbaston	1982
299	D.J. Bicknell (130) & G.P. Thorpe (171)	*v.* Worcestershire	Worcester	1993
260	D.J. Bicknell (146) & G.P. Thorpe (152)	*v.* Kent	Canterbury	1995
256*	G.P. Howarth (179*) & R.D.V. Knight (103*)	*v.* Cambridge University	Fenner's	1978

3rd Wicket

413	D.J. Bicknell (186) & D.M. Ward (263)	*v.* Kent	Canterbury	1990
301	G.P. Thorpe (114) & D.M. Ward (294*)	*v.* Derbyshire	The Foster's Oval	1994
297	J.H. Edrich (226*) & K.F. Barrington (113)	*v.* Middlesex	The Oval	1967

267	R.J. Gregory (164) & H.T. Barling (233*)	*v.* Nottinghamshire	The Oval	1947
263	D.G.W. Fletcher (194) & H.S. Squires (154)	*v.* Nottinghamshire	Trent Bridge	1947
261	B. Constable (96) & P.B.H. May (163)	*v.* Nottinghamshire	Trent Bridge	1958
4th Wicket				
250	T.H. Clark (165) & R.E.C. Pratt (90)	*v.* Kent	The Oval	1953
244	L.B. Fishlock (253) & M.R. Barton (103)	*v.* Leicestershire	Leicester (GR)	1948
238	H.S. Squires (117) & J.F. Parker (129)	*v.* Hampshire	Bournemouth	1948
230	K.F. Barrington (150*) & M.D. Willett (117)	*v.* Kent	Gravesend	1964
226	Younis Ahmed (138*) & G.R.J. Roope (109)	*v.* Leicestershire	Leicester (GR)	1971
5th Wicket				
288	A.D. Brown (265) & A.J. Hollioake (116)	*v.* Middlesex	Lord's	1999
262	A.D. Brown (177) & Nadeem Shahid (150)	*v.* Sussex	The AMP Oval	2002
253*	D.J. Bicknell (235*) & A.D. Brown (134*)	*v.* Nottinghamshire	Trent Bridge	1994
252	A.J. Stewart (158) & M.A. Lynch (115)	*v.* Kent	Canterbury	1985
247*	J.F. Parker (108*) & E.R.T. Holmes (122*)	*v.* Nottinghamshire	Trent Bridge	1947
6th Wicket				
220	G.P. Thorpe (190) & A.J. Hollioake (123)	*v.* Worcestershire	The Foster's Oval	1994
215	M.R. Ramprakash (131) & B.C. Hollioake (118)	*v.* Yorkshire	The Oval	2001
210	M.R. Ramprakash (218) & R. Clarke (153*)	*v.* Somerset	Taunton	2002
200	M.J. Stewart (107) & D. Gibson (98)	*v.* Leicestershire	The Oval	1965
7th Wicket				
262	C.J. Richards (172*) & K.T. Medlycott (153)	*v.* Kent	The Oval	1987
206	A.J. Stewart (106) & A.J. Tudor (116)	*v.* Essex	The Oval	2001
181	A.J. Hollioake (129) & B.P. Julian (117)	*v.* Northamptonshire	The Foster's Oval	1996
180*	M.A. Lynch (144*) & C.J. Richards (44*)	*v.* Middlesex	The Oval	1985
8th Wicket				
205	I.A. Greig (291) & M.P. Bicknell (42)	*v.* Lancashire	The Foster's Oval	1990
198	K.F. Barrington (108*) & J.C. Laker (113)	*v.* Gloucestershire	The Oval	1954
197	H.T. Barling (146) & A.V. Bedser (126)	*v.* Somerset	Taunton	1947
189*	N.J. Falkner (101*) & K.T. Medlycott (117*)	*v.* Cambridge University	Banstead	1984
173	B. Constable (70) & J.C. Laker (100)	*v.* Cambridge University	Guildford	1949
171	A.J.W. McIintyre (127*) & E.R.T. Holmes (88)	*v.* Hampshire	Guildford	1948
168	D.M. Smith (115) & R.P. Baker (91)	*v.* Hampshire	Portsmouth	1978
150	R.D. Jackman (62) & Intikhab Alam (100)	*v.* Sussex	The Oval	1973
9th Wicket				
161	G.J. Whittaker (129) & W.S. Surridge (87)	*v.* Glamorgan	The Oval	1951
155	S.J. Storey (107) & R.D. Jackman (83)	*v.* Glamorgan	Cardiff (SG)	1973
129	M.R. Ramprakash (279*) & I.D.K. Salisbury (65)	*v.* Nottinghamshire	Whitgift School	2003
10th Wicket				
172	A. Needham (134*) & R.D. Jackman (60)	*v.* Lancashire	Old Trafford	1982
141	A.D. Brown (295*) & Saqlain Mushtaq (66)	*v.* Leicestershire	Oakham	2000
138	R.I. Jefferson (136) & D.A.D. Sydenham (15*)	*v.* Northamptonshire	Northampton	1963
116	M.P. Bicknell (79*) & Saqlain Mushtaq (54)	*v.* Lancashire	Old Trafford	2000
109*	M.P. Bicknell (85*) & I.D.K. Salisbury (30*)	*v.* Leicestershire	Leicester (GR)	2001
107	M.R. Ramprakash (279*) & Saqlain Mushtaq	*v.* Nottinghamshire	Whitgift School	2003
100	A.J. Hollioake (117*) & J.E. Benjamin (32)	*v.* Warwickshire	Edgbaston	1995

BOWLING RECORDS

NINE OR MORE WICKETS IN AN INNINGS

10-54	G.A.R. Lock	v. Kent	Blackheath	1956	
10-88	C. Laker	v. Australians	The Oval	1956	(1)
9-17	P.J. Loader	v. Warwickshire	The Oval	1958	
9-28	P.J. Loader	v. Kent	Blackheath	1953	
9-45	M.P. Bicknell	v. Cambridge University	The Foster's Oval	1988	
9-47	M.P. Bicknell	v. Leicestershire	Guildford	2000	
9-57	P.I. Pocock	v. Glamorgan	Cardiff (SG)	1979	
9-70	D.A.D. Sydenham	v. Gloucestershire	The Oval	1964	
9-77	G.A.R. Lock	v. Oxford University	Guildford	1960	

THIRTEEN OR MORE WICKETS IN A MATCH

16-83	G.A.R. Lock	v. Kent	Blackheath	1956
16-119	M.P. Bicknell	v. Leicestershire	Guildford	2000
15-97	J.C. Laker	v. MCC	Lord's	1954
15-182	G.A.R. Lock	v. Kent	Blackheath	1958
14-69	A.V. Bedser	v. Glamorgan	Cardiff (AP)	1956
14-111	P.J. Loader	v. Worcestershire	Worcester	1954
14-113	R. Harman	v. Derbyshire	Ilkeston	1968
13-46	A.V. Bedser	v. Nottinghamshire	The Oval	1952
13-69	G.A.R. Lock	v. Hampshire	Bournemouth	1953
13-82	G.A.R. Lock	v. Middlesex	The Oval	1955
13-113	P.J. Loader	v. Kent	Blackheath	1953
13-122	P.I. Pocock	v. Hampshire	Portsmouth	1979
13-128	G.G. Arnold	v. Gloucestershire	The Oval	1967
13-130	G.A.R. Lock	v. Lancashire	Old Trafford	1955
13-144	G.A.R. Lock	v. Nottinghamshire	Trent Bridge	1956

TEN WICKETS IN A MATCH ON DEBUT

10-73	H.R.A. Kelleher	v. Worcestershire	The Oval	1955

FIVE WICKETS IN AN INNINGS ON DEBUT

5-81	J.W.J. McMahon	v. Lancashire	The Oval	1947
5-51*	P. Westerman	v. Gloucestershire	The Oval	1949
5-23	H.R.A. Kelleher	v. Worcestershire	The Oval	1955
6-35***	J. Cumbes	v. Oxford University	The Parks	1968
6-28**	I.J. Curtis	v. Oxford University	The Oval	1983
6-80	M.W. Patterson	v. South Africa "A"	The Foster's Oval	1996

* *Obtained in the opponent's second innings, having bowled in the first* ** *Debut for team, having previously played first-class cricket*

FOUR WICKETS IN FOUR BALLS

G.P. Butcher	v. Derbyshire	The Foster's Oval	2000
P.I. Pocock	v. Sussex	Eastbourne	1972

HAT-TRICKS

G.G. Arnold		*v.* Leicestershire	Leicester (GR)	1974
A.V. Bedser		*v.* Essex	The Oval	1953
G.P. Butcher		*v.* Derbyshire	The Foster's Oval	2000
S.T. Clarke	(2)	*v.* Nottinghamshire	The Oval	1980
		v. Essex	Colchester	1987
D. Gibson		*v.* Northamptonshire	Northampton	1961
A.H. Gray		*v.* Yorkshire	Sheffield (Abbeydale Park)	1985
R. Harman	(2)	*v.* Kent	Blackheath	1963
		v. Derbyshire	Ilkeston	1968
Intikhab Alam		*v.* Yorkshire	The Oval	1972
R.D. Jackman	(2)	*v.* Kent	Canterbury	1971
		v. Yorkshire	The Oval	1972
J.C. Laker	(3)	*v.* Gloucestershire	Gloucester (Wagon Works)	1951
		v. Warwickshire	The Oval	1953
		v. Cambridge University	Guildford	1953
P.J. Loader		*v.* Leicestershire	The Oval	1963
G.A.R. Lock		*v.* Somerset	Weston-super-Mare	1955
J. Ormond		*v.* Middlesex	Guildford	2003
P.I. Pocock	(2)	*v.* Worcestershire	Guildford	1971
		v. Sussex	Eastbourne	1972
Saqlain Mushtaq	(2)	*v.* Middlesex	Lord's	1997
		v. Sussex	Hove	1999
S.J. Storey		*v.* Glamorgan	Swansea	1965

WICKETKEEPING RECORDS

MOST DISMISSALS IN AN INNINGS

Total	**Ct**	**St**				
7	7	0	A. Long	*v.* Sussex	Hove	1964
6	6	0	G.N.G. Kirby	*v.* Cambridge University	Guildford	1949
6	6	0	R. Swetman	*v.* Kent	The Oval	1960
6	6	0	R. Swetman	*v.* Somerset	Taunton	1960
6	6	0	A. Long	*v.* Lancashire	Old Trafford	1967
6	5	1	A. Long	*v.* Northamptonshire	The Oval	1968
6	6	0	C.J. Richards	*v.* Warwickshire	The Foster's Oval	1988
6	6	0	A.J. Stewart	*v.* Lancashire	Southport	1988
6	6	0	A.J. Stewart	*v.* Leicestershire	Leicester (GR)	1989
6	6	0	A.J. Stewart	*v.* Glamorgan	The Foster's Oval	1993
6	6	0	G.J. Kersey	*v.* Durham	Stockton-on-Tees	1996

MOST DISMISSALS IN A MATCH

Total	**Ct**	**St**				
11	11	0	A. Long	*v.* Sussex	Hove	1964
11	11	0	A.J. Stewart	*v.* Leicestershire	Leicester (GR)	1989
10	9	1	C.J. Richards	*v.* Sussex	Guildford	1987
10	9	1	A.J. Stewart	*v.* Lancashire	The AMP Oval	2002
9	6	3	C.J. Richards	*v.* Glamorgan	Cardiff (SG)	1987
9	9	0	A.J. Stewart	*v.* Glamorgan	The Foster's Oval	1993
9	9	0	G.J. Kersey	*v.* Durham	Stockton-on-Tees	1996

8	8	0	C.J. Richards	*v.* Derbyshire	The Oval	1987
8	8	0	C.J. Richards	*v.* Warwickshire	The Foster's Oval	1988
8	7	1	G.J. Kersey	*v.* Essex	The Foster's Oval	1993
8	8	0	G.J. Kersey	*v.* Durham	The Foster's Oval	1995
8	8	0	J.N. Batty	*v.* Northamptonshire	Guildford	2002

MOST DISMISSALS IN A SEASON

Total	Ct	St	Wicketkeeper	Matches	Season
91	74	17	A. Long	32	1962
87	66	21	A.J.W. McIntyre	30	1949
81	61	20	A.J.W. McIntyre	28	1955
80	73	7	R. Swetman	33	1961
78	69	9	A. Long	29	1964
74	61	13	A.J.W. McIntyre	29	1950
71	55	16	A.J.W. McIntyre	31	1952
70	59	11	A. Long	31	1968
68	61	7	A. Long	23	1965
65	61	4	A. Long	25	1970
65	60	5	G.J. Kersey	15	1995
64	59	5	G.S. Mobey	30*	1946
64	58	6	C.J. Richards	17*	1987
63	56	7	A. Long	26	1971
62	59	3	C.J. Richards	24	1980
62	61	1	C.J. Richards	18	1988
61	52	9	R. Swetman	28	1959

* *Mobey and Richards each played one further match not keeping wicket*

FIELDING RECORDS

MOST CATCHES IN AN INNINGS

7	M.J. Stewart	*v.* Northamptonshire	Northampton	1957
6	G.P. Thorpe	*v.* Kent	The Foster's Oval	1998
5	G.A.R. Lock	*v.* Lancashire	Old Trafford	1953
5	W.S. Surridge	*v.* Lancashire	The Oval	1955
5	G.R.J. Roope	*v.* Cambridge University	Fenner's	1980

MOST CATCHES IN A MATCH

8	G.A.R. Lock *(5 off his own bowling)*	*v.* Warwickshire	The Oval	1957
7	J.F. Parker	*v.* Kent	Blackheath	1952
7	G.A.R. Lock	*v.* Lancashire	Old trafford	1953
7	W.S. Surridge	*v.* leicestershire	The Oval	1955
7	M.J. Stewart	*v.* Northamptonshire	Northampton	1955
7	G.P. Thorpe	*v.* Kent	The Foster's Oval	1998
6	W.S. Surridge	*v.* Glamorgan	Cardiff (AP)	1956
6	R.E.C. Pratt	*v.* Sussex	Hastings	1956
6	M.J. Stewart	*v.* Sussex	Hove	1961
6	G.A.R. Lock	*v.* Australians	The Oval	1961 (2)

6	M.J. Edwards	*v.* Kent	Maidstone	1967
6	M.J. Edwards	*v.* Essex	Colchester	1970
6	G.R.J. Roope	*v.* Nottinghamshire	Trent Bridge	1970

MOST CATCHES IN A SEASON

Total	Fielder	Matches	Year
77	M.J. Stewart	34	1957
64	K.F. Barrington	35	1957
59	G.R.J. Roope	27	1971
58	G.A.R. Lock	27	1957
58	M.J. Stewart	33	1958
55	W.S. Surridge	28	1955
54	W.S. Surridge	31	1956
54	K.F. Barrington	32	1958
53	M.J. Edwards	31	1967
52	M.J. Stewart	24	1955
52	M.J. Stewart	33	1959
51	W.S. Surridge	31	1952
50	G.A.R. Lock	29	1952
48	W.S. Surridge	31	1953
44*	G.R.J. Roope	20	1981
43	G.A.R. Lock	27	1955
43	G.A.R. Lock	25	1961
43	G.R.J. Roope	20	1976
42	G.R.J. Roope	26	1970
41	M.J. Edwards	21	1966
41	G.R.J. Roope	23	1979
40	M.J. Stewart	29	1960

* *Includes 8 catches as wicketkeeper*

SURREY CAREER RECORDS OF PLAYERS WHO HAVE REPRESENTED THE COUNTY IN LIMITED-OVERS MATCHES

	Career	M	I	NO	Runs	HS	Ave	100	50	Balls	R	W	Ave	Best	4wI	Econ	SR	Ct	St
Alikhan, R.I.	1990	1	1	0	22	22	22.00	-	-									-	
Amin, R.M.	1997-2002	4	1	1	0	0*	-	-	-	84	97	2	48.50	2-43	-	6.92	42.0	1	
Arnold, G.G.	1963-1989	153	93	36	472	24*	8.28	-	-	7,850	4031	228	17.67	5-9	12	3.08	34.4	34	
Atkins, P.D.	1988-1993	7	7	1	154	82	25.66	-	2									1	
Aworth, C.J.	1974-1976	18	18	0	289	67	16.05	-	1									2	
Azhar Mahmood	2002-2003	21	19	2	424	98	24.94	-	3	958	759	32	23.71	6-37	3	4.75	29.9	6	
Baker, R.P.	1973-1978	45	24	10	190	48*	13.57	-	-	1,769	1,238	37	33.45	4-39	2	4.19	47.8	12	
Barnett, A.A.	1995	1	1	0	0	0	0.00	-	-	30	35	0				7.00		-	
Barrington, K.F.	1963-1968	14	14	2	399	70*	33.25	-	3	108	132	4	33.00	3-41	-	7.33	27.0	5	
Barucha, Z.	1995	1	1	0	0	0	0.00	-	-									2	
Batty, G.J.	1998-2001	22	21	5	450	83*	28.12	-	3	717	591	15	39.40	4-36	1	4.94	47.8	6	
Batty, J.N.	1997-2003	87	61	15	695	55	15.10	-	1	-	-	-	-	-	-	-	-	90	15
Bell, M.A.V.	1998	7	5	2	43	16	14.33	-	-	258	275	6	45.83	3-36	-	6.39	43.0	1	
Benjamin, J.E.	1992-1999	138	49	25	192	25	8.00	-	-	6,548	4,580	146	31.36	4-19	4	4.19	44.8	22	
Benning, J.G.E.	2002-2003	3	3	0	41	25	13.66	-	-	96	101	6	16.83	4-43	1	6.31	16.0	2	
Bicknell, D.J.	1987-1999	161	157	23	5,243	135*	39.12	7	34	78	76	3	25.33	1-11	-	5.84	26.0	39	
Bicknell, M.P.	1986-2003	311	157	68	1,382	66*	15.52	-	2	14,944	9,898	394	25.12	7-30	14	3.97	37.9	73	
Bishop, I.E.	1999-2001	12	6	5	23	15*	23.00	-	-	523	335	14	23.92	4-34	1	3.84	37.3	1	
Boiling, J.	1991-1994	84	36	16	223	24	11.15	-	-	3,952	2,787	86	32.40	5-24	2	4.23	45.9	29	

	Career	M	I	NO	Runs	HS	Avge	100	50	Balls	R	W	Avge	Best	4wI	Econ	SR	Ct	St
Brown, A.D.	1990-2003	287	277	15	8,423	268	32.14	15	36	333	344	10	34.40	3-39	-	6.19	33.3	93	
Bryson, R.E.	1992	13	5	2	60	20	20.00	-	-	583	499	18	27.72	4-31	2	5.13	32.3	-	
Bullen, C.K.	1985-1991	104	59	30	667	93*	23.00	-	1	4,411	3,149	92	34.22	5-31	1	4.28	47.9	62	
Butcher, A.R.	1971-1986	259	243	24	6,264	140	28.60	5	41	3,421	2,200	67	32.83	5-19	3	3.85	51.0	65	
Butcher, G.P.	1999-2002	17	16	4	241	37	20.08	-	-	309	344	5	68.80	2-49	-	6.67	61.8	2	
Butcher, M.A.	1991-2003	149	132	25	2,962	104	27.68	1	16	2,527	2,210	49	45.10	3-23	-	5.24	51.5	47	
Carberry, M.A.	2001-2002	10	9	1	68	20	8.50	-	-									5	
Cheatle, R.G.L.	1980-1981	16	4	3	2	2*	2.00	-	-	671	478	22	21.72	4-34	1	4.27	30.5	7	
Clarke, R.	2001-2003	33	32	5	656	98*	24.29	-	4	921	919	22	41.77	3-48	-	5.98	41.8	11	
Clarke, S.T.	1979-1989	160	96	25	876	45*	12.33	-	-	7,981	4,398	212	20.74	5-23	10	3.30	37.6	46	
Clinton, G.S.	1979-1990	175	161	14	5,112	146	34.77	4	32	32	12	0	-	-	-	2.25		30	
Constable, B.	1963-1964	2	2	0	4	4	2.00	-	-									1	
Cosh, N.J.	1969	3	3	0	41	25	13.66	-	-									1	
Cousins, D.M.	1999	3	2	1	2	1*	2.00	-	-	162	125	4	31.25	2-38	-	4.62	40.5	1	
Cuffy, C.E.	1994	9	1	1	2	2*	-	-	-	516	387	8	48.37	4-43	1	4.50	64.5	2	
Cumbes, J.	1969-1970	10	4	0	2	1	0.50	-	-	490	368	16	23.00	3-18	-	4.50	30.6	2	
Cummins, A.C.	1995	1	1	0	20	20	20.00	-	-	66	58	0	-	-	-	5.27	-	-	
Curtis, I.J.	1983	6	3	2	4	4	4.00	-	-	168	121	2	60.50	1-35	-	4.32	84.0	-	
de la Peña, J.M.	1994-1995	3	3	3	2	2*	-	-	-	108	107	2	53.50	2-46	-	5.94	54.0	-	
Doughty, R.J.	1985-1987	22	14	2	179	36	14.91	-	-	816	651	11	59.18	2-46	-	4.78	74.1	3	
Edrich, J.H.	1963-1978	149	144	18	4,487	108*	35.61	1	37									43	
Edwards, M.J.	1964-1974	92	88	8	1,549	108*	19.36	1	7									27	
Falkner, N.J.	1984-1987	13	12	1	254	58	23.09	-	2									3	
Feltham, M.A.	1983-1992	149	101	30	1,128	61	15.88	-	2	6,515	5,115	159	32.16	5-28	3	4.71	40.9	37	
Gibson, D.	1963-1969	18	15	9	104	29*	17.33	-	-	1,015	585	16	36.56	3-42	-	3.45	63.4	-	
Giddins, E.S.H.	2001-2002	46	20	10	37	13*	3.70	-	-	2,135	1,576	59	26.71	5-20	2	4.42	36.1	13	
Gray, A.H.	1985-1990	31	12	6	118	24*	19.66	-	-	1,488	1,049	46	22.80	4-21	2	4.22	32.3	3	
Greenidge, C.G.	1998-2001	17	5	3	6	3*	3.00	-	-	602	544	10	54.40	2-17	-	5.42	60.2	7	
Greig, I.A.	1987-1992	118	96	27	1,462	75	21.18	-	4	3,200	2,564	95	26.98	5-30	2	4.80	33.6	31	
Hansell, T.M.G.	1975-1977	7	4	0	47	26	11.75	-	-									1	
Harman, R.	1964	1	0							53	50	3	16.66	3-50	-	5.66	17.6	-	
Hollioake, A.J.	1992-2003	226	198	26	4,816	117*	28.00	2	22	7,308	6,607	304	21.73	6-17	23	5.42	24.0	69	
Hollioake, B.C.	1996-2001	106	89	9	1,968	98	24.60	-	10	3,856	3,217	121	26.58	5-10	2	5.00	31.8	34	
Hooper, J.M.M.	1970-1972	17	17	0	275	40	16.17	-	-	36	46	2	23.00	2-46	-	7.66	18.0	4	
Howarth, G.P.	1971-1984	170	160	4	3,765	122	24.13	2	17	123	110	7	15.71	4-16	1	5.36	17.5	47	
Intikhab Alam	1969-1981	185	159	29	2,439	62	18.76	-	5	5,739	3,867	131	29.51	6-25	3	4.04	43.8	38	
Jackman, R.D.	1968-1982	261	161	51	1,387	46	12.60	-	-	12,991	8,273	399	20.73	7-33	17	3.82	32.5	43	
Jefferson, R.I.	1964-1966	6	5	0	42	21	8.40	-	-	414	223	8	27.87	3-44	-	3.23	51.7	-	
Jesty, T.E.	1985-1987	61	53	11	1,267	112	30.16	1	8	1,052	809	22	36.77	4-23	1	4.61	47.8	15	
Julian, B.P.	1996	24	16	3	233	41	17.92	-	-	960	839	33	25.42	4-46	1	5.24	29.0	11	
Kendrick, N.M.	1990-1994	10	6	4	42	24	21.00	-	-	477	385	11	35.00	3-21	-	4.84	43.3	3	
Kenlock, S.G.	1994-1995	21	5	1	13	9	3.25	-	-	896	797	30	26.56	5-15	3	5.33	29.8	6	
Kennis, G.J.	1995	2	2	0	12	7	6.00	-	-									1	
Kersey, G.J.	1993-1996	29	19	1	292	50	16.22	-	1									30	4
Knight, R.D.V.	1969-1984	161	149	15	3,121	92*	23.29	-	18	5,856	3,889	147	26.45	4-19	2	3.98	39.8	45	
Knott, J.A.	1997-1998	10	8	0	142	98	17.75	-	1	6	7	0	-	-	-	7.00	-	15	
Lewis, C.C.	1996-1997	36	28	12	591	68*	36.93	-	2	1,630	1,073	56	19.16	4-21	1	3.94	29.1	19	
Lewis, R.M.	1969-1973	14	12	1	149	50	13.54	-	1	24	25	0	-	-	-	6.25	-	3	
Ligertwood, D.G.C.	1992	1	0															-	1
Loader, P.J.	1963	1	1	0	1	1	1.00	-	-	90	35	3	11.66	3-35	-	2.33	30.0	-	
Long, A.	1963-1975	127	99	27	1,067	71	14.81	-	1									111	22
Lynch, M.A.	1977-1994	312	280	36	6,833	136	28.00	5	39	563	471	13	36.23	2-2	-	5.01	43.3	120	
Mack, A.J.	1975-1977	32	11	3	26	16	3.25	-	-	1,330	1,035	25	41.40	3-34	-	4.66	53.2	2	
Mackintosh, K.S.	1981-1983	14	7	2	36	12	7.20	-	-	493	365	15	24.33	4-37	1	4.44	32.8	3	

	Career	M	I	NO	Runs	HS	Avge	100	50	Balls	R	W	Avge	Best	4wI	Econ	SR	Ct	St
Marriott, D.A.	1967	2	1	1	2	2*	-	-	-	90	35	2	17.50	2-25	-	2.33	45.0	-	
Medlycott, K.T.	1985-1991	57	37	9	399	44*	14.25	-	-	1,743	1,424	49	29.06	4-18	3	4.90	35.5	16	
Miller, D.J.	2002	1	1	0	1	1	1.00	-	-	42	32	0	-	-	-	4.57	-	-	
Monkhouse, G.	1981-1986	90	45	19	341	27	13.11	-	-	4,194	2,940	101	29.10	3-20	-	4.20	41.5	20	
Muggleton, A.N.	1995	1	1	0	7	7	7.00	-	-	48	57	0	-	-	-	7.12	-	-	
Murphy, A.J.	1989-1994	89	22	12	37	9*	3.70	-	-	4,274	3,183	110	28.93	6-26	2	4.46	38.8	6	
Murtagh, T.J.	2001-2003	23	16	7	54	14*	6.00	-	-	1,148	963	31	31.06	4-31	1	5.03	37.0	4	
Mushtaq Ahmed	2002	1	1	0	16	16	16.00	-	-	54	19	1	19.00	1-19	-	2.11	54.0	-	
Nadeem Shahid	1995-2003	114	104	21	2,214	109*	26.67	2	10	264	235	4	58.75	3-30	-	5.34	66.0	35	
Needham, A.	1978-1986	61	48	9	743	55	19.05	-	3	1,143	882	30	29.40	4-32	1	4.62	38.1	16	
Newman, S.A.	2001-2003	9	9	0	128	37	14.22	-	-									1	
Nowell, R.W.	1995	5	3	2	17	15*	17.00	-	-	162	113	1	113.00	1-35	-	4.18	162.0	3	
Ormond, J.	2002-2003	23	9	3	44	14*	7.33	-	-	1,077	898	26	34.53	3-46	-	5.00	41.4	5	
Owen-Thomas, D.R.	1970-1979	69	63	13	1,078	66	21.56	-	3									24	
Parsons, A.B.D.	1963	1	1	0	2	2	2.00	-	-									1	
Pauline, D.B.	1981-1985	38	32	6	629	92	24.19	-	4	696	552	17	32.47	3-34	-	4.75	40.9	8	
Payne, I.R.	1977-1984	48	31	11	303	56*	15.15	-	1	1,542	1222	50	24.44	5-21	4	4.75	30.8	10	
Pearson, R.M.	1996	23	7	5	35	12*	17.50	-	-	862	762	18	42.33	3-33	-	5.30	47.8	2	
Peters, N.H.	1988-1989	12	6	4	7	4*	3.50	-	-	551	360	13	27.69	2-16	-	3.92	42.3	1	
Pigott, A.C.S.	1994-1996	35	18	10	139	19*	17.37	-	-	1,735	1274	47	27.10	3-31	-	4.40	36.9	9	
Pocock, P.I.	1966-1986	318	157	61	696	22	7.25	-	-	15,003	9081	326	27.85	4-11	7	3.63	46.0	58	
Porter, J.J.	2001	1	1	0	23	23	23.00	-	-									-	
Rackemann, C.G.	1995	13	6	3	37	15*	12.33	-	-	595	513	12	42.75	3-36	-	5.17	49.5	-	
Ramprakash, M.R.	2001-2003	52	51	11	2,231	107*	55.77	4	18	173	170	4	42.50	2-19	-	5.89	43.2	14	
Ratcliffe, J.D.	1995-2002	86	70	11	1,258	82	21.32	-	7	1,478	1,127	35	32.20	4-44	1	4.57	42.2	22	
Richards, C.J.	1977-1988	240	177	43	2,744	113	20.47	3	8									182	49
Robinson, J.D.	1988-1992	54	46	10	705	55*	19.58	-	2	1,487	1,161	26	44.65	3-46	-	4.68	57.1	15	
Robson, A.G.	1990-1991	4	0							186	165	8	20.62	3-42	-	5.32	23.2	-	
Roope, G.R.J.	1966-1982	277	256	45	6,092	120*	28.87	2	29	4,817	3,650	125	29.20	5-23	3	4.54	38.5	127	2
Rose, F.A.	2003	2	1	0	1	1	1.00	-	-	102	78	2	39.00	1-33	-	4.58	51.0	-	
Roshier, P.G.	1995	1	1	0	1	1	1.00	-	-	60	61	1	61.00	1-61	-	6.10	60.0	-	
Sadiq, Z.A.	1987-1989	24	20	0	251	53	12.55	-	1									10	
Salisbury, I.D.K.	1997-2003	92	59	17	552	34*	13.14	-	-	3,648	2,775	90	30.83	4-17	3	4.56	40.5	35	
Sampson, P.J.	2001-2003	11	7	2	29	16	5.80	-	-	468	415	12	34.58	3-42	-	5.32	39.0	4	
Saqlain Mushtaq	1997-2003	85	46	17	339	38*	11.68	-	-	4,004	2,792	106	26.33	4-17	6	4.18	37.7	16	
Sargeant, N.F.	1990-1995	15	7	2	58	22	11.60	-	-									12	
Scott, B.J.M.	2002	1	1	0	4	4	4.00	-	-									-	
Skinner, L.E.	1971-1977	86	73	11	1,141	89	18.40	-	4									65	14
Smith, A.W.	1993-1995	36	26	7	545	58	28.68	-	2	678	593	15	39.53	3-25	-	5.24	45.2	19	
Smith, D.M.	1973-1988	170	151	30	3,689	110*	30.48	2	15	1,259	985	23	42.82	4-29	1	4.69	54.7	61	
Smith, W.A.	1964-1970	22	19	2	403	64	23.70	-	2									7	
Stewart, A.J.	1981-2002	321	300	38	9,667	167*	36.89	14	63	4	8	0	-	-	-	12.00	-	270	30
Stewart, M.J.	1963-1972	75	72	2	1,172	101	16.74	1	3	1	4	0	-	-	-	24.00	-	24	
Storey, S.J.	1963-1976	124	114	7	1,552	56	14.50	-	1	5,189	3,156	115	27.44	5-35	2	3.64	45.1	41	
Sydenham, D.A.D.	1964-1965	8	2	0	8	8	4.00	-	-	528	262	13	20.15	4-6	1	2.97	40.6	3	
Taylor, D.J.S.	1966-1967	2	1	0	2	2	2.00	-	-									1	
Taylor, N.S.	1984-1985	5	3	1	11	9*	5.50	-	-	184	148	2	74.00	1-30	-	4.82	92.0	1	
Thomas, D.J.	1977-1987	144	101	22	1,468	72	18.58	-	6	6,361	4,577	136	33.65	4-13	2	4.31	46.7	24	
Thorpe, G.P.	1988-2003	236	219	36	7,473	145*	40.83	9	52	517	465	12	38.75	3-21	-	5.39	43.0	98	
Tindall, R.A.E.	1963-1966	10	10	1	218	73	24.22	-	2	132	118	2	59.00	1-25	-	5.36	66.0	5	
Townsend, G.T.J.	1995	1	1	0	10	10	10.00	-	-									1	
Tudor, A.J.	1995-2003	58	39	10	324	29*	11.17	-	-	2,589	1,979	86	23.01	4-26	4	4.58	30.1	14	
Verrinder, A.O.C.	1974-1976	3	3	1	2	2	1.00	-	-	120	105	1	105.00	1-43	-	5.25	120.0	-	
Waller, C.E.	1971-1972	5	2	1	2	2*	2.00	-	-	132	96	3	32.00	2-34	-	4.36	44.0	-	

	Career	M	I	NO	Runs	HS	Avge	100	50	Balls	R	W	Avge	Best	4wI	Econ	SR	Ct	St
Waqar Younis	1990-1993	57	24	6	152	39	8.44	-	-	2,820	1,889	112	16.86	5-26	8	4.01	25.1	9	
Ward, D.M.	1984-2002	229	200	31	5,178	112	30.63	5	32									100	3
Ward, I.J.	1996-2003	126	119	12	2,952	108	27.58	1	19	149	181	2	90.50	2-27	-	7.28	74.5	22	
Waterman, P.A.	1983-1985	10	5	3	27	17*	13.50	-	-	450	370	3	123.33	1-25	-	4.93	150.0	2	
Willett, M.D.	1964-1966	8	8	2	188	46*	31.33	-	-	255	171	5	34.20	2-20	-	4.02	51.0	3	
Willis, R.G.D.	1969-1971	32	15	6	81	24	9.00	-	-	1,435	886	49	18.08	6-49	1	3.70	29.2	8	
Wilson, P.H.L.	1978-1982	43	14	4	43	18*	4.30	-	-	1,941	1,412	59	23.93	5-21	3	4.36	32.8	4	
Younis Ahmed	1966-1978	195	188	21	4,917	113	29.44	2	31	37	29	1	29.00	1-6	-	4.70	37.0	54	

BATTING RECORDS

HIGHEST INDIVIDUAL SCORES

Cheltenham & Gloucester Trophy

268	A.D. Brown	*v.* Glamorgan	The AMP Oval	2002
146	G.S. Clinton	*v.* Kent	Canterbury	1985
145*	G.P. Thorpe	*v.* Lancashire	The Foster's Oval	1994
135*	D.J. Bicknell	*v.* Yorkshire	The Oval	1989
129	M.A. Lynch	*v.* Durham	The Oval	1982
125*	A.J. Stewart	*v.* Essex	The Foster's Oval	1996

Benson and Hedges Cup

167*	A.J. Stewart	*v.* Somerset	The Foster's Oval	1994
160	A.J. Stewart	*v.* Hampshire	The Foster's Oval	1996
121*	G.S. Clinton	*v.* Kent	The Foster's Oval	1988
119	D.J. Bicknell	*v.* Hampshire	The Foster's Oval	1990
117*	A.D. Brown	*v.* Sussex	Hove	1996
115*	G.R.J. Roope	*v.* Essex	Chelmsford	1973

National League

203	A.D. Brown	*v.* Hampshire	Guildford	1997
157*	A.D. Brown	*v.* Leicestershire	Leicester (GR)	1997
142*	A.D. Brown	*v.* Middlesex	The Foster's Oval	1994
136	M.A. Lynch	*v.* Yorkshire	Bradford	1985
133	A.D. Brown	*v.* Yorkshire	Scarborough	1994
130	A.D. Brown	*v.* Nottinghamshire	Trent Bridge	2001
126*	G.P. Thorpe	*v.* Nottinghamshire	Guildford	2000
125	D.J. Bicknell	*v.* Durham	Durham Univ.	1992
125	A.J. Stewart	*v.* Lancashire	The Foster's Oval	1990

HIGHEST PARTNERSHIPS

Cheltenham & Gloucester Trophy

286	1st	I.J. Ward & A.D. Brown	*v.* Glamorgan	The AMP Oval	2002
180	3rd	G.P. Thorpe & D.M. Ward	*v.* Lancashire	The Foster's Oval	1994
170	4th	G.P. Thorpe & D.M. Ward	*v.* Northumberland	Jesmond	1989
166	5th	M.A. Lynch & G.R.J. Roope	*v.* Durham	The Oval	1982
164*	1st	D.J. Bicknell & A.J. Stewart	*v.* Dorset	The Foster's Oval	1993
161	1st	J.D. Radcliffe & A.J. Stewart	*v.* Buckinghamshire	The Foster's Oval	1998

Benson and Hedges Cup

212	2nd	A.J. Stewart & G.P. Thorpe	*v.* Lancashire	The Foster's Oval	1993
185	2nd	A.J. Stewart & B.C. Hollioake	*v.* Somerset	The Foster's Oval	1998
159*	4th	D.M. Smith & T.E. Jesty	*v.* Worcestershire	The Oval	1987
159	2nd	A.J. Stewart & B.C. Hollioake	*v.* Kent	Lord's	1997
158	3rd	A.J. Stewart & G.P. Thorpe	*v.* Leicestershire	The Foster's Oval	1997
155	1st	J.H. Edrich & G.R.J. Roope	*v.* Essex	Chelmsford	1973
154	1st	D.J. Bicknell & M.A. Lynch	*v.* Minor Counties	The Foster's Oval	1992

National League

218	1st	A.R. Butcher & G.P. Howarth	*v.* Gloucestershire	The Oval	1976
203	2nd	D.J. Bicknell & G.P. Thorpe	*v.* Gloucestershire	The Oval	1995
200	3rd	A.J. Stewart & G.P. Thorpe	*v.* Glamorgan	The Oval	1989
190	2nd	D.J. Bicknell & Nadeem Shahid	*v.* Derbyshire	Derby	1995
189	2nd	A.D. Brown & G.J. Batty	*v.* Nottinghamshire	Trent Bridge	2001
187	2nd	A.R. Butcher & R.D.V. Knight	*v.* Leicestershire	Leicester	1983
184	1st	D.J. Bicknell & A.D. Brown	*v.* Yorkshire	The Oval	1995
181	4th	I.J. Ward & A.J. Hollioake	*v.* Glamorgan	The Foster's Oval	2000

BOWLING RECORDS

BEST BOWLING PERFORMANCES

Cheltenham & Gloucester Trophy

7-33	R.D. Jackman	*v.* Yorkshire	Harrogate	1970
6-22	R.D. Jackman	*v.* Hampshire	Southampton	1982
6-26	A.J. Murphy	*v.* Glamorgan	Swansea	1994
6-32	R.D. Jackman	*v.* Northamptonshire	The Oval	1980
6-49	R.G.D. Willis	*v.* Middlesex	The Oval	1970

Benson and Hedges Cup

5-15	S.G. Kenlock	*v.* Ireland	The Foster's Oval	1995
5-21	P.H.L. Wilson	*v.* Oxford & Cambridge Univs.	The Oval	1979
5-23	S.T. Clarke	*v.* Kent	The Oval	1980
5-25	S.T. Clarke	*v.* Oxford & Cambridge Univs.	The Oval	1983
5-28	M.A. Feltham	*v.* Combined Univs.	Fenner's	1989

National League

7-30	M.P. Bicknell	*v.* Glamorgan	The Oval	1999
6-17	A.J. Hollioake	*v.* Kent	Canterbury	2003
6-25	Intikhab Alam	*v.* Derbyshire	The Oval	1974
6-34	R.D. Jackman	*v.* Derbyshire	Derby	1972
6-37	Azhar Mahmood	*v.* Essex	The AMP Oval	2003

MOST ECONOMIC BOWLING

Cheltenham & Gloucester Trophy

O	M	R	W				
12	6	9	2	C.E. Cuffy	*v.* Glamorgan	Swansea	1994
12	7	9	1	S.T. Clarke	*v.* Northamptonshire	The Oval	1980
12	5	11	1	P.I. Pocock	*v.* Lancashire	Old Trafford	1977
12	5	13	3	S.J. Storey	*v.* Glamorgan	Swansea	1970

O	M	R	W				
12	8	13	2	S.J. Storey	*v.* Hertfordshire	The Oval	1971
12	6	13	3	R.D.V. Knight	*v.* Ireland	The Oval	1984

Benson and Hedges Cup

O	M	R	W				
11	6	5	2	Intikhab Alam	*v.* Glamorgan	Cardiff (SG)	1975
11	5	7	2	A.R. Butcher	*v.* Yorkshire	Bradford	1976
11	5	11	1	G.G. Arnold	*v.* Essex	The Oval	1972
11	4	11	3	A.R. Butcher	*v.* Lancashire	Old Trafford	1974

National League

O	M	R	W				
8	2	7	1	P.I. Pocock	*v.* Northamptonshire	Tring	1978
8	4	8	4	R.D. Jackman	*v.* Northamptonshire	Northampton	1976
7	2	7	1	A.J. Tudor	*v.* Hampshire	Southampton	2000
8	5	9	0	G.R.J. Roope	*v.* Gloucestershire	Sunbury-on-Thames	1972

N.B. Over the years there have been many sponsors for the limited-overs matches. The current Cheltenham and Gloucester Trophy started in 2001 taking over from the NatWest Trophy from 1981 to 2000 and the Gillette Cup which ran from 1963 to 1980. The National League started in 2003, the previous leagues being the John Player Special League (1969-1986), the Refuge Assurance League (1987-1991), AXA Equity & Law League (1993-1998), CGU National League (1999) & Norwich Union National League (2000-2002).

TEAM RECORDS

RESULTS OF FIRST-CLASS MATCHES 1946-2003 AGAINST EACH OPPONENT

Opponents	**HOME**				**AWAY**				**ALL**
	W	**D**	**L**	**Total**	**W**	**D**	**L**	**Total**	**Total**
Derbyshire	16	18	1	35	12	11	9	32	67
Durham	5	0	0	5	4	0	1	5	10
Essex	17	19	12	48	10	26	12	48	96
Glamorgan	12	18	6	36	13	13	9	35	71
Gloucestershire	18	13	6	37	15	15	9	36	76
Hampshire	18	19	5	42	18	12	11	41	83
Kent	20	26	8	54	14	30	10	54	108
Lancashire	16	19	7	42	7	23	12	42	84
Leicestershire	16	18	7	41	14	21	6	41	82
Middlesex	17	23	11	51	16	21	15	52	103
Northamptonshire	12	15	9	36	14	16	9	39	75
Nottinghamshire	23	16	3	42	16	17	9	42	84
Somerset	19	14	6	39	12	15	11	38	77
Sussex	22	19	7	48	20	20	8	48	96
Warwickshire	16	11	8	35	12	13	12	37	72
Worcestershire	15	16	5	36	8	17	10	35	71
Yorkshire	20	19	8	47	10	18	17	45	92
MCC	0	0	1	1	8	10	6	24	25
Cambridge University	10	8	0	18	15	13	0	28	46
Cambridge UCCE	0	0	0	0	0	1	0	1	1
Loughborough UCCE	0	1	0	1	0	0	0	0	1
Oxford University	11	8	1	20	3	8	0	11	31
Australians	2	6	6	14	0	0	0	0	14
Indians	2	4	3	9	0	0	0	0	9

New Zealanders	2	4	1	7	0	0	0	0	7
Pakistanis	0	4	3	7	0	0	0	0	7
South Africans	0	3	2	5	0	0	0	0	5
Sri Lankans	1	1	0	2	0	0	0	0	2
West Indians	0	6	2	8	0	0	0	0	8
Zimbabweans	0	2	0	2	0	0	0	0	2
Combined Services	1	4	0	5	0	0	0	0	5
India 'A'	0	1	0	1	0	0	0	0	1
New South Wales	0	1	0	1	0	0	0	0	1
Rest of Engalnd	0	0	2	2	1	0	0	1	3
Rhodesia	0	0	0	0	0	1	1	2	2
Scotlnad	1	0	0	1	0	0	0	0	1
South Africa 'A'	0	0	1	1	0	0	0	0	1
Sri Lanka 'A'	1	0	0	1	0	0	0	0	1
Totals	313	336	131	780	242	321	177	740	1,520

** It is generally agreed by the Association of Cricket Statisticians and Historians that abandoned matches are not included in the total of games played. During this period 9 Surrey matches have been abandoned, 2 against Essex, 2 against Lancashire and 1 against each of Derbyshire, Hampshire, Leicestershire, Warwickshire and West Indians.*

HIGHEST AND LOWEST SCORES BY SURREY AGAINST EACH COUNTY

Opponents	Highest	Venue	Year	Lowest	Venue	Year
Derbyshire	570-6 dec.	The Oval	1994	77	Ilkeston	1978
Durham	652-9 dec.	The Oval	1995	85	Chester-le-Street	2000
Essex	613-6 dec.	The Oval	1990	14	Chelmsford	1983
Glamorgan	701-9 dec.	Cardiff (SG)	2001	50	Cardiff (AP)	1948
Gloucestershire	475	The Oval	1995	77	Cheltenham	1955
Hampshire	591	Southampton	1998	64	Basingstoke	1986
Kent	648	Canterbury	1990	53	Blackheath	1950
Lancashire	707-9 dec.	The Oval	1990	86	The Oval	1952
Leicestershire	576	The Oval	1947	71	The Oval	1961
Middlesex	585	Lord's	1999	49	Lord's	1977
Northamptonshire	607	Northampton	2001	89	The Oval	1963
Nottinghamshire	706-4 dec.	Trent Bridge	1947	79	Trent Bridge	1977
Somerset	608-6 dec.	Taunton	2002	102	The Oval	1961
Sussex	575-8 dec.	The Oval	2002	83	Hove	1958
Warwickshire	544	Edgbaston	2002	61	The Oval	1962
Worcestershire	536-7 dec.	Worcester	1982	57	The Oval	1958
Yorkshire	549	The Oval	1997	42	Bramall Lane	1948

HIGHEST AND LOWEST SCORES AGAINST SURREY BY EACH COUNTY

Opponents	Highest	Venue	Year	Lowest	Venue	Year
Derbyshire	469	The Oval	1996	52	The Oval	1949
Durham	377	Stockton-on-Tees	1996	91	Chester-le-Street	1998
Essex	597	The Oval	1946	60	The Oval	1980
Glamorgan	450	The Oval	1995	31	The Oval	1957
Gloucestershire	438	The Oval	1951	52	Gloucester	1956
Hampshire	603-7 dec.	Southampton	1994	48	Guildford	1946
Kent	535	Canterbury	2003	57	The Oval	1954

Lancashire	863 (9)	The Oval	1990	27	Old Trafford	1958
Leicestershire	636-4 dec.	Leicester	2003	56	The Oval	1956
Middlesex	537-2 dec.	The Oval	1947	51	The Oval	1954
Northamptonshire	529-9	The Oval	1958	59	Northampton	1995
Nottinghamshire	475-8 dec.	Guildford	1989	40	The Oval	1955
Somerset	558	Taunton	1996	36	Weston-super-Mare	1955
Sussex	451-5 dec.	Hove	1960	70	Hove	1958
Warwickshire	470	Edgbaston	1995	45	The Oval	1953
Worcestershire	446-7	Guildford	1979	25	The Oval	1954
Yorkshire	495-9 dec.	The Oval	1992	43	The Oval	1973

HIGHEST TOTALS IN LIMITED-OVERS CRICKET BY SURREY

National League	375-4	Yorkshire	Scarborough	1994
Gillette Cup/Nat West/C & G	438-5	Glamorgan	The Oval	2002
Benson and Hedges Cup	361-8	Nottinghamshire	The Oval	2001

HIGHEST TOTALS IN LIMITED-OVERS CRICKET AGAINST SURREY

National League	316	Kent	The Oval	2003
Gillette Cup/Nat West/C&G	429	Glamorgan	The Oval	2002
Benson and Hedges Cup	318-8	Kent	Canterbury	1995

LOWEST TOTALS IN LIMITED-OVERS CRICKET BY SURREY

National League	64	Worcestershire	Worcester	1978
Gillette Cup/Nat West/C&G	74	Kent	The Oval	1967
Benson and Hedges Cup	89	Nottinghamshire	Trent Bridge	1984

LOWEST TOTALS IN LIMITED-OVERS CRICKET AGAINST SURREY

National League	44	Glamorgan	The Oval	1999
Gillette Cup/Nat West Trophy	76	Yorkshire	Harrogate	1970
Benson and Hedges Cup	63	Hampshire	Southampton	1997

If you are interested in purchasing
other books published by Tempus, or in case you have
difficulty finding any Tempus books in your local bookshop,
you can also place orders directly through our website

www.tempus-publishing.com